FRANTIC COMEDY

8 Plays of Knockabout Fun

Anthologies edited by Marvin Kaye

Sweet Revenge *10 Plays of Bloody Murder*
Lovers and Other Monsters
Haunted America
Devils & Demons
Ghosts
Masterpieces of Terror and the Supernatural
13 Plays of Ghosts and the Supernatural
Weird Tales™: *The Magazine That Never Dies*
Witches & Warlocks
Fiends and Creatures
Brother Theodore's Chamber of Horrors

FRANTIC COMEDY

8 Plays of Knockabout Fun

Selected by
MARVIN KAYE

*With an Introduction by
Tony Tanner*

Garden City, New York

CONTENTS

PREFACE

Victor Borge once told me that he thinks it shameful that statues in town squares throughout Europe and America honor politicians, warhounds and sometimes a tragic artist like Brahms, Goethe or Ibsen, but rarely, if ever, a comedian.

America has produced its fair share of comedic geniuses, yet far too many of its critics, educators and cultural funding institutions still undervalue the importance of the antic muse, despite a preponderance of evidence that the best work of a Larry Gelbart, Buster Keaton, Daniel Pinkwater, Neil Simon, Mark Twain or Kurt Vonnegut is more trenchant and longer relevant to the human condition than the obsolescent narcissism that constitutes much of our "serious" literature. Pagliaccio has always peeped through the eyeholes of the masks of both Comedy and Tragedy, but it took the Twentieth Century to stamp the face of these siblings on the same coin, not back to back, but composite.

Comedy's traditional disprizement owes much to its democratic lack of manners. While Tragedy revels in the revelation of lofty character, Comedy is no respecter of persons; it spares neither cabbageheads nor kings and their crapulent ideologies. The plight of King Lear harrows us from a safe aesthetic distance, but King Ubu's japeries smash down the fourth wall to remind us, even as we're laughing, that the jokes are at our personal expense. The authors of the eight theatrical comedies in this collection are merciless in their raillery against such hallowed institutions as the law, marriage, parental authority, romantic love, social classes and, especially, conventional morality.

When FRANTIC COMEDY was first proposed for publication by The Fireside Theatre, the subtitle I had in mind was "From commedia dell'arte to doorslammers," but I soon decided that commedia *lazzi* are too skeletal to make interesting reading. As for doorslammers, I considered obtaining rights for "Run for Your Wife," a riotously funny, thoroughly offensive British farce slaughtered by the same New York newspaper reviewers who later heaped praise on what I considered a particularly feeble native American farce. The peculiar mind-set that produces criticism contemptuous of the peasant wisdom of audiences is examined by Tony Tanner in his splendid introduction. At any rate, the discovery of a genuine doorslammer by none other than Charles Dickens changed my mind and satisfied my need.

FRANTIC COMEDY chiefly consists of farces, which academicians distinguish from comedies by applying the plot vs. character criterion. True, stock figures abound—clever servants and gullible masters, quack doctors and tyrannical fathers, pert maids and princesses, clowns and bawds and magistrates—but with the transfiguring wit of masters like Molière, Goldoni or Gilbert, caricature is frequently synonymous with percipient characterization.

Three of the following selections were edited and adapted to a greater degree than is my usual practice in anthologies I have prepared for The Fireside Theatre. I wanted to present playable scripts that would be both relevant and accessible to contemporary audiences.

A note to readers and producers alike: these eight comedies are highly visual in nature. When reading them, do bear in mind that much unspecified, but necessary comic business must be invented by the actors during rehearsal. And don't forget that farce needs to be performed with the breakneck pace of a Marx Brothers movie!

—MARVIN KAYE
New York City 1992

INTRODUCTION

The first three years of my professional life were spent with the Oldham Repertory Theatre Company. Oldham is a small industrial town in the North of England and stands, quite frankly, in the shadow of Manchester, an imposing neighbor city. Manchester had a theatre company too, which produced a new show every four weeks and was accounted in consequence, very grand. Our turnover was a little more hectic, we had an opening every Monday night. They did Anouilh, Cocteau and Restoration comedy. We did thrillers, chillers and the latest West End hits. We also did Anouilh, Shakespeare, Shaw, Molière and just about everyone else you can think of since we had thirty more titles per year to find than they did.

One genre that the audience never tired of was North Country comedy. This, to put it simply was frantic comedy with a north country accent, so I discovered quite early in my career that rehearsing farce was just as arduous as rehearsing Othello. To begin with I cannot remember a North country comedy that did not have at least three doors in the set. These doors were continually opening and closing. Often there were windows as well that admitted new characters and discharged old ones. Wardrobes, too, were in evidence. Wardrobes large enough to conceal at least one person, often two or more. Tables with floor-length cloths upon them, tables that got up and moved around, tables that were quite literally turned, when the need arose. All this stuff took time to organize. In "Little Lies," an adaptation of Pinero's "The Magistrate" that I staged at Wyndham's Theatre in London, a whole buffet supper on a cart was eaten by people onstage and someone concealed behind a curtain, simultaneously. That took a whole morning. You can see then that in frantic comedy, what is done is every bit as important as what is said. And in the doing and the saying timing is everything, and often this timing can only be guessed at before the audience is included in the performance. One actress that I knew told of her early experience with Ralph Lynn, one of the most famous of English farceurs. At one point in the play he delivered a line that got a gigantic laugh. She opened her mouth to respond. They were standing at the time, she said, almost nose to nose onstage. "Wait," he hissed at her without moving his lips in best ventriloquial style. She waited. Then opened her mouth to speak. "Wait," he hissed again. Again she waited. The laugh abated slightly. She tried again. "Wait" came one last time. She sweated and waited. "Now," said Mr. Lynn. She spoke and the house fell in. The lesson is obvious: no matter how "frantic" the comedy may become, the actor must remain the very opposite.

My dictionary defines "frantic" as being "driven out of one's mind, as with grief, fear or rage. . . ." Few emotions onstage at least, are more amusing than anger, but the primary fuel of "frantic comedy" is, of course, fear. Usually the fear of potential discovery. This fear produces enormous pressure. And this pressure sets in motion a series of "frantic" defensive actions, which in turn produce endless circumlocutions of action and reaction, usually on the part of characters who have no idea what the hero or heroine is hoping to achieve, or indeed at times who in blazes they actually are, since so many lies are told and since so often people are pretending to be persons they are not. Sometimes even, persons of another sex. The aforementioned lies are usually told to the person from whom it is most important to conceal the truth. This person is usually a grouch. In farcical comedy there are no real villains, you see, only grouches. Often these grouches are authority figures: fathers, policemen, magistrates, even mothers-in-law. Sometimes they are quite simply the person to whom one is married.

This spouse, however, never discovers the awful truth, so everything always comes out right in the end. Happy endings are an essential ingredient of "frantic comedy." If the audience can't be sure that everything will turn out well, they cannot enjoy the absurd contortions their leading characters must perform to escape discovery. A happy ending is as important an element in farce as an unhappy ending is essential to tragedy. It colors each word and deed: no matter how many lies are told or how many cliffs hung from, the audience must know that their hero or heroine will prevail in the end, and that reconciliation and reassurance will be the order of the day as the curtain falls.

This reconciliation and/or reassurance usually implies success on the part of the central figure in keeping some particular skeleton firmly stashed in the closet.

It comes as no surprise, therefore, to learn that most of these "frantic" comedies emanate from the nineteenth century or earlier. So many of the great farceurs—Feydeau, Pinero—wrote at a time when the notion of "respectability" was of supreme importance to the middle class. Especially the middle class of European societies. Frantic efforts to preserve this respectability have produced some of the greatest examples of the genre. One important reason for the dearth of frantic comedy now is the increasingly liberal climate enjoyed by most western societies. In a world in which people are "coming out" about so many aspects of their private behavior which, till now may have existed, but which could not be proclaimed, it is difficult to write about people being caught in any kind of societal pressure, at least one of which splendid fun can be made. The tradition of writing farce, however, is still very much alive in France ("La Cage aux Folles") and England ("Noises Off") and almost non-existent in America, which from the very beginning has prided itself on being a more open society where conventional respectability has never meant as much as a sort of splendid (if possible) money-producing individualism.

Italy, too, has a great tradition of frantic comedy, emanating from the commedia dell'arte which is alive today in the plays of Dario Fo and which reached its early apogee in the work of Carlo Goldoni. "The Servant of Two Masters" is the one undoubted masterpiece in this collection and if you don't know it, you should meet its delicious contrivances for the first time on the page without any forewarnings from me.

Incidentally, the servant in the title, Truffaldino, is a part I played in that same weekly repertory company where my career and this foreword started. As young and cocksure as I was, I realized even then that a week was not really long enough time in which to stage a ballet with words. But they laughed, anyway. And my addiction to that particular sound grew more profound by the moment. I'm serious. One can get hooked on laughter. Then follows the eternal struggle to hang on to the truth of whatever absurd situation the author has strung about you, instead of doing or saying something, anything to keep that laughter going. I remember in my very young days, reeling offstage enmeshed in the sheets of an unraveled toilet roll. It was a new piece of business I had improvised that night. A senior actor was waiting in the wings. "That wasn't funny," he said shortly. "It was silly." He was right. I don't think I was ever silly again. One can be silly in a frantic comedy, but one has to be real, since most laughter is based on recognition. Recognition of something already observed or experienced. And something already observed or experienced is by definition "real." And if the audience doesn't recognize it, they don't laugh.

In spite of the appalling difficulties and disciplines involved in comic acting, actors don't seem to win awards for funny performances. Neither on film nor in the theatre.

This phenomenon is not new. Comedy has always been undervalued. When Louis the Fourteenth asked Boileau who, in his opinion, was the greatest writer of the age, that eminent (and smart) critic replied "Molière." The King was surprised. This, in spite of the fact that Louis was Molière's greatest fan and most valued patron. I suppose the King's answer might have been Racine or Corneille, tragedians both.

Even today such snobbery persists. One English farce after another has been bounced from the Broadway stage by critical disclaim. Admittedly these farces are usually characterized by a great deal of sexual innuendo and cheerful vulgarity, but still they are put together with immense skill and usually played and directed with equal accomplishment. I had the misfortune to star in the American company of one of these: "No Sex Please We're British," which ran for twelve years in Britain and for twelve minutes in New York. Interestingly enough, I had, when I saw the play in London, approached several Americans in the audience to elicit their reaction. They loved the piece. But after two weeks of previews in New York, during which the play was greeted with howls of laughter, the reviewers turned their noses up and their thumbs down, so the house immediately fell silent.

Don't let us fall silent. When we think something is funny, let's laugh out loud. We shall be pumping life blood into the actors in front of us and at the same time giving thanks to these playwrights, not only for their skill and good humor, but also because many of the plays they wrote are already of historical importance. Yes, that's the way it was then, but even then there were authors and audiences who longed to make fun of and perhaps throw off the corsets that bound them all.

—TONY TANNER
Los Angeles, California
December 1992

ASSININE

by
Plautus
Freely revised and adapted by Marvin Kaye

The plot of Burt Shevelove–Larry Gelbart–Stephen Sondheim's howlingly funny musical, "A Funny Thing Happened on the Way to the Forum," was based on the comedies of Titus Maccius PLAUTUS (circa 255–184 B.C.) who, in turn, borrowed from the Greeks.

Born in Sarsina, Plautus went to Rome early in his life and pursued a career in the theatre. His twenty extant comedies include "The Haunted House" ("Mostellaria"); "The Maenechmi" ("The Twins"), which was revamped by Shakespeare as "The Comedy of Errors" and also influenced Carlo Goldoni's "The Venetian Twins," and ASSININE ("Asinaria"), whose two conniving slaves bring to mind Shevelove–Gelbart's Pseudolus and Hysterium, as ably portrayed by Zero Mostel and Jack Gilford.

ASSININE is freely adapted and streamlined from a 1913 translation by Paul Nixon, Dean of Bowdoin College, Maine. I eliminated most of Nixon's stage directions, which do not appear in Plautus, and have converted pounds to drachmae (the original specifies "viginti minas") because the action is set in Athens. "Asinaria" is based on a Greek play by Demophilus, which Plautus conjecturally saw performed a generation earlier.

A slightly variant version of *Assinine* with the roles of Parasitus and Diabolus combined was first produced on April 15, 1992, at the Amsterdam Room, New York, with the following cast:

DEMAENETUS	Marvin Kaye
ARTEMONA	Melissa Berman
ARGYRIPPUS	Jon Koons
LIBANUS	Toby Sanders
LEONIDA / DIABOLUS	R. J. Lewis
CLEARETA	Barbara Gallow
PHILAENIUM	Barbara Pratt
A TRADER	Trey Birkhead

CAST OF CHARACTERS

DEMAENETUS, an elderly Athenian
ARTEMONA, his wife
ARGYRIPPUS, their son
LIBANUS ⎱ slaves of Demaenetus
LEONIDA ⎰
CLEARETA, a procuress
PHILAENIUM, her courtesan daughter
DIABOLUS, a young Athenian
PARASITUS, Diabolus's aide
A trader

Athens. A street running in front of the houses of DEMAENETUS *and* CLEARETA. *There is a narrow lane between the two houses.* DEMAENETUS *emerges from his house, hobbling on a cane. He is followed by his slave,* LIBANUS.

LIBANUS: You want to talk to me about your son?

DEMAENETUS: Yes, Libanus, I do.

LIBANUS: Before I say one word, sir, promise me something.

DEMAENETUS: What?

LIBANUS: No, you have to promise me before I say one word.

DEMAENETUS: Well, I promise.

LIBANUS: No, you've got to swear it, too. Swear by your grey hairs and by your wife, who made them grey, that if you break your word to me, you've got to live with her another forty years.

DEMAENETUS: What a wretched thought! All right, I swear it. Now what have I sworn to?

LIBANUS: Not to beat me if I talk about your son.

DEMAENETUS: Oh, Libanus, you were never in danger. I'm not angry because you haven't kept me informed. I won't fly into a rage at what my son, Argyrippus, has been up to, like other fathers might. As a matter of fact, I already know he's been having a fling with that wench next door, Philaenium. Right?

LIBANUS: Well . . . yes, sir, he has.

DEMAENETUS: Are you aiding my son in this affair? Come on now, I've given you my word.

LIBANUS: Yes, sir. So has my fellow slave, Leonida.

DEMAENETUS: Good. I'm grateful to you both.

LIBANUS: You are?

DEMAENETUS: Yes, but—look here, now you've got to promise *me* something.

LIBANUS: The servant promising the master? This is priceless! *(To* DEMAENETUS*)* My lips are sealed, sir.

DEMAENETUS: What I'm about to tell you must never reach my wife's ears. You know what she's like.

LIBANUS: You know it better, sir, but we get plenty of it.

DEMAENETUS: Libanus, it's my opinion that if parents indulged their children more than they usually do, their offspring would be much more affectionate than they usually are. I loved my father. He was very good to me. Once, he actually dressed himself up like a shipmaster so he could swindle a slave dealer out of a girl I was in love with. Now there was a father! I want to be like him.

LIBANUS: Well, now's the time. Argyrippus is feeling very glum.

DEMAENETUS: So I've noticed. What can I do to help him?

LIBANUS: Probably nothing. He's upset because the presents he's able to give his lover, Philaenium, fall far short of his promises.

DEMAENETUS: I see. The lad needs money.

LIBANUS: A lot of it.

DEMAENETUS: Then he shall have it.

LIBANUS: But—

DEMAENETUS: No matter that his mother usurps the role of father, too, and keeps a tight rein on the purse strings. My son shall be provided for.

LIBANUS: But how—

DEMAENETUS: There are slaves and slaves. I sold myself for a dowry. But my boy shall fare better. He needs money for his mistress? Go out and get him some!

LIBANUS: Me?! How'm I going to manage that?

DEMAENETUS: Cheat me out of it.

LIBANUS: That's ridiculous! You're telling me to steal clothes from the naked.

DEMAENETUS: Then cheat my wife. Get Leonida to help you. Two smart slaves can pull off any swindle.

LIBANUS: What happens to us if your wife finds out? Will you protect us?

DEMAENETUS: As far as I'm able.

LIBANUS: Well, that's reassuring. *(To audience)* I'll tell you something . . . after this peek into my master's heart, there's never a free citizen I'll ever fear again. *(Pause)* Women, that's something different. *(To* DEMAENETUS*)* All right, I'll do it. By tonight, Argyrippus'll be back in the sack. Where will you be if I need to find you?

DEMAENETUS: At the forum with Archibulus, the banker. And where will you be?

LIBANUS: Wherever I damn well please. *(He exits)*

DEMAENETUS: A bigger rascal than that one can't be found. But he's wily as can be. He'll get the job done.

(DEMAENETUS *exits. The doors of* CLEARETA*'s house burst open and* ARGYRIP-PUS *hurtles violently out into the street)*

ARGYRIPPUS: So you're throwing me out? I rescued you both from the gutter, set you up comfortably—but now that I've exhausted my capital, this is my reward? I ought to report you to the authorities—you and your ungrateful daughter! . . . No, that's unfair. Philaenium doesn't deserve my anger. It's her mother I hate. Revenge, witch! Do you hear me?

CLEARETA *(emerging from her house):* Do I hear you? Who doesn't? Kindly lower your voice!

ARGYRIPPUS: I'll say what I please out here, seeing as I couldn't do it inside.

CLEARETA: Insult me all you want, what do I care? Your heart's fastened to my daughter with one of Cupid's spikes through it.

ARGYRIPPUS: Ingrate! I rescued you from loneliness and poverty.

CLEARETA: History bores me. Tell me what happens next.

ARGYRIPPUS: You're never satisfied! I give you a present, and a minute later you're devising some new demand.

CLEARETA: What about the way you're always fooling with my daughter? Are you ever satisfied? You do what you want with her and a minute later you want her again.

ARGYRIPPUS: Well, I paid you what you asked.

CLEARETA: And you got what you paid for. Give and take. First you give, then you take.

ARGYRIPPUS: You don't treat me with courtesy.

CLEARETA: Women in my line don't like that word, "treat." Here's how it works, sonny: no pay, no lay.

ARGYRIPPUS: You use a different kind of eloquence on me now that I've been fleeced. Before, when I visited you with money and presents, your household was wreathed in smiles. You'd tell me I was the only man in the world good enough for your little girl.

CLEARETA: I'll tell you that again when you can afford it. If not—

ARGYRIPPUS: If not . . . what?

CLEARETA: I'll sell her to someone else.

ARGYRIPPUS: Wait, don't do that! Listen! What would it cost to have her all to myself for a whole year?

CLEARETA *(laughing):* Are you mad? Why should I bother trying to answer that?

ARGYRIPPUS: Because I still have some resources left.

CLEARETA: I doubt that. Still—you *have* been a good customer. Let me think about this. A whole year?

ARGYRIPPUS: And all that time, no man but me is to come near her.

CLEARETA: If that's what you want, I'll exchange all the men servants in the house for maids. Only it's going to cost you—let me see—eight hundred drachmae.

ARGYRIPPUS: Eight HUNDRED drachmae?

CLEARETA: That's the toll. Pay it, and our doors and arms are open wide. If not, all portals are shut. *(She exits)*

ARGYRIPPUS: It's all over with me if I don't get hold of eight hundred drachmae. I'll go to the forum and beg from everyone I know. If I can't negotiate a friendly loan, I'll have to borrow from a usurer.

(ARGYRIPPUS *exits.* LIBANUS *enters*)

LIBANUS: Time's-a-flying, and I still haven't figured out how to get my hands on that cash. Shake off this sluggishness, sloth, and save your master's ass! But how? Who should I swindle?

(LEONIDA *rushes in without seeing* LIBANUS)

LEONIDA: Libanus! Where are you? Wait'll you hear! Where's the young master?

LIBANUS: Why's he so happy? Probably robbed another house.

LEONIDA *(still not seeing him):* Libanus! If we miss this chance, we'll both of us regret it! I need a partner!

LIBANUS: Here I am, jailbait!

LEONIDA: There you are, you professional whipping post!

LIBANUS: Lascivious codpiece!

LEONIDA: Connoisseur of colons!

LIBANUS: I love you, too. Leonida, what's this big chance you're yammering about?

LEONIDA: How'd you like to help out young master Argyrippus with his love affair?

LIBANUS: Funny you should mention that. Go on.

LEONIDA: Some unexpected good luck is coming our way—but it's mixed with bad luck, too.

LIBANUS: What do you mean?

LEONIDA: I mean, we need grit and guile, if we're to bring this off and not get skinned alive.

LIBANUS: If it's just my back at risk, I'll sack the Treasury. What's the scam?

LEONIDA: Where's the master?

LIBANUS: The old one's at the forum and, last I knew, the young one's still carousing at Cleareta's.

LEONIDA: Good enough. Now, listen, do you remember when Saurea, our mistress's steward, sold some Arcadian asses to that merchant from Pella?

LIBANUS: I remember. So?

LEONIDA: So the merchant sent the money to pay for them with a young trader who just arrived here in Athens.

LIBANUS: Wow! Where is he?

LEONIDA: On his way here to turn over the money to Saurea. Now get this, Libanus . . . I'm at the barber's, when this young fellow asks me if I know a man named Demaenetus, son of Strato. I say yes, I'm his servant. I tell him where our house is—

LIBANUS: And? And?

LEONIDA: And he says he's got eight hundred drachmae for some asses that a friend of his bought and he's supposed to hand it over to a steward named Saurea, but he doesn't know him . . . although he *does* know Demaenetus. So-o . . .

LIBANUS: So? So?

LEONIDA: So I tell him, he's in luck, I'm the steward he's looking for. He says, "Well, I'm not personally acquainted with this Saurea and I don't know what he looks like, so don't be offended if I ask you to go find your master and if *he* says you're Saurea, I'll be glad to give you the money."

LIBANUS: Perfect! The old man took me aside earlier and asked me to get my hands on some cash for Argyrippus's sake. I'll run to the forum and get him, so he can back you up when you say you're Saurea.

LEONIDA: Too late! Here comes the trader!

LIBANUS: Do something before he really runs into Saurea!

LEONIDA: Okay, but listen . . .

LIBANUS: What?

LEONIDA: If I'm going to imitate Saurea, I'll have to boss you around, like he does.

LIBANUS: What do you mean, boss me around?

LEONIDA: Well, to be convincing, I might have to—slap you around a little. If I do, don't get mad, it's nothing personal.

LIBANUS: You'd better not try it, pal.

LEONIDA: But if I do, Libanus, you've got to play along!

LIBANUS: All right, all right, I agree . . . to get even.

LEONIDA: Here he is. Keep him busy. I'll be right back. (LEONIDA *runs off as the* TRADER *enters*)

TRADER: According to directions, this must be the house where Demaenetus lives. If Saurea the steward is in there, maybe he'll hear me knock.

LIBANUS: Hey, there! Who's that battering down our door? We're not deaf!

TRADER: Are you crazy? I haven't even touched your door!

LIBANUS: Well, don't. It's a fellow servant like me and I love my fellow servants.

TRADER: If you answer all callers like this, it'll never be battered off its hinges.

LIBANUS: So what's your business?

TRADER: I want to see Demaenetus.

LIBANUS: He's not in.

TRADER: How about his steward, Saurea?

LIBANUS: He went to the barbershop.

TRADER: I met him there. He's not back yet?

LIBANUS: Not yet. What do you want him for?

TRADER: I have to give him eight hundred drachmae.

LIBANUS: Oh, that must be for the asses.

TRADER: That's right. Look here, what does Saurea look like?

LIBANUS: Average height—reddish hair—potbellied—and the ugliest scowl you'd ever want to see.

TRADER: That's him, all right.

LIBANUS: Yes, and here he comes now.

TRADER: Good Lord! Look at him! He must be in a foul mood!

(Enter LEONIDA, *pretending to be in a rage)*

LEONIDA: I'm furious! I told Libanus to meet me at the barbershop, but he never came. By God, I'll teach his hide and shanks!

TRADER: What a domineering bully!

LIBANUS: Oh, I'm in for it!

LEONIDA: Ah, there you are, slave! Or perhaps you've been given your freedom without my knowing it?

LIBANUS: Please, sir! I'm sorry, sir!

LEONIDA: I'll give you good reason to be sorry. *(He slaps him)* Why didn't you meet me at the barber's?

LIBANUS: This gentleman delayed me.

LEONIDA: I don't care if God Almighty delayed you! *(Slap)*

LIBANUS *(to the* TRADER): Stranger, I'm a dead man!

TRADER: Please, Saurea, for my sake, spare him!

LEONIDA: Get out of my way and let me murder the rascal! I have to tell him things a hundred times. Look! Didn't I tell you to clean this crap away from the door? Look at those columns! What about those spider webs? You force your master to live in a pigpen! *(Slap)*

LIBANUS: Help! Protect me, stranger!

TRADER: What can *I* do?

LEONIDA: And another thing . . . where's the money for that wine I sold yesterday to Exaerambus?

LIBANUS: Exaerambus just brought his banker here himself.

LEONIDA: Well, that's better. Last time I trusted him, I barely got the money out of him a year afterward. It looks like I finally taught him that he's got to pay his bills promptly!

LIBANUS *(to* TRADER): See, when he gets his way, he's calmer.

TRADER: Yes. Maybe I can talk to him now. Saurea, how soon can you spare me a minute?

LEONIDA: What? Ah, it's you again. Splendid! I was so wrought up before, I actually didn't recognize you. Sorry about that.

TRADER: That's all right. So where's Demaenetus?

LEONIDA: Not in yet. But give me the money you brought and your account with us will be all settled.

TRADER: I can't do that till Demaenetus identifies you.

LIBANUS: Don't stir him up again! I'll get the worst of it.

TRADER: I will only pay him in the presence of his master.

LIBANUS: For my sake, give it to him, puh-lease! If our old man finds out his steward's word was doubted, he'll be so furious, *he'll* take it out on me, too! Please give it to him!

TRADER: But I'm a stranger. I don't know Saurea personally.

LIBANUS: Let me do the honors. Saurea, stranger. Stranger, Saurea.

LEONIDA: He's all puffed up with self-importance because he's got our eight hundred drachmae. What does he expect me to do for it, lick his boots? To hell with him! Go home, stranger. I wouldn't touch that money now if you got down on your hands and knees and begged me.

TRADER: Why, you arrogant slave!

LEONIDA: How dare you talk to me that way? *(He slaps* LIBANUS*)*

LIBANUS *(to* TRADER*)*: No more insults—I can't take it! Will you p-l-e-a-s-e give him the money?!

LEONIDA: Stop pleading with that shameless wretch! *(Slap)*

TRADER: How dare you insult a free man, slave? Just wait till I talk to Demaenetus!

LEONIDA: What's that, you vulture? You think I'm afraid of my master? If you're so anxious to see him, come on, I'll take you to him right now. He's at the forum.

TRADER: Look, I'm sorry we're all in such a temper. But even if we were the best of friends, I couldn't hand over all this money to a stranger. Like they say, "To a stranger, a man's not a man, he's a wolf."

LEONIDA: Well, I'm sorry for all the howling I've done. Let's go to the forum and straighten this mess out.

(As they start to leave, LIBANUS *draws* LEONIDA *aside)*

LIBANUS *(showing his fist)*: I owe you, partner. *(They exit)*

*(*CLEARETA *and* PHILAENIUM *enter from their house)*

CLEARETA: Daughter, I told you no! Don't you have any respect for my authority?

PHILAENIUM: How can I, when you suggest the things you do?

CLEARETA: But I'm your mother.

PHILAENIUM: I don't find fault with mothers that do right, only those that do wrong.

CLEARETA: You glib little hussy!

PHILAENIUM: All part of the profession you taught me, Mom. The tongue learns to tempt, the body learns to tease.

CLEARETA: I meant to scold you, but now you're turning on me!

PHILAENIUM: Not really. That *would* be disrespectful. But it's cruel of you to separate me from the man I love.

CLEARETA: Love?! Is that all you've learned from me? I told you to stay away from Argyrippus. What's he given us lately? Pretty speeches. But witty words aren't gold pieces; you can't spend them. Sure, he promises to make you rich, but in the meantime, for all the help he is, we could starve.

PHILAENIUM: I'd sooner do without food than him.

CLEARETA: Men that give you things, you treat with contempt. Why can't you fall in love with one of them?

PHILAENIUM: Because my heart's not free, Mother. Even the shepherd who pastures other people's sheep may have one ewe lamb of his own to build happy hopes upon. Do let me love Argyrippus. He's the only man I want.

CLEARETA: Inside with you, you shameless minx!

PHILAENIUM: You've trained me . . . to be . . . obedient, Mother.

(PHILAENIUM *exits sadly, followed by* CLEARETA. LIBANUS *and* LEONIDA *enter from the direction of the forum.* LEONIDA *carries a purse*)

LIBANUS: All praise to Divine Treachery! We've defied the whip, the shackle, chain and cell and brought off our swindle! All hail to me! I'm a hero. I know how to tolerate a smack across the chops!

LEONIDA: You ought to, villain, you've been smacked enough. You've cheated friends, lied to our master, broken into houses and swiped whatever you could lay your hands on—

LIBANUS: Come on, Leonida, don't be modest. The list of your own villainies is as long as my codpiece.

LEONIDA: But was there ever any better game than the one we just played? Old Demaenetus makes a pretty rogue himself, doesn't he? Pretending I'm Saurea . . . giving that poor guy hell for not being willing to trust me in his absence—

LIBANUS: Shush! Look . . . Philaenium's sneaking out to meet Master Junior. Let's have some fun with them.

LEONIDA: Shh. Sneak back here . . . let's eavesdrop.

(They *withdraw into the background as* PHILAENIUM *meets* ARGYRIPPUS *by the doorway of her mother's house*)

PHILAENIUM: Stay with me!

ARGYRIPPUS: How can I? Your mother said this was to be my last hour with you; she's ordered me home.

LIBANUS: He's been thrown out of the house again.

PHILAENIUM: If I lose you, I'll die of misery.

ARGYRIPPUS: Come on, release me. Let me go.

LEONIDA: He talks a good game, but holds her tight.

ARGYRIPPUS: Farewell. Be happy. We'll meet again—

PHILAENIUM: When? Where?

ARGYRIPPUS: In the world to come. I mean to die soon.

PHILAENIUM: And leave me here to mourn? No! I'll die as well.

ARGYRIPPUS: Ah, sweeter than the sweetest nectar!

PHILAENIUM: Hold me tight! Tighter! If we could only be buried together like this!

LEONIDA: Whew, I pity a man in love.

LIBANUS: There's worse things.

LEONIDA: Name one.

LIBANUS: How about a slave hanging upside down by his heels?

LEONIDA: It feels about the same.

LIBANUS: Come on, let's surprise them . . .

(The slaves station themselves on either side of the lovers, who are still intertwined)

LEONIDA: Hi, there, you two. *(The startled lovers leap apart)* This lady must be made of smoke.

ARGYRIPPUS: Smoke? What do you mean?

LEONIDA: Well, your eyes are watering.

LIBANUS: Hi, there, Philaenium.

PHILAENIUM: God grant you all your wishes, Libanus.

LIBANUS: Amen!

PHILAENIUM: What did you wish for?

LIBANUS: Wine that doesn't stop . . . ditto ditto, your wazoo!

ARGYRIPPUS: Hold your tongue, scoundrel!

LIBANUS: Wishing it for you, sir, WHY OH YOU, not me!

ARGYRIPPUS: Thanks. It's no use, though. This lady's mother threw me out. I can't find a penny anywhere, let alone eight hundred drachmae. Meanwhile, young Diabolus promised he'd pay that amount for the privilege of having her for an entire year. That's the power and futility of eight hundred drachmae: a year of bliss for Diabolus, an early grave for me.

LIBANUS: Hold on—has Diabolus paid Cleareta yet?

PHILAENIUM: Not yet.

LIBANUS: Then cheer up, the both of you.

LEONIDA *(aside):* Libanus! Let's make them beg for it!

LIBANUS *(aside):* Right you are! *(To* ARGYRIPPUS*)* Listen, sir, the two of us happen to be your slaves, we don't deny that, but if we could give you eight hundred drachmae, what would you call us then?

ARGYRIPPUS: Free! I'd call you fellow citizens!

LEONIDA: That's all? Citizens? How about patrons?

ARGYRIPPUS: For eight hundred drachmae, I'd call you gods.

LEONIDA: There's eight hundred drachmae in this purse.

ARGYRIPPUS: O Mighty Savior and Holy Sovereign of Love! Now give me the money, quick, before Diabolus shows up and beats me to it.

LEONIDA: Wait. Philaenium, this money's going right to you, isn't it?

PHILAENIUM: Well, yes—me *and* my mother. Why?

LEONIDA: Since that's the way it's headed, anyhow, you might as well ask me for it directly.

PHILAENIUM: May I please have the purse, Leonida?

LEONIDA: Coax me.

PHILAENIUM: Leonida, apple of my eye, blushing rosebud, my secret heart's desire—

ARGYRIPPUS: That's enough! Give her the money!

LEONIDA: I've always wanted some sweet young thing to call me her itsy-bitsy-witsy wittle sparrow . . .

PHILAENIUM: My itsy-bitsy-witsy wittle sparrow.

LEONIDA: My little lambykin . . .

PHILAENIUM: My little lambykin.

LEONIDA: I've always wanted a pretty little lady to grab me by the ears and go moushy-moushy-moush with her lips.

ARGYRIPPUS: You expect a kiss from her, too, you toad-wart?!

LEONIDA: RICH toad-warts expect a lot of things.

PHILAENIUM: "Need knows no shame." Here's your kiss . . . now grant our prayers and help us!

LEONIDA: Thanks, that was almost worth eight hundred. I only wish the purse were mine to give—

ARGYRIPPUS: What, villain? Have you been making fools of us?

LEONIDA: No, sir, not at all. If it was up to me, I'd hand it over at once. But I've only been holding it for Libanus here. He's the one you have to ask.

ARGYRIPPUS: I'm glad.

PHILAENIUM: Glad?

ARGYRIPPUS: Libanus is a decent sort, not like *that* thief and scalawag! *(To* LIBANUS*)* Be a good sport now, Libanus, and give us the money. We're so very much in love.

LIBANUS: Tell the lady to ask me for it.

PHILAENIUM: Do I have to call you things, too, and kiss you?

LIBANUS: I don't know. Give it a try.

PHILAENIUM: Which?

LIBANUS: Both.

PHILAENIUM: Libanus precious, my little pot of gold, my little ducky-wucky, my lovey-dovey tootsie-wootsie, I love you beyond belief. I'll do anything you want—now give us that money! *(She kisses him wildly)*

LIBANUS *(breaking free):* Not bad . . . but not real. I changed my mind. I want something else entirely.

ARGYRIPPUS: *What?!*

LIBANUS: When you were a little boy, master, remember how you used to climb up on my back and ask for horsey-rides?

ARGYRIPPUS: Yes.

LIBANUS: Well, now it's your turn.

ARGYRIPPUS: Damnation! It's wrong for a master to tote his slave!

LIBANUS: Even a slave who's toting eight hundred drachmae?

ARGYRIPPUS: I'm bending over.

LIBANUS: Attaboy! You must be the smartest horse in Athens!

ARGYRIPPUS: Get up and be quick about it! (LIBANUS *gets on his back and rides him)* Stop kicking me!

LIBANUS: I forgot my spurs. Whoa, that's enough. Too rough. *(Dismounts)* More like riding a jackass.

ARGYRIPPUS: All right, the two of you have had your fun at our expense. Now's the time to pay up.

LEONIDA: You've both been good sports. You deserve the truth.

LIBANUS: Yes. Your father told us to give this money to you—

ARGYRIPPUS: You brought it just in the nick of time!

LIBANUS: Hold on a second. Your father instructed me to give you this purse on one condition . . .

ARGYRIPPUS: What?

LIBANUS: You're not going to like it.

ARGYRIPPUS: Name it!

LIBANUS: He wants to spend tonight with this lady himself.

LEONIDA: Complete with wine and dinner.

ARGYRIPPUS: We . . . we'll do what he asks.

LEONIDA: You sure you can tolerate your Pop all over her?

ARGYRIPPUS: What choice do I have? Go bring the old man here.

LEONIDA *(indicating* CLEARETA's *house):* He's already inside, waiting. He sneaked in the back way, so your mother wouldn't find out. It'd be bad enough if she discovered what he's up to . . . but if she ever heard about these eight hundred drachmae—

ARGYRIPPUS: Shh! Don't even think about it!

(They all enter CLEARETA's *house. Enter* DIABOLUS *and* PARASITUS)

DIABOLUS: Come on, show me the contract you drew up between me and my mistress Philaenium and the Madam, her mother.

PARASITUS: Madam will shudder when she hears the terms.

DIABOLUS: Well, Parasitus, reel 'em off.

PARASITUS: "Diabolus, son of Glaucus, gives to Cleareta, Madam, a present of eight hundred drachmae so that through the coming year, her daughter Philaenium shall spend her days and nights with him."

DIABOLUS: And not with anyone else!

PARASITUS: I should put that in?

DIABOLUS: Put it down in a good, firm hand.

PARASITUS: All right . . . it's in. "She is to admit no other male outsider to her house, not even a relative. She must hang a sign on the door saying that she's busy."

DIABOLUS: That's good.

PARASITUS: "Said Philaenium must not speak to any other man. If her glance accidentally falls on a man other than Diabolus, she must immediately be blinded."

DIABOLUS: Severe, but just. Go on.

PARASITUS: "Said Philaenium may call upon any goddess she chooses for favor, but upon no god, and if this contradicts her religious scruples, she must so inform the aforesaid Diabolus, so he may offer up the necessary prayer on her behalf."

DIABOLUS: I call that generous.

PARASITUS: "Said Philaenium must never lick her lips in public and if she should happen to cough, she mustn't let her boobies bobble."

DIABOLUS: That's in the interest of propriety.

PARASITUS: "Finally, the Madam, her mother, must never drop in on Diabolus, nor may she utter a single abusive word to him. If such a word should accidentally pass her lips, her penalty shall be—no wine for twenty days."

DIABOLUS: Excellent! A splendid document! Follow me in, so I may present it to them. (*They enter* CLEARETA's *house. The sound of wrangling within, then the pair re-emerge*) How dare they abuse me so?! Do they think they can insult me like this, and get away with it?

PARASITUS: The son I can understand, but the old man, too?!

DIABOLUS: Demaenetus thinks he can play young rake with my mistress, does he? By God, I'll go right to Artemona, his wife, and spill the whole sordid mess!

PARASITUS: Wait—it'll look better if I tell her for you.

DIABOLUS: You're right. She might think I'm just acting out of jealousy.

PARASITUS: Whereas I can tell her out of pity and regard for her own good name. Don't worry, Diabolus. For your sake, I'll stir things up plenty.

(*Exit* DIABOLUS. PARASITUS *enters* DEMAENETUS's *house.* CLEARETA's *doors open to reveal both* ARGYRIPPUS *and* DEMAENETUS *on banquet couches.* PHILAENIUM *sits beside the old man)*

DEMAENETUS: You don't mind it, do you, son, her being on the couch here with me?

ARGYRIPPUS: As the man who loves her, I don't like it at all, but as a dutiful son, I'm doing my best not to mind.

DEMAENETUS: Forget about filial duty. I want you to love me, boy.

ARGYRIPPUS: I do, Dad.

DEMAENETUS: Can't you look happier when you say it?

ARGYRIPPUS: I'm doing my best.

DEMAENETUS: I'd hate to see your worst.

ARGYRIPPUS: Here now . . . see? I'm smiling.

DEMAENETUS: I hope my enemies see smiles like that every night in their sleep!

(ARTEMONA *storms out of* DEMAENETUS*'s house.* PARASITUS *emerges directly behind her)*

ARTEMONA: But where would my husband get eight hundred drachmae in the first place? You not only expect me to believe he paid a fortune to a loose woman, but that he's in there right now carrying on like an old goat in front of his own son!

PARASITUS: Never trust me in another thing divine or human if I've made any of this up.

ARTEMONA: I thought my husband was the very paragon of men: worthy, moral, devoted to his wife!

PARASITUS: Now you know the truth.

ARTEMONA: We'll see about that. Although . . . it would explain why he goes out to dinner so often. If he's truly at a harlot's, corrupting our child . . . I'll turn his life into a living hell.

PARASITUS *(he peeps through* CLEARETA*'s door):* Well, *ecce homo!*

ARTEMONA: What?

PARASITUS: Behold your man!

ARTEMONA *(peeping through the door):* That scoundrel!

ARGYRIPPUS: Papa, when's that kiss going to end?

DEMAENETUS: Sorry, lad—this little gal is something else! And wicked! Know what she wants me to do? Steal your mother's favorite cloak and give it to her as a gift.

ARTEMONA: So that's what happened all those times I accused my maids of swiping things from me!

ARGYRIPPUS: Order me more wine, Pop. My glass is dry again.

DEMAENETUS: Hey! More wine! And you, Philaenium, how about another naughty, naughty, naughty kiss?

PARASITUS: You hear that?

ARTEMONA: My ears work perfectly.

PARASITUS: Look how he's kissing her!

ARTEMONA: My eyes work perfectly, too. Shut up!

DEMAENETUS: My dear, your breath's *so* sweet . . .

PHILAENIUM: As sweet as your wife's?

DEMAENETUS: My wife's breath? God forbid! Rather than kiss her again, I'd sooner slurp water from a privy.

ARTEMONA: We'll discuss *that* remark at length.

ARGYRIPPUS: Look here, Dad—don't you love my mother?

DEMAENETUS: Certainly I love her . . . when she's far away.

ARGYRIPPUS: But what about when she's near?

DEMAENETUS: I try to remind myself that life is short.

ARTEMONA: It's quite long enough for the revenge I'm planning.

PARASITUS: What are you going to do to him?

ARTEMONA: For starters? Kiss him to death.

ARGYRIPPUS: Pop, here's the dice. Your throw.

ARTEMONA: On top of everything else, gambling?!

DEMAENETUS: In the name of Philaenium's divine kisses . . . ha!

ARTEMONA: That's enough! *(She bursts into the house)*

ARGYRIPPUS: Mother!

ARTEMONA: I'll deal with you later, whelp!

DEMAENETUS: Oh, God, I'm dead!

PARASITUS: Is there an undertaker in the house? *(He exits)*

ARTEMONA: How dare you entertain my husband here?

PHILAENIUM: Take him home, with my blessings.

ARTEMONA: Get up, worm!

DEMAENETUS: I'm afraid to budge!

ARTEMONA: Get up before I breathe on you!

DEMAENETUS: My dear, your breath is like perfume!

ARTEMONA: Then your nose is in for quite a treat. You degenerate, come on home and steal my cloak.

PHILAENIUM: He never really promised me he would.

DEMAENETUS: OW! Let go!

ARTEMONA: I'm dragging your ear out of this den of vice. If you want to come with it, that's entirely up to you.

DEMAENETUS: But they were just about to serve dinner!

ARTEMONA: After I rip your heart out, you won't be hungry.

DEMAENETUS: Help! *(She pulls him across stage and out)*

PHILAENIUM: That's a shame. I was beginning to get used to his naughty, naughty, naughty kisses.

ARGYRIPPUS: Will this one do, instead? *(He kisses her)*

PHILAENIUM: Mmm . . . like father, like son.

(As they kiss, DEMAENETUS *runs back out, pursued by his wife)*

DEMAENETUS *(to audience):* Don't look at me like that! I haven't done anything up here that you haven't seen before, or tried yourselves, or at least thought about. Now don't be hardhearted—she's getting ready to beat me up, but you people can save me. How? Easy! The next time you see me . . . applaud like hell!

(Curtain.)

THE LOVE DOCTOR

by
Molière
Freely revised and adapted
by Marvin Kaye

THE LOVE DOCTOR is based on "L'Amour Médecin" by Jean-Baptiste Poquelin (1622–73), the French comic playwright far better known by his pseudonym, MOLIÈRE.

The son of a court furnisher, Molière was educated by the Jesuits. When he was twenty-one, he entered the theatrical profession; a few years later he began "playing the sticks," touring French provinces for many years before attracting the patronage of the king.

Molière's thirty comedies sharply criticize hypocrisy with a masterful combination of high wit and low comedy. Such uproarious fare as "The Imaginary Invalid," "The Would-Be Gentleman," "The Miser," "The Pseudo-Intellectual Women" and "Tartuffe" delight audiences with their finely balanced mixture of clever dialogue and pure slapstick.

At the invitation of the king to whip up an entertainment for the court, Molière wrote, rehearsed and performed "L'Amour Médecin" in five days. My adaptation is so free as to border on the licentious, but Molière does not enlist my usual scruples for maintaining the pristine purity of a fellow writer's artistic vision. Molière was a plagiarist. As Edmond Rostand accurately points out in "Cyrano de Bergerac," Molière stole an entire scene, virtually word for word, from an unpublished comedy by Cyrano's historical prototype, Savinien II de Cyrano.

CAST OF CHARACTERS

SGANARELLE

LUCINDA, Sganarelle's daughter

LISETTE, Lucinda's maid

CLITANDER, Lucinda's lover

LUCRECE, Sganarelle's niece

MADEMOISELLE AMINTE, Sganarelle's neighbor

REDEW
LAPIDARE } merchants

DOCTORS BLABBER, BLEEDER, GRUMBLE, MUMBLE and
LASTGASP

A quack

A notary

SGANARELLE *is discovered at his home in Paris with* LUCRECE, *his niece; his neighbor* AMINTE *and the merchants,* REDEW *and* LAPIDARE. SGANARELLE *is frantically pacing.*

SGANARELLE: What am I going to do? I only had one wife and now she's dead.

REDEW: But you only get one at a time.

SGANARELLE: And now I don't have any. True, I argued with her all the time. If she walked into the room right now, in two seconds we'd be fighting. But still, I miss her. What's worse, my daughter Lucinda is so down in the dumps, I'm worried for her health. That's why I asked you all to stop by—*(indicating each in turn)*—my niece Lucrece, neighbor Aminte and you, my fellow merchants. Tell me how to cheer up my daughter.

REDEW: Fix up her room. Redecorate it tastefully.

LAPIDARE: Better yet, buy her some jewels.

AMINTE: Don't be silly. She's mooning over that chap, Clitander. Marry them off.

LUCRECE: What a horrible idea! My cousin's too frail. Childbirth would kill her. Send her to a convent, uncle, if you want to save her life.

SGANARELLE: Why, you scoundrels! Redew, you tell me to redecorate, and you're an upholsterer. *(To* LAPIDARE*)* "Buy her jewels," you say, Lapidare, and guess what business you're in? *(To* AMINTE*)* Your lover is interested in my daughter. No wonder you tell me to marry her to Clitander! *(To* LUCRECE*)* And you, my own flesh and blood, you're worst of all! You know I have no intention of letting my daughter marry anybody, but that's not good enough for you, is it? You think if she were exiled to a convent, you might have a chance of becoming my heir. You're all rascals and scavengers! Get out of my house! *(The four swiftly exit.* SGANARELLE *muses alone)* I'm baffled. How can I help my poor child? *(Enter* LUCINDA*)* Ah, there you are. *(She sighs)* Sad, Lucinda? What's wrong? Is there anything I can do? *(She sighs)* You're breaking my heart, child! Tell Daddy what's wrong. I'll make it better. *(She heaves her deepest sigh yet, which makes him lose his temper)* Now cut that out! I'm not a mindreader. Tell me what's wrong and Daddy will try to fix it! *(She maintains a sullen silence)* Is there anything I can buy you, Lucinda, to make you feel better? The necklace you liked last week? *(She shakes head)* Maybe your bedchamber's too drab? Would you like it redecorated? *(She shakes head. He grows angry)* What if I pack you off to the Convent of the Sad Virgin?

LUCINDA *(gasping):* No!

SGANARELLE *(slyly):* I don't suppose it's just that you'd like to get married? *(She nods vigorously)* No, I didn't think that was it.

(Enter LISETTE, LUCINDA*'s maid)*

LISETTE: Well, master, have you figured out what ails her?

SGANARELLE: No. She's driving me crazy.

LISETTE: Let me give it a try. Mistress Lucinda, maybe you're too shy to talk to your father, but you can't be afraid to talk to me. Just whisper what's wrong. (LUCINDA *murmurs in her ear)* I thought so. The secret's out, master. She's as good as cured—

SGANARELLE *(interrupting):* I understand what's wrong. She's an ungrateful wretch. Nothing I do is good enough for her. Let her act stubborn, then.

LUCINDA: But, Daddy—

SGANARELLE: I don't want to hear any more.

LISETTE: But, master, all she wants—

SGANARELLE: All she wants is to worry me to death.

LISETTE: All she wants is a man.

SGANARELLE *(pretending not to hear):* I've had enough of her moods.

LISETTE: All she wants is a man.

SGANARELLE: I'm really angry at her.

LISETTE: A man.

SGANARELLE: Extremely upset.

LISETTE: A man!

SGANARELLE: Even if she changes her mind and decides to tell me what's wrong, it's too late now—

LISETTE: A *man!*

SGANARELLE: I positively refuse to listen. *(He exits)*

LISETTE *(shouting after him):* A *man!* A MAN! A *MAN!*

LUCINDA: Save your breath. I told you Daddy doesn't want to hear a word about my marrying Clitander.

LISETTE: Well, after all, he *is* a stranger.

LUCINDA: With the most eloquent eyes! The first time we saw each other, Lisette, we fell in love.

LISETTE: He told you so?

LUCINDA: We've never spoken a word.

LISETTE: Then how can you possibly know—

LUCINDA *(interrupting):* Because Clitander asked for my hand in marriage, only Daddy told him no. See why I'm upset?

LISETTE: Yes, but cheer up, mistress, I'm going to help you.

LUCINDA: How? There's no talking to my father.

LISETTE: Leave him to me. *I'll* handle him.

LUCINDA: How?

LISETTE *(under her breath):* God only knows. *(Aloud)* Let's go to your room . . . I'll figure something out.

(As they exit, SGANARELLE *re-enters)*

SGANARELLE *(to the audience):* I worked too hard all my life making a fortune and raising a daughter to hand them both over to the first clown who asks for them. Sometimes it's smart to play dumb.

*(*LISETTE *runs in, seemingly upset. She pretends she doesn't see* SGANARELLE*)*

LISETTE *(running about frantically):* O tragedy! O horror!

SGANARELLE *(trying to catch her):* Good God, what's wrong?

LISETTE *(same business):* My poor master!

SGANARELLE *(same):* What's wrong?

LISETTE *(same):* Unhappiest of fathers!

SGANARELLE *(catching up with her):* What happened to Lucinda?

LISETTE: Sorrow, sorrow!

SGANARELLE: What's wrong?!

LISETTE: Calamity, calamity!

SGANARELLE: *What's wrong?!!*

LISETTE: Disaster, di—

SGANARELLE *(furiously):* WHAT IN HOLY HELL IS WRONG?!!!

LISETTE: Ah, master, your daughter, overcome by grief, ran to her room and opened up the window. You know the one I mean—the window high above the river!

SGANARELLE: No!

LISETTE: Yes! "Daddy is angry at me," she said. "I'm too wicked to live." Then she threw herself—

SGANARELLE: Into the river?!

LISETTE: Onto her bed. She began to cry. Suddenly, her piteous tears stopped. Her eyes closed, her face went white. Her broken heart stopped beating—

SGANARELLE: Lucinda is dead?

LISETTE: I shook her hard and brought her back to life. But if we don't help her right away, she won't last long.

SGANARELLE: Send for a doctor immediately!

LISETTE: I already thought of that—

SGANARELLE *(not hearing her):* One is not enough! Quick—bring as many doctors as you can find! *(To audience)* Is there a doctor in the house? *(Runs out)* Help!

LISETTE *(with a shrug):* This is going to be harder than I thought . . .

(SGANARELLE *hurries back in, followed by four physicians:* DOCTORS BLABBER, BLEEDER, MUMBLE *and* LASTGASP)[1]

SGANARELLE: Walk this way, gentlemen. *(He indicates exit* LUCINDA *used. They cross and exit, imitating his walk)*[2]

LISETTE: Four doctors! Why four doctors?

SGANARELLE: Four times the chance of saving my daughter's life.

LISETTE: Four times as good a chance of killing her.

SGANARELLE: Doctors don't kill people!

LISETTE: Wait and see.

SGANARELLE: Oh, be still, you foolish girl! *(The doctors re-enter)* Well, gentlemen, what's the matter with my child?

BLEEDER: We've examined the patient. She's absolutely foul.

SGANARELLE: Foul? My daughter *foul?!*

BLEEDER: Harrumph! Her system is foul. She's sick as a dog.

SGANARELLE: Oh, dear!

BLEEDER: My colleagues and I must hold a consultation.

SGANARELLE: Lisette, hurry up and bring chairs.

LISETTE *(she does so):* A chair for you, Dr. Bleeder—

SGANARELLE: How do you know this doctor's name?

LISETTE: I met him a few days ago at your niece's house.

BLEEDER: That's right. I treated your niece's coachman.

LISETTE: Treated him to a coffin.

BLEEDER *(offended):* I beg your pardon?

LISETTE: He's dead.

BLEEDER: He can't be dead! The illness I treated him for lasts two to three weeks. He's only been in bed six days.

LISETTE *(shaking her head):* Mm-mmm. Four days. The other two—*(She points downward)*

BLEEDER *(furious):* I'll have you know, the treatment I gave him was recommended by Hippocrates!

LISETTE: The coachman's probably giving *him* hell right now.

SGANARELLE: That's enough sauce, Lisette! Go tend to your mistress! *(To the doctors)* We'll give you privacy to consult. *(One of the doctors coughs meaningfully)* Oh, I almost forgot . . . *(He pays each doctor then, taking* LISETTE *by the ear, steers her out. A long silence. Each doctor coughs importantly)*

LASTGASP: It's getting harder and harder to make my rounds.

BLEEDER: I know what you mean. Paris is getting too big.

---

[1] These may be the same actors who played AMINTE, LAPIDARE, LUCRECE and REDEW.

[2] Three excuses for this hoary gag: 1) It works. 2) Molière means the doctors to be burlesque figures, like the Marx Brothers. 3) I have an execrable sense of humor.—mk

LASTGASP: I've got a great horse. That's how I get around.

BLEEDER: A horse? Bah. I use a mule. It's incredible how far he can carry me in a day.

LASTGASP: My horse can go just as far and twice as fast.

BLEEDER: Possibly. But what do you think about the brouhaha between Doctor Thunderhoney and Doctor Blight? The whole faculty's taking sides.

LASTGASP: I support Doctor Blight.

BLEEDER *(nodding):* So do I. Thunderhoney had no business disputing the opinion of a colleague with seniority.

LASTGASP: He was right, though.

BLEEDER: So what? Blight was the physician of record. His treatment killed the patient, but that's besides the point. It's a matter of professional courtesy!

(SGANARELLE re-enters)

SGANARELLE: Gentlemen, my daughter's fading fast! How do you propose to treat her?

BLEEDER *(nodding to LASTGASP):* I defer to you, Doctor Lastgasp.

LASTGASP: No, no, Doctor Bleeder, you speak first.

BLEEDER: After you, sir.

LASTGASP: After you.

BLEEDER *(indicating the others):* Perhaps Doctor Blabber or Doctor Mumble would care to go first . . .

SGANARELLE: Will *somebody* please say *something?!* *(All four doctors talk at once, ad lib)* ONE AT A TIME!!!

BLEEDER: My opinion is, your daughter's blood is too hot. We have to bleed her.

LASTGASP: I don't think so. She's got bad things inside her.

SGANARELLE: How do we get them out?

LASTGASP: We have to make her throw up.

BLEEDER: I wouldn't do that. It might kill her.

LASTGASP: Well, bleeding would certainly finish her off.

BLEEDER: Nonsense!

LASTGASP: You bled that coachman.

BLEEDER: What about that lad you sent to his Maker yesterday?

LASTGASP: I don't have to sit here and take this. *(To SGANARELLE)* I gave you my advice. Induce vomiting.

BLEEDER: If you do, your daughter will be dead by tomorrow morning. Bleed her! *(Storms out)*

LASTGASP: If you do, she won't make it to morning! *(Exits)*

SGANARELLE: Now what do I do? *(To the remaining doctors)* I'm not a doctor. How am I supposed to know which treatment will save my daughter? Gentlemen, help me out here!

MUMBLE *(speaking v-e-r-y slowly):* We-e-e-e-ell, if you ask me—and you are —asking me—it's my considered opinion (and practice)—in cases like this—to proceed cautiously—carefully. Never do anything in haste. That's how to avoid making fatal mistakes.

SGANARELLE *(addressing* BLABBER*):* Do you agree with that?

BLABBER *(swiftly, but with a bad stutter):* A-a-a-a-absolutely! You've g-g-g-g-got to be v-v-very care-care-care-care-careful. M-m-m-make one f-f-f-f-false m-m-move and it's b-b-b-b-bye-bye p-p-patient! You've g-g-g-got to th-th-think this over v-v-very care-care-care-

SGANARELLE: I get the message!

MUMBLE *(same):* We-e-e-e-ell, since you've asked my opinion—it's my considered opinion—that your daughter's condition is chronic—and if you don't do anything about it—dangerous.

SGANARELLE: But what should I do?

BLABBER: In m-m-my opinion, we've g-got to l-l-loosen her up.

SGANARELLE: How?

BLABBER: G-g-g-g-give her an em-em-em-em-em-

SGANARELLE: An emetic?

BLABBER *(shaking his head):* An em-em-em-em-em-

SGANARELLE: Enema?

BLABBER *(blurting it out):* Emulsion! In a little syr-syr-syr-

SGANARELLE: Syringe?

BLABBER: Syrup.

MUMBLE *(same as before):* I agree—with Dr. Blabber's treatment. But *do* understand—your daughter—still—might—die.

BLABBER: B-b-but at least you'll know you d-d-d-did everything you c-c-c-c-could for her.

SGANARELLE *(ironically):* We-e-e-e-ell, since you've given me your opinion —it's my c-c-c-considered opinion—that you should both go to Hell!!! *(The doctors exit in a huff. To the audience)* How do you like that? Their advice isn't worth beans . . . and I paid good money for it!

(A QUACK *enters the theatre, singing)*

THE QUACK: I'm a curator of skills. I will cure you of your ills
               With my inexpensive pills—they are priceless!
               I've elixir that will ease any virulent disease—
               If you rub it on your cheese you'll be miceless!
               I can cure you, dinna doubt,
               Of the vapors, cough or gout,
               So just haul your money out:

Buy a box or bag or bottle.
If a minor ache you'd nix, buy a little of *this* mix;
If a major pain you'd fix, then buy a lottle! *(Exits)*

SGANARELLE *(chasing after him):* Wait! I'll buy whatever you've got . . . one of everything!

(Enter DOCTORS BLEEDER, GRUMBLE *and* LASTGASP*)*

GRUMBLE: You two should be ashamed of yourselves, arguing in front of a patient! It's bad enough that anybody can read the history of medicine and see how many disagreements there were amongst physicians of antiquity. All we've got is our pose. Lose that and what's left? Not that you're hurting me. I've had a profitable career and salted away a tidy sum, but if you want to do the same, remember, people have got to trust us. That's how we make a buck.

BLEEDER: In principle, I agree, but in practice, I'm furious.

LASTGASP: Look, I'm willing to compromise. *(To* BLEEDER*)* If you'll back up my diagnosis this time, I'll agree with whatever you prescribe for your next patient.

GRUMBLE: That's a handsome offer, Bleeder.

BLEEDER: Good enough for me. *(To* LASTGASP*)* Let's shake on it. (LASTGASP *and* BLEEDER *shake hands)*

LISETTE *(entering):* You doctors wouldn't look so pleased if you'd seen what I just saw.

GRUMBLE: What was that?

LISETTE: A fight. A man died, and guess what?

GRUMBLE: What?

LISETTE: The man who killed him wasn't even a doctor! *(She laughs at them as they leave, incensed)*

BLEEDER *(sticking his head back in):* Just you wait . . . we'll get YOU someday.

LISETTE: I'll die first! (BLEEDER *smiles at that notion and exits.* LISETTE *calls to someone offstage)* Come on in—my master's busy talking to some quack. (CLITANDER *enters, dressed like a doctor)*

CLITANDER: So how do I look, Lisette?

LISETTE: Terrific. My mistress fell for you one-two-three, and now I see why. I'm determined to liberate Lucinda from her father's tyrannic rule.

CLITANDER: How?

LISETTE: Easy . . . *(She whispers to him; he laughs)* Here he comes now. Wait in the other room till I call you. (CLITANDER *exits as* SGANARELLE *re-enters)*

SGANARELLE: Remarkable how cheap that fellow's remedies are.

LISETTE: Master, rejoice!

SGANARELLE: What?

LISETTE: Rejoice!

SGANARELLE: What for?

LISETTE: Rejoice, and I'll tell you.

SGANARELLE: Tell me some good news, and I'll rejoice.

LISETTE: No, rejoice first, then I'll tell you why.

SGANARELLE *(exasperated):* What do you expect, a song and dance?

LISETTE: That'd be nice.

SGANARELLE *(singing and dancing):* I'm doing what you said I should
Despite the fact I'm tired.
Your reason why had best be good
Or else I swear you're fired!

(Stops) Now what am I so blankety-blank happy about?

LISETTE: Your daughter is cured!

SGANARELLE: Cured?!

LISETTE: As good as cured. I found a new doctor.

SGANARELLE *(disappointed):* I've had my bellyful of doctors.

LISETTE: Not like this one. He's different.

SGANARELLE: How?

LISETTE: I'll show you . . . (LISETTE *waves offstage. Enter* CLITANDER) This is
Doctor Love.

SGANARELLE: He's too young.

LISETTE: He's old enough. Talk to him.

SGANARELLE: I've begun to think all doctors are scoundrels.

CLITANDER: I agree.

SGANARELLE: You do?

LISETTE: Except for him.

SGANARELLE: Hush! *(To* CLITANDER) My daughter is sick. I suppose you'll
want to bleed her or purge her or—

CLITANDER *(shakes his head):* No, no, I don't employ such techniques. My
treatment is entirely different.

SGANARELLE: In what way?

CLITANDER: I use the power of language to cure.

SGANARELLE: The—*what?*

CLITANDER: I weave a spell of words to charm the sufferer. A single dose
restores the ecstasy of health.

SGANARELLE *(interested):* A single dose? That can't cost too much.

CLITANDER: "Who chooseth me must give and hazard all he hath."

SGANARELLE: I knew it! Another money-leech!

CLITANDER: Sir, I spoke metaphorically. I charge no fees.

SGANARELLE: From one extreme to the other! How do you survive?

CLITANDER: I was born wealthy. I justify it with public service.

SGANARELLE: Dangerous idea. It'll never catch on.

LISETTE: Look, master, here comes Lucinda! The mere presence in the house of this marvelous physician has prompted her to quit her bedchamber.

(LUCINDA *enters*)

CLITANDER *(holding* SGANARELLE*'s wrist):* Hm. She's very sick.

SGANARELLE: How can you tell that from taking MY pulse?

CLITANDER: Father and daughter are one flesh.

LISETTE: Master, we'd better leave them alone with each other.

SGANARELLE: What for?

LISETTE: The doctor has to examine her . . . *(coughs)* privately.

SGANARELLE *(embarrassed):* Oh . . . yes, of course. *(To* CLITANDER*)* I'll be close by, in case you need me. (CLITANDER *nods.* SGANARELLE *and* LISETTE *exit)*

CLITANDER *(in a stage whisper):* I don't know what to say! When only our eyes spoke, I was eloquent. Now I'm dumb.

LUCINDA: Who needs words? *(They move nearer)*

SGANARELLE *(peeping in):* Why's he so close to her?

LISETTE: He's about to palpate. Don't watch. *(She yanks him offstage)*

CLITANDER: Will you always love me?

LUCINDA: Ever and ever. Will you?

CLITANDER: My whole life through! Kiss me! *(They kiss)*

SGANARELLE *(re-entering):* So how's she doing? She looks lots better.

CLITANDER *(taking him aside;* sotto voce*):* That's just temporary. She's suffering from a debased urge to get married. Of course, that would be the worst thing you could let her do.

SGANARELLE *(to audience):* What a wise doctor!

CLITANDER: People afflicted with such a delusion will never relinquish it willingly. I had to pretend to her that I'm not a doctor, but a young man about to ask you for her hand in marriage. As soon as she thought she was going to be betrothed, her eyes brightened and her spirits soared.

SGANARELLE: But what happens when she learns there's not going to be a ceremony?

CLITANDER: Her condition is still too chancy for that. It would be dangerous for her to learn the truth.

SGANARELLE: What do you recommend?

CLITANDER: For now, we must encourage her notion that she and I are about to be wed. Once she's healthy again, I'll induce a long-range therapy to destroy her delusions.

SGANARELLE: Brilliant! *(To* LUCINDA*)* Child, this gentleman wants to marry you. I've told him it's all right.

LUCINDA: Oh, Daddy, truly?

SGANARELLE: Truly.

CLITANDER *(to* SGANARELLE*)*: Note her color immediately improves.

LUCINDA *(to* CLITANDER*)*: You really want to marry me?

CLITANDER: I certainly do.

LUCINDA: My father actually agrees?

CLITANDER *(to* SGANARELLE*)*: Look at her eyes light up.

SGANARELLE: Yes, my darling daughter, yes!

LUCINDA: I'm afraid to believe this is true. *(To* CLITANDER*)* Why are you all dressed up like a doctor?

CLITANDER *(winking at* SGANARELLE*)*: I've been in love with you for a long time, but didn't know how to reach you. These doctor's robes are just a trick to fool your father.

SGANARELLE *(to audience, laughing):* Have you ever seen such a smart doctor?!

LUCINDA *(to* CLITANDER*)*: Now I understand. You're so clever!

SGANARELLE *(to audience, laughing):* Have you ever seen such a gullible girl?

CLITANDER *(on his knees):* Lucinda, will you marry me?

LUCINDA: If my father accepts you, how can I possibly refuse?

SGANARELLE *(dotingly to audience):* She's always been a good girl.

CLITANDER: With this ring, I thee wed. *(To* SGANARELLE*)* It has psychotherapeutic properties.

SGANARELLE *(sagaciously):* Oh, of course!

LUCINDA: Now all we need is a notary.

SGANARELLE: A . . . what?

LUCINDA *(frowning):* A notary! To draft the marriage contract.

SGANARELLE: But . . . ahhh—

CLITANDER *(whispering to* SGANARELLE*)*: She's growing pale again. We mustn't contradict her. She'll suffer a relapse.

SGANARELLE *(reluctantly):* Well, if it's absolutely necessary . . . *(Calls)* Lisette! (LISETTE *enters with a* NOTARY)

LISETTE: Yes, master?

SGANARELLE: Go fetch a notary.

LISETTE: He's here.

SGANARELLE *(gaping at* NOTARY, *then regarding* CLITANDER *suspiciously):* What's going on here?

CLITANDER *(drawing him aside):* This young man works for me. I anticipated your daughter might do this, so rather than cause you the embarrassment—and expense—of sending for a real notary, if the need arose I instructed my apprentice to pose as one.

SGANARELLE *(to audience):* Have you ever seen such a marvelous doctor? *(To* NOTARY*)* So you're a notary, sir?

NOTARY: That's what I am. How may I serve you?

SGANARELLE: By drawing up a marriage contract right away.

NOTARY: Tell me the names of the bride and her father.

SGANARELLE *(to* NOTARY, *who writes):* L-U-C-I-N-D-A, daughter of *(slowly)* S . . . G . . . uh—*(Hesitates)*

LISETTE *(swiftly):* A-N-A-R-E-L-L-E!

SGANARELLE: As a dowry, I give her half my estate. *(Winking at* CLITANDER*)* Write that down, Notary.

LUCINDA: Thank you, Daddy!

NOTARY: It's writ. I've got the bridegroom's signature already. As soon as you and the bride sign it, the wedding's official.

SGANARELLE *(taking contract, suddenly suspicious):* How did you manage to write so much so fast?

*(*LISETTE *claps a hand over* NOTARY*'s mouth)*

CLITANDER *(drawing* SGANARELLE *aside):* He prepared it in advance.

SGANARELLE *(pointing to contract):* But it looks real.

CLITANDER: It is. I bought a blank contract from a real notary.

SGANARELLE: Why?

CLITANDER: Your daughter's too smart to be fooled by a fake one.

SGANARELLE: But how did you know before you even examined her—

LUCINDA: Oh! Oh! I'm feeling sick again!

LISETTE: Master, your daughter's going to faint!

CLITANDER: She's having a relapse!

SGANARELLE: My darling child! No!

CLITANDER: Quickly . . . sign the contract, before it's too late!

SGANARELLE: All right, I'm signing it! *(Runs to* LUCINDA *and puts the contract in her hands)* Lucinda, look! All you've got to do is sign this, and you're a bride!

LUCINDA: I . . . I don't . . . have . . . enough strength left.

SGANARELLE: Here, Daddy will help you . . . *(He guides her hand)* There! *(Crooning)* Now you're all-ll-ll married!

LUCINDA *(jumping up and throws her arms round* SGANARELLE*):* Oh, Daddy, thank you, thank you! You've made me the happiest woman in the world!

SGANARELLE *(overjoyed):* It's the cure of the century!

CLITANDER *(taking* LISETTE*'s hand):* Yes, but now it's time for the long-range therapy I told you about.

SGANARELLE *(to* LISETTE): To cure her of her romantic delusions.

LISETTE: Marriage will do that.

SGANARELLE *(to* LISETTE): Marriage? What are you talking about? This wasn't real.

CLITANDER: Come, my bride, our carriage is waiting.

SGANARELLE: A carriage? What for?

CLITANDER: Her long-range therapy begins abroad.

(CLITANDER *exits with* LUCINDA, *who blows a kiss to her father and* LISETTE *as she goes)*

SGANARELLE *(calling after them):* Abroad? Abroad?! Who's paying for this trip?

LISETTE *(aside):* You are, master, with half of your estate.

SGANARELLE: What kind of therapy requires foreign travel?

LISETTE: I know all about it. It's a very old cure.

SGANARELLE: It is? What do you call it?

LISETTE: A honeymoon.

(SGANARELLE *looks horrified. Curtain.)*

THE SERVANT OF TWO MASTERS

by
Carlo Goldoni
Adapted by Marvin Kaye

CARLO GOLDONI (1709–93), a native of Venice, is one of Italy's most important dramatists, yet few of his two hundred and fifty plays (one hundred and fifty of them comedies) have been translated into English. His work includes such masterpieces as "The Benevolent Despot," "The Fan," "The Mistress of the Inn" and "The Venetian Twins," historically significant as the first play in which commedia dell'arte actors trepidatiously, at the playwright's insistence, performed without masks . . . and were a great success.

When Goldoni took up residency in Paris, the French nicknamed him "the Italian Molière." There is indeed a stylistic resemblance to Molière in Goldoni's later works, but THE SERVANT OF TWO MASTERS, an earlier composition, is thoroughly Italianate. It employs—and humanizes —several stock commedia characters, notably Pantalone, whose archetypal miserliness is subdued, though far from gone. Now he loves his daughter almost as much as his fortune.

The titular Truffaldino, a transmogrification of Punch, is one of literature's great comic servants and possibly the first example in the history of domestic employment of "moonlighting."

CAST OF CHARACTERS

PANTALONE, a merchant of Venice
CLARICE, his daughter
SMERALDINA, her maid
LOMBARDI, a doctor
SILVIO, his son
BEATRICE, a woman of Turin, disguised
FLORINDO, a gentleman of Turin
BRIGHELLA, an innkeeper
TRUFFALDINO, the servant of two masters
Two porters
A waiter

ACT I

Scene One

A town square in Venice. PANTALONE'*s house is at one side, the Eagle Inn at the other.* SILVIO *and* CLARICE *are holding hands in a public declaration of their intent to wed. With them are* PANTALONE, DOCTOR LOMBARDI, SMERALDINA *and* BRIGHELLA.

PANTALONE *(indicating each as he names them):* Today marks the betrothal of my child Clarice to young Silvio, son of the estimable Doctor Lombardi. Two witnesses are customary, so I've asked my friend and neighbor, Brighella, proprietor of the Eagle Inn, to act in that capacity with my daughter's maid, Smeraldina.

SMERALDINA *(aside):* I'd rather be getting married myself.

PANTALONE: Now it's time for you children to exchange vows.

SILVIO: My heart and hand are yours, Clarice.

CLARICE: My hand and heart are yours, Silvio.

SILVIO: I vow to be your loving husband.

CLARICE: I vow to be your loving wife.

LOMBARDI: That makes it official. No changing your minds now.

SILVIO: No danger of that. I'm supremely happy. Though I can't answer for my beloved bride Clarice.

CLARICE: Silvio, you wrong me! I've always loved you!

SILVIO: But you *were* betrothed to another . . .

CLARICE: That was only because I'm an obedient daughter.

PANTALONE: That's true, sir. I was the one who arranged for Clarice to marry Signor Federigo Rasponi of Turin.

BRIGHELLA: I knew Federigo Rasponi. A fine young man with a remarkable sister, Beatrice.

PANTALONE: Remarkable? How?

BRIGHELLA: For one thing, she could ride a horse as good as a man—and always did it dressed in trousers.

LOMBARDI: Good God!

BRIGHELLA *(to* PANTALONE): How well did you know Federigo?

PANTALONE: We never actually met. I'd been doing business with him, and my bankers spoke so highly of him that I decided to make him my son-in-law, sight unseen. But I just got word that he's been killed in a duel—

BRIGHELLA: What was Federigo fighting about?

PANTALONE: Something to do with his sister. *(To* SILVIO) So that's how I'm able to offer Clarice to you.

SILVIO: I'll do my best to make her happy, sir.

CLARICE: Father, with your permission . . . ?

PANTALONE: What?

CLARICE: Silvio and I would like to be excused.

PANTALONE: What?

CLARICE: We'd like to retire.

PANTALONE: Where to?

CLARICE: My room.

PANTALONE: No, no, no, not just yet, you little lovebirds.

LOMBARDI: There's still the blessing of the priest to come.

PANTALONE: Yes, and a fancy dinner at Brighella's inn—

(Enter TRUFFALDINO)

TRUFFALDINO: Ladies and gentlemen, I bring you greetings!

PANTALONE: Greetings? Who from?

TRUFFALDINO (indicating CLARICE): Who might this lovely lady be?

PANTALONE: Why—my daughter.

SMERALDINA: She just exchanged her marriage vows.

TRUFFALDINO: My condolences. Who might you be?

SMERALDINA: I'm her maid.

TRUFFALDINO: Well, I suppose I should offer my congratulations.

PANTALONE: But why? What do you want? Who sent you?

TRUFFALDINO: Please, sir, take it easy! Three questions at a time is too
   much for a poor soul like me to handle.

PANTALONE (to the doctor): The man's an ass!

LOMBARDI: Or pretending to be.

TRUFFALDINO (to SMERALDINA): Are you getting married, too?

SMERALDINA: Don't I wish!

PANTALONE: Will you please either tell us who you are or go away?

TRUFFALDINO: Oh, you want to know I am? I'm a servant. (To SMERALDINA)
   So marriage appeals to you, hm?

PANTALONE: Whose servant?

TRUFFALDINO: What?

PANTALONE: Whose . . . servant . . . are . . . you?

TRUFFALDINO: My master's.

LOMBARDI: Look here, sir, where is your master?

TRUFFALDINO: At the inn. He sent me on ahead to greet you.

PANTALONE: Who did?

TRUFFALDINO: My master did.

PANTALONE: WHAT'S YOUR MASTER'S NAME?!

TRUFFALDINO: Oh, didn't I say that? Federigo Rasponi of Turin. (Shocked
   silence) Now if that's all, I'll go and—

PANTALONE: Hold on there! What was that name?

TRUFFALDINO: My name is Truffaldino Battocchio of Bergamo.

PANTALONE: Who cares? What's your master's name?

TRUFFALDINO: Signor Federigo Rasponi of Turin. Why do you all look so surprised?

PANTALONE: Because he's dead!

TRUFFALDINO: Who's dead?

PANTALONE: Federigo Rasponi!

TRUFFALDINO: Good God, he must've had an accident! *(Rushes out)*

PANTALONE: What do you think? Is he a scoundrel or a dolt?

LOMBARDI: Equal parts of both, I suspect.

BRIGHELLA: He's more likely to be a dolt than dishonest.

PANTALONE: What makes you think that?

BRIGHELLA: He comes from Bergamo.

PANTALONE: Good point.

SMERALDINA *(aside):* Personally, I like him.

CLARICE *(to* SILVIO*):* What if he *is* still alive?

SILVIO: What if he is? You're mine now!

TRUFFALDINO *(returning):* I'm really upset. Is this the way Venetian gentlemen behave to poor, hard-working servants? For shame!

PANTALONE: What's the matter with you?

TRUFFALDINO: Did you or did you not just tell me that Signor Federigo Rasponi is dead?

PANTALONE: I did.

TRUFFALDINO: Why?

PANTALONE: Because he's dead!

TRUFFALDINO: He is not! I just saw him.

PANTALONE: Federigo Rasponi?

TRUFFALDINO: Yes.

PANTALONE: Of Turin?

TRUFFALDINO: Yes.

PANTALONE: You're out of your mind!

LOMBARDI: Calm down, Pantalone. Let's meet this chap who seems to have risen from the dead.

PANTALONE: Yes, go and fetch him, young man.

TRUFFALDINO: Gladly!

*(*TRUFFALDINO *exits.* BEATRICE *enters, disguised as a man.* BRIGHELLA *starts)*

BEATRICE: Signor Pantalone, in business you always used me with the utmost courtesy, but today you've treated my servant shabbily and kept me waiting forever.

PANTALONE: Look, sir, meaning no offense, but—who *are* you?

BEATRICE: Why, Federigo Rasponi of Turin.

PANTALONE: Well, sir, we're glad to see you alive.

BEATRICE: So that's what this is all about! You must have heard the report that I'd been slain in a duel.

PANTALONE: We did.

BEATRICE: I was wounded, that's all. As soon as I was well enough to travel, I started off for Venice. Now I'm here and we can proceed with our nuptial plans.

PANTALONE: Excuse me for not taking you at your word, but I was told by quite reliable sources that you—that Federigo Rasponi—is dead.

BEATRICE: I understand. We never met before, so it's only natural for you to want proof of my identity. *(She hands him some letters)* These are letters from several of our mutual business associates, including the manager of the bank that we both use in Turin.

CLARICE: Ah, Silvio, all is lost.

SILVIO: Before I lose you, I'll lose my life.

(While PANTALONE *inspects the letters,* BEATRICE *notices* BRIGHELLA *for the first time. She stiffens)*

BEATRICE: Excuse me, sir . . . your face looks familiar.

BRIGHELLA: I think I recognize you, too—*sir.* My name is Brighella Gaviochi. I run that inn.

BEATRICE: Excellent. I'll stay there, if you have the room.

BRIGHELLA: My establishment will be honored—*sir.*

BEATRICE *(to* PANTALONE): Still skeptical? This man knows me.

PANTALONE: You do?

BRIGHELLA: I've known—Federigo Rasponi—for years.

CLARICE: Father, is this gentleman really Signor Rasponi?

PANTALONE: He seems to be. He almost got here too late.

LOMBARDI: What do you mean, "almost?"

BEATRICE: Sir, may I ask who that young woman is?

PANTALONE: Her? That's my daughter.

BEATRICE: My bride-to-be?

PANTALONE: Er—yes.

BEATRICE: Madame, it's an honor to meet you at last.

CLARICE *(stiffly):* Likewise, I'm sure.

BEATRICE: Your daughter is somewhat aloof, sir.

CLARICE: Somewhat.

BEATRICE *(sees* SILVIO): Is this man one of your relatives?

PANTALONE: He's my nephew!

SILVIO: I am not! I'm his daughter's intended husband.

BEATRICE: I beg your pardon! She's been promised to me.

PANTALONE: When I heard you were dead, I told my daughter she could marry Silvio. But you're alive, so we'll go ahead with our original plans. I'm sorry to disappoint you, Silvio, but you see the spot I'm in.

SILVIO: We exchanged our vows in front of witnesses. Anyone who tries to part us will confront my sword.

LOMBARDI: My son *shall* wed her! The law's on our side! (LOMBARDI *and* SILVIO *exit*)

BEATRICE: And what about you, fair lady? Where do you stand?

CLARICE: Did you happen to notice a shriveled-up old peddler selling dried fruit on the street corner?

BEATRICE: Yes, I did. Why?

CLARICE: I would sooner marry him than you! *(She exits)*

PANTALONE: Stop! You little vixen, how dare you—

BEATRICE: Peace, Signor Pantalone, it's not the moment to be harsh with her. A time will come when she'll think better of me. But for now, let's turn aside from affairs of the heart and concentrate on business.

PANTALONE: Good idea. My books are ready for your inspection. When does the rest of the merchandise arrive?

BEATRICE: Tomorrow.

PANTALONE: Your money will be waiting for you promptly.

BEATRICE: Could you let me have a little in advance? I don't travel with much cash, for fear of highway robbery.

PANTALONE: Very sensible of you. I'll send some money to your lodgings. You're staying with my friend Brighella?

BEATRICE: That's right. But don't trouble yourself. I'll send my servant. He's honest. You met him.

PANTALONE: Oh, yes . . . but it's no trouble at all.

(Enter SMERALDINA)

SMERALDINA: Sir, you'd better come home and talk to my mistress.

PANTALONE: I suppose I must. *(To BRIGHELLA)* Take good care of Signor Federigo. *(To BEATRICE)* Till we meet again. *(He exits with SMERALDINA)*

BRIGHELLA: All right now, Signora Beatrice, what is all of this about? Why are you pretending to be your brother? I know that he's really dead.

BEATRICE: Yes, Florindo Aretusi killed him in a duel.

BRIGHELLA: What was the fight about?

BEATRICE: Me. Florindo and I want to get married, but my brother objected. They fought. Federigo fell.

BRIGHELLA: Where's Florindo now? In jail?

BEATRICE: No, he fled here to Venice.

BRIGHELLA: So that's what you're doing here?

BEATRICE: That's one reason. The other's harsh reality.

BRIGHELLA: Meaning?

BEATRICE: Meaning how do I survive if I can't collect the money Signor Pantalone owes my brother?

BRIGHELLA: But Pantalone is my friend! I can't hold my tongue while you cheat him.

BEATRICE: I'm not. The money's due my brother. I'm his heir.

BRIGHELLA: Hm. You're absolutely right. Then why not tell the truth, instead of performing this strange charade?

BEATRICE: Because I'm a woman. If Pantalone knew the truth, he'd act like my guardian and dole out my money.

BRIGHELLA: Would that be so terrible?

BEATRICE: Yes. Without total control of the cash due me, I can't locate Florindo and help him.

BRIGHELLA: So that's what's behind all this!

BEATRICE: Yes. Will you keep my secret? Please?

BRIGHELLA: As long as I can do so honorably.

BEATRICE: That's all I ask. Now where did Truffaldino go?

BRIGHELLA: That man's an ass. Where'd you find him?

BEATRICE: During my journey to Venice. He does behave foolishly at times, but he's honest and loyal.

BRIGHELLA: Well, that's something. Come on, let me show you to your room.

(They exit. TRUFFALDINO *enters)*

TRUFFALDINO: This is ridiculous. It's half past twelve and I haven't had a bite to eat. Other masters that I worked for would go to an inn like this as soon as we got into town, but this one—oh, no! He leaves his luggage on the dock and runs off to see people. I'm supposed to hang around waiting for him, but if I had a few cents to my name, I'd go inside and have something to eat. Unfortunately, I'm broke.

(A PORTER *enters, lugging a trunk, followed by* FLORINDO)

PORTER: This is too heavy. I can't carry it a foot farther.

FLORINDO: Just a few more steps. I'll stop at that inn.

PORTER *(drops trunk):* Good for you. I'm stopping right here.

TRUFFALDINO: Here's a chance to earn my dinner! *(To* FLORINDO) Can I be of assistance, sir? My name is Truffaldino.

FLORINDO: Thank you. Carry my trunk into that inn, please.

TRUFFALDINO: Glad to. *(He picks it up)* It's not that heavy.

(As TRUFFALDINO *exits with the trunk, the* PORTER *approaches* FLORINDO *with his hand out)*

FLORINDO: Well, what do you want?

PORTER: My pay.

FLORINDO: What for?

PORTER: For carrying your trunk.

FLORINDO: The dock's not thirty feet from where you dropped it. How much is that worth? *(Gives him a coin)*

PORTER: A penny? Are you trying to insult me?

FLORINDO: All right, here's one more. That's enough.

PORTER: No, sir, it isn't. I want more!

FLORINDO: You do, eh? *(He smacks him)* Is THAT enough?

PORTER: Yes, sir. Goodbye!

(He runs off as TRUFFALDINO *re-enters)*

TRUFFALDINO: Everything's ready, sir. Your trunk's inside and, if you like, the owner's got a room waiting for you.

FLORINDO: Can you recommend this place?

TRUFFALDINO: I've heard it's got good beds and the kitchen certainly smells promising.

FLORINDO: Tell me, sir, what business are you in?

TRUFFALDINO: Me? I'm a servant.

FLORINDO: Whose?

TRUFFALDINO: Well—

FLORINDO: I ask because I could use a servant myself, while I'm in Venice.

TRUFFALDINO: You could?

FLORINDO: I'll pay fair wages and meals included, of course.

TRUFFALDINO: Of course.

FLORINDO: If you're free, you could start right now.

TRUFFALDINO: In time for lunch?

FLORINDO: Certainly. What do you say?

TRUFFALDINO: I say—at the moment, I'm without a master.

FLORINDO: Well, now you have one. *(He gives him some money)* Begin by finding out whether any letters have arrived on the post from Turin in the name of Florindo Aretusi.

TRUFFALDINO: While I'm doing that, will you see that dinner is ready and waiting when I get back?

FLORINDO *(laughing):* Yes. I'll order something as saucy as your tongue. *(He exits)*

TRUFFALDINO: Thus I improve my income and finally get something to eat! My other master, the one who doesn't have a beard, is nowhere to be seen, so I might as well go and check the post for Signor Florindo.

(Enter BEATRICE)

BEATRICE: There you are. I've been looking all over for you. Fetch my trunk from the dock. Bring it to my room.

TRUFFALDINO: Which is where?

BEATRICE: Right here.

TRUFFALDINO: *This* inn?

BEATRICE: Yes. And check the post from Turin to see if there are letters for me or my sister, Beatrice. *(Exits)*

TRUFFALDINO: Well, here's a complication. Both masters staying at the same inn. Can I pull it off? Double wages and twice as much to eat . . . the worst that can happen is one of them will find out and fire me, but I'll still have the other job. It's worth a try. Let's see . . . the trunk can wait. First I'll check the Turin post on behalf of both masters.

(Enter SILVIO*)*

SILVIO: Excuse me. Where's your master?

TRUFFALDINO *(confused):* My master? Which?

SILVIO: Where is he?

TRUFFALDINO: Well, he's staying at this inn.

SILVIO: I want to talk to him. Call him out.

TRUFFALDINO: But—

SILVIO: What are you waiting for?

TRUFFALDINO: If you could just give me a name—

SILVIO: Tell him Silvio Lombardi demands to see him.

TRUFFALDINO: No, you don't understand. I have to know—

SILVIO: You heard all you need to know. Now get a move on.

TRUFFALDINO: But—

SILVIO: Move! Or else!

TRUFFALDINO: I'm moving! *(Aside)* I'll send out whichever master I run into first. *(He exits into the inn)*

SILVIO: We'll see about this! If Rasponi insists on marrying Clarice, he'll have to fight another duel and this time Signor Federigo might not be so lucky.

(Enter TRUFFALDINO, *followed by* FLORINDO*)*

TRUFFALDINO: There's the hothead I told you about, sir.

FLORINDO: I never set eyes on him before. What's he want?

TRUFFALDINO: Beats me. I'll go see about your mail. *(He exits)*

FLORINDO: Sir, you wanted to see me?

SILVIO: Me? You? What for?

FLORINDO: I was told you asked for me in no uncertain terms.

SILVIO: Who told you that?

FLORINDO: The fellow heading off in that direction.

SILVIO: That figures. I told him I wanted to see his master.

FLORINDO: Well, that's me.

SILVIO: You're his master?

FLORINDO: Yes.

SILVIO: I'm sorry. This is my fault. Your servant's a dead ringer for a man I met this morning.

FLORINDO: An honest mistake. No need to apologize.

SILVIO: Are you new in town?

FLORINDO: Yes. I just arrived from Turin.

SILVIO: Turin? The man I'm waiting for comes from Turin.

FLORINDO: Oh? What's his name?

SILVIO: Federigo Rasponi. Do you know him?

FLORINDO: Only too well. What quarrel did you have with him?

SILVIO: He's trying to take away the woman I love.

FLORINDO: Set your mind at ease. Federigo Rasponi is dead.

SILVIO: That's what we all thought till he arrived today.

FLORINDO: God forbid! Look, I know he's dead.

SILVIO: He showed up today. The innkeeper recognized him.

FLORINDO *(aside):* He must've survived the duel, after all.

SILVIO: I'm surprised you haven't run into him yet.

FLORINDO: Venice is a big place.

SILVIO: But you're both staying at the Eagle Inn!

FLORINDO: He's here, too?!

SILVIO: Yes.

FLORINDO: So am I.

SILVIO: Anyway, I'm sorry I troubled you. If you do run into him, though, tell him for his own good, he'd better forget about marrying Clarice.

FLORINDO: You may depend on me, sir.

SILVIO: By the way, I'm Silvio Lombardi.

FLORINDO: Pleased to meet you. I'm—Orazio Ardenti. *(They shake hands.* SILVIO *exits)* If he's really still alive, I'd better hurry back to Turin before Beatrice thinks I ran out on her.

(TRUFFALDINO *enters, carrying* BEATRICE*'s trunk)*

TRUFFALDINO: Whoops! There's my other master. How do I explain this trunk? *(He puts it just offstage)*

FLORINDO: Ah, Truffaldino, there you are. Will you come with me when I travel to Turin?

TRUFFALDINO: Turin? When are you going there?

FLORINDO: Immediately. *(Sees his consternation)* Don't be upset. We'll have dinner first.

TRUFFALDINO: Well, that's a relief. After dinner, we'll talk.

FLORINDO: Did you go to the post?

TRUFFALDINO: Yes, sir. *(He produces three letters, then pauses)*

FLORINDO: Well, let me have them.

TRUFFALDINO *(aside):* Damn! I've got letters for both masters, but I don't know which is which!

FLORINDO: Come on, what are you waiting for?

TRUFFALDINO: It's like this. I met a servant I used to work with in Bergamo. Since I was going to the post anyway, I told him I'd see if there was any mail for *his* master. There was. One of these belongs to him.

FLORINDO: So what's the problem? Keep it and give me the rest.

TRUFFALDINO: The problem is, I don't know how to read.

FLORINDO: Then give them to me. I'll return the one that isn't mine. *(He takes the letters and looks at them)* Here it is. *(Aside)* Good Lord, it's a letter to Beatrice! "Beatrice Rasponi, Venice." She's here!

TRUFFALDINO: Is that the letter for my friend's master?

FLORINDO: Yes. Look here, what's your friend's name?

TRUFFALDINO: His name? Uh . . . Pasquale.

FLORINDO: Who's his master?

TRUFFALDINO: How should I know?

FLORINDO: You have to know—you picked up his mail!

TRUFFALDINO: No, he wrote it for me on a piece of paper.

FLORINDO: Let me see the paper.

TRUFFALDINO: I lost it.

FLORINDO: Oh, hell!

TRUFFALDINO *(aside):* I'm improvising like mad!

FLORINDO: Where is this Pasquale staying in Venice?

TRUFFALDINO: I don't know.

FLORINDO: Then how can you give him his master's letter?

TRUFFALDINO: We're meeting at the Piazza. Now can I have it back?

FLORINDO: I have to open it first.

TRUFFALDINO: No, don't! It's wrong to open other people's mail!

FLORINDO: This letter's addressed to someone I'm involved with. I have the right to open it. *(He does so)*

TRUFFALDINO: If you say so, sir.

FLORINDO *(reads letter):* "Dear Madame Rasponi, your decision to leave Turin has provoked gossip. Everyone thinks you're going to rendezvous with Florindo. Legal authorities found out you're dressed as a man. They ordered your arrest. I'm posting this by an indirect route. Your devoted servant, Antonio."

TRUFFALDINO: I don't care what he says. You shouldn't read other people's mail!

FLORINDO: What a state of things! Federigo alive, Beatrice disguised as a man and both of them in Venice! The lady certainly loves me. Truffaldino!

TRUFFALDINO: Sir?

FLORINDO: Find this Pasquale and bring him here at once!

TRUFFALDINO: I'll do what I can. Give me back the letter.

FLORINDO *(doing so):* This matter's very important to me. Hurry and there's money in it for you and Pasquale both.

TRUFFALDINO: How do I explain his master's letter being open?

FLORINDO: Make something up. Say it was an accident. *(Exits)*

TRUFFALDINO: Two masters, and not a meal between them! Meanwhile, how can I give this to Master Number One? "Make something up." I'm worn out, making things up. Let me think—Grandma used to seal letters with a slice of chewed-up bread. *(He goes into the inn and comes out with a small piece of bread)* It's a shame to waste this . . . *(he bites off a bit, chews and swallows it)* Damn! I forgot! *(He chews and puts the mess on the letter)* All right, all sealed. Now to deliver it—wait, I forgot the trunk!

(As he gets it, BEATRICE *emerges from the inn)*

BEATRICE: That my trunk?

TRUFFALDINO: Yes, sir.

BEATRICE: Take it to my room . . . wait. Did I get any letters?

TRUFFALDINO: One.

BEATRICE *(taking it):* This has been opened.

TRUFFALDINO: Opened?! It can't be!

BEATRICE: It was opened and stuck together with bread.

TRUFFALDINO: But who would do that?

BEATRICE: Suppose you tell me!

TRUFFALDINO: All right, I confess. I did it by accident.

BEATRICE: What kind of accident?

TRUFFALDINO: There was a letter for me, too. I opened yours, thinking it was mine.

BEATRICE: Why would you do that?

TRUFFALDINO: I can't read.

BEATRICE: Then why—oh, never mind. No one else saw this?

TRUFFALDINO *(indignantly):* Absolutely not!

BEATRICE *(reads):* Oh, dear. I hope he told the truth this time. *(To* TRUFFALDINO) Here, take my keys, go to my room and unpack my things. When I get back, we'll have dinner.

TRUFFALDINO: That'd be nice. *(He takes the trunk into the inn)*

BEATRICE *(aside):* I'd better remind Pantalone about my money.

(As BEATRICE *crosses to* PANTALONE'*s house,* PANTALONE *emerges from it, but they do not see one another. She exits into his house.* PANTALONE *crosses to the inn as* TRUFFALDINO *comes out for the trunk)*

TRUFFALDINO: So far, so good. I'm managing this mess rather well!

PANTALONE: Hey, you!

TRUFFALDINO: Now what?! *(Puts down the trunk)* Yes, sir?

PANTALONE: Is your master in?

TRUFFALDINO: Sorry, he's out.

PANTALONE: Will he be back soon?

TRUFFALDINO: I suppose.

PANTALONE: Well, he told me you were honest . . . *(He hands a purse to* TRUFFALDINO) Please give him this money.

TRUFFALDINO: Give *who* this money?

PANTALONE: Your master. *(Murmurs)* What an idiot! *(He exits)*

TRUFFALDINO: WHICH master?! *(Perplexed)* Now what do I do?

*(*FLORINDO *enters)*

FLORINDO: Did you find Pasquale for me?

TRUFFALDINO: Not yet. Sir, does anyone owe you any money?

FLORINDO: As a matter of fact, yes. This morning, I presented a letter of credit to a merchant. Why?

TRUFFALDINO *(hands him the purse):* Then this must be yours.

FLORINDO *(looks inside):* A sizable sum. How'd you get this?

TRUFFALDINO: An old man gave it to me.

FLORINDO: Just like that? What did he say?

TRUFFALDINO: To give it to my master.

FLORINDO: Well, that's what you did. Thanks.

TRUFFALDINO *(aside):* I hope I got this one right.

FLORINDO: Are you ready for dinner now?

TRUFFALDINO: Am I? You bet!

FLORINDO: Let's order our meal, then afterward you can resume your search for Pasquale.

(They exit. CLARICE *bursts out of her house with* PANTALONE *following)*

PANTALONE: Now look, I gave my word and that's that. You're going to marry Signor Rasponi.

CLARICE: If I have to, I will, but I won't like it.

PANTALONE: The first time I mentioned Signor Federigo, you didn't object. If you had, I would have listened.

CLARICE: I'm a dutiful daughter. I held my tongue.

PANTALONE: Then why don't you hold it now?!

CLARICE: Signor Federigo is hateful.
PANTALONE: Forget about Silvio and Federigo won't look so bad.
CLARICE: I can't! I won't!

(SMERALDINA *enters*)

SMERALDINA: Master, Signor Rasponi has been waiting to see you.
PANTALONE: Excuse me, child! *(He goes inside)* Signor!
SMERALDINA: Mistress, you've been crying!
CLARICE *(crossing away from her)*: Well, of course I have!
SMERALDINA: I wonder where that adorable Truffaldino went to?

(PANTALONE *and* BEATRICE *come out*)

BEATRICE: You say you gave my servant the money?
PANTALONE: You told me he was honest.
BEATRICE: Well, he is. I'll get it from him soon. But look at your daughter
   . . . her eyes are all red.
PANTALONE: Talk to her. Maybe you can cheer her up. *(He snaps his fingers*
   at SMERALDINA *and the two of them exit)*
BEATRICE: Dear lady—
CLARICE: Don't call me "dear."
BEATRICE: If you'll just listen to me, I think—
CLARICE: Every word you say makes me hate you more.
BEATRICE: Hear me out. I promise you'll be pleased.
CLARICE: Silvio pleases me. You don't.
BEATRICE: Look, can you keep a secret?
CLARICE: Not yours.
BEATRICE: I'll tell you, anyway.
CLARICE: I'm not listening.
BEATRICE: I don't want to marry you, either.
CLARICE: I'm listening. *(Frowns)* Why not?
BEATRICE: Because I love someone else. *Now* will you promise to keep my
   secret?
CLARICE: Yes, with all my heart.
BEATRICE: Federigo Rasponi really was killed in that duel.
CLARICE: Then who are you?
BEATRICE: His sister Beatrice.
CLARICE: What?! You're a woman?
BEATRICE: Give me your hand. *(She guides it to her bosom)*
CLARICE: You *are* a woman! Wait till I tell Silvio!
BEATRICE: Not yet! You promised.
CLARICE: I did. But how long will this masquerade continue?
BEATRICE: Not long. So . . . are we friends now?

CLARICE: Absolutely! *(They embrace.* PANTALONE *enters)*

PANTALONE *(misunderstanding):* Splendid, splendid! *(To* CLARICE) I knew you'd change your mind, child. We'll hold the wedding immediately.

CLARICE: Father! There's no need to rush things!

PANTALONE: Come, come now, hugging one another in public? It's obvious neither of you can contain yourselves.

BEATRICE: Signor, you forget we've got business pending, not to mention the marriage settlement to work out.

PANTALONE: Those things won't take long. But very well, we'll put off the wedding till tomorrow. Now I'd better go tell Signor Silvio what's what.

CLARICE: No, don't upset him!

PANTALONE: Would you rather have two husbands? Signor, till we meet again . . . *(He exits)*

CLARICE: You've got to tell him the truth!

BEATRICE: As soon as I can.

(They exit. FLORINDO *comes out of the inn, pursued by* TRUFFALDINO)

FLORINDO *(aside):* I've no appetite. I've got to find Beatrice!

TRUFFALDINO: Sir, where on earth are you going?

FLORINDO: I've important business to take care of.

TRUFFALDINO: But we were just about to order dinner!

FLORINDO: Order it for me. I'll be back soon. *(He exits)*

TRUFFALDINO: I'll never get anything to eat today!

(He exits. SILVIO *and his father enter)*

SILVIO: Will you please stop following me?

LOMBARDI: Not till I know what you're up to.

SILVIO: I'm going to have a talk with Clarice's father.

LOMBARDI: In the temper you're in? Absolutely not! Leave him to me. I'll talk to him.

SILVIO: But—

LOMBARDI: Did you hear me? Go somewhere and wait for me.

SILVIO: I'll be at the druggist's. Talk some sense into Signor Pantalone. If you don't, I will! *(Exits)*

LOMBARDI: Hmph. I've got my own temper to contend with.

*(*PANTALONE *enters)*

PANTALONE: There you are, Doctor! You weren't at home.

LOMBARDI: Ah, you came to tell us that your daughter will be Silvio's wife, after all? Excellent!

PANTALONE: Well, actually—

LOMBARDI: No need to apologize. I feel sorry for you. The position you were placed in was dreadful.

PANTALONE: That's true, but—

LOMBARDI: You didn't even realize how deeply you wounded my family's honor. But all's forgiven now.

PANTALONE: That's very good of you, but—

LOMBARDI: Your contract with Rasponi did not involve your daughter directly, but ours did.

PANTALONE: That's true, but—

LOMBARDI: Therefore our claim holds greater legal weight.

PANTALONE: I'm not a lawyer, but then again, neither are—

LOMBARDI: So now let's talk about the dowry.

PANTALONE: Will you allow me to get a word in edgewise?!

LOMBARDI: Of course, of course.

PANTALONE: She's not going to marry Silvio. I won't break my word. Furthermore, Clarice now agrees with me.

LOMBARDI: This is outrageous! Today's contract had your full consent. My son expects you to annul Rasponi's contract, but now that you tell me she's changed her mind, too, frankly, I don't want such a dishonorable girl in my family! Good day, sir! *(He storms out)*

PANTALONE: Bah! Rasponis are socially superior to the Lombardis and, besides, Federigo's rich.

(SILVIO *enters, obviously upset*)

SILVIO: A word with you, sir. Is what my father said true?

PANTALONE: Since when has your father ever lied to you?

SILVIO: You're telling me Rasponi's going to marry Clarice?

PANTALONE: That's right, sir.

SILVIO: And you have the nerve to tell me this to my face?

PANTALONE: I *beg* your pardon?

SILVIO: And so you should, you villainous lowlife!

PANTALONE: How dare you address a man of my years like that?

SILVIO: Your age is no excuse for dishonoring my family. *(Drawing sword)* I'm tempted to skewer you, sir.

PANTALONE: Help! He's going to murder me! (BEATRICE *runs out and stands between them)* Son-in-law! Just in the nick of time!

BEATRICE: Leave him alone!

SILVIO: Gladly, sir. I'd much rather fight with you.

BEATRICE *(draws sword):* So be it!

PANTALONE: Help!

(PANTALONE *runs inside, slamming the door.* BEATRICE *and* SILVIO *fight. She wins. As he falls down, he loses his sword. She places the tip of her sword against his breast.* CLARICE *runs out)*

CLARICE: Stop! Don't kill him!

BEATRICE: Since it's you who ask me, I'll spare him. Remember I showed him mercy and keep the promise you made me. (CLARICE *nods.* BEATRICE *exits)*

CLARICE: Are you all right?

SILVIO *(rising):* How can I be all right? You betrayed me!

CLARICE: How?

SILVIO: You've agreed to marry Federigo Rasponi.

CLARICE: Never! You're the only husband for me.

SILVIO: Liar! Rasponi just referred to your promise to him.

CLARICE: That's an entirely different promise.

SILVIO: Is it?

CLARICE: It is.

SILVIO: Well, what is it?

CLARICE: I can't tell you.

SILVIO: Why not??

CLARICE: I gave—Federigo—my word I wouldn't.

SILVIO: But you mustn't keep secrets from me.

CLARICE: Don't ask me to reveal it. I can't.

SILVIO: And I'm supposed to believe you're not involved with him? Get away from me, you lying jade!

CLARICE: Silvio, I love you!

SILVIO: I detest you, woman.

CLARICE *(picking up his sword):* Why don't you just use this? It'll hurt less. *(She aims the point at her breast.* SMERALDINA *runs in)*

SMERALDINA: Stop! Are you crazy? *(She snatches the sword from* CLARICE *and rounds on* SILVIO) Were you really going to let her? Madame, this coldhearted brute doesn't deserve you. He's a devil—let him go to Hell!

CLARICE: Why, that's where I am now. He hates me. Someday he'll find out that I'm blameless—then, when it's too late, he'll remember how I cried for him and he'll shed tears as bitter as these. *(Exits)*

SMERALDINA: How can you stand there, not batting an eye? She almost killed herself!

SILVIO: She was just putting on a show for my sake.

SMERALDINA: So that's what you think? Men! A woman even suspected of infidelity is branded for life, but meanwhile, men are unfaithful day in, day out. Do you know why?

SILVIO: Why?

SMERALDINA: Because you men make the laws—and get away with murder! *(She throws down his sword and exits)*

SILVIO *(picking it up):* I still don't think she really meant to kill herself. She was just trying to make me feel sorry for her. Meanwhile, she's given her heart to Signor Federigo—but not for long. I'll fight him again. Next time he won't be so lucky! *(Exits. Curtain.)*

Scene Two

An antechamber at the inn. Doors lead to the kitchen and two private dining rooms. TRUFFALDINO *is discovered.*

TRUFFALDINO: What good is it, having two masters when neither one of 'em ever eats? Wait! Here's Master Number Two.

(FLORINDO enters)

FLORINDO: Truffaldino, have you found Pasquale yet?

TRUFFALDINO: You told me that could wait till after we ate.

FLORINDO: All right, let's get it over with. Did you order?

TRUFFALDINO: How could I? You ran out. Dinner would've gone cold.

FLORINDO: What's the difference? I'm not hungry.

TRUFFALDINO: With all the running around you do, you should eat.

FLORINDO: I suppose so. Very well, go ahead and order a meal. If I'm not here when it's ready, eat without me, then find Pasquale. *(He gives him the purse and a set of keys)* This money weighs a ton. Put it in my trunk and be sure to lock it.

TRUFFALDINO: Right away. I'll bring you back the key.

FLORINDO: No need. I trust you. Now don't forget—

TRUFFALDINO: To find Pasquale?

FLORINDO: Yes. *(He exits)*

TRUFFALDINO: I'm almost starting to believe this Pasquale exists!

(Enter BEATRICE)

BEATRICE: Truffaldino!

TRUFFALDINO: Oh, God, what now? *(To her)* Sir?

BEATRICE: Did Signor Pantalone give you a purseful of money?

TRUFFALDINO: Well . . . yes.

BEATRICE: So give it to me.

TRUFFALDINO: It . . . it's yours?

BEATRICE: Of course it's mine. Didn't he tell you so?

TRUFFALDINO: He said I should give it to my master.

BEATRICE: Well? How many masters do you have?

TRUFFALDINO: Uh—here. *(He hands her the purse)*

BEATRICE: Is all the money still here?

TRUFFALDINO: I never touched a single coin!

BEATRICE *(aside):* All the same, I'm going to count it.

TRUFFALDINO *(aside):* This is going to be a problem later.

BEATRICE: Truffaldino, I've invited Signor Pantalone to dine with me shortly.

TRUFFALDINO: To *dine?*

BEATRICE: Certainly. It's after two o'clock. I should think you'd be hungry by now.

TRUFFALDINO: Me, hungry? What a novel notion! *(Aside)* I was beginning to think this one never ate.

BEATRICE: Ask the innkeeper to prepare a simple meal for us.

TRUFFALDINO: What would you like?

BEATRICE: Nothing fancy. Five or six dishes. You decide. Here, take this bill of exchange and put it in my room. Don't lose it. It's worth four thousand ducats.

TRUFFALDINO *(takes paper from her):* I'll be careful with it.

BEATRICE: I'll be back soon with Signor Pantalone. *(Exits)*

TRUFFALDINO: Dinner can't be whipped up in ten seconds! I'll put this paper away later. *(Calls)* Signor Brighella!

(BRIGHELLA *enters)*

BRIGHELLA: Yes, Truffaldino? What can I do for you?

TRUFFALDINO: Can you fix dinner for my master and a guest?

BRIGHELLA: Certainly. How many courses? Two?

TRUFFALDINO: How many dishes per course?

BRIGHELLA: How many do you want?

TRUFFALDINO: Five or six dishes, at least. Eight would be better.

BRIGHELLA: Eight per course?! If you say so.

TRUFFALDINO: Show me how you set the table.

BRIGHELLA: Talk to my waiter about that.

TRUFFALDINO: You don't know how it's done?

BRIGHELLA *(irritated):* Of course I know! Eight dishes? They go here, here, here, here, here, here, here, here.

TRUFFALDINO: What about in the center?

BRIGHELLA: The center? I suppose we could put the sauce there.

TRUFFALDINO: Obviously, you've never been a servant.

BRIGHELLA *(amused):* All right. You show me how.

TRUFFALDINO: You do it like this . . . *(Kneeling, he tears off bits of BE-ATRICE's bill of exchange to demonstrate)* See? Here, here, here, here, here, here, here and here.

(BEATRICE *enters with* PANTALONE)

BEATRICE: Truffaldino, what are you doing on the floor?

TRUFFALDINO: Showing the innkeeper how to lay a table.

BEATRICE: With my bill of exchange?!

TRUFFALDINO: Oh, Lord! *(He collects pieces)* I got carried away. I'll reassemble it, sir. *(Aside)* God knows how.

BEATRICE: You deserve to be whipped!

PANTALONE: Don't get upset, son-in-law, it's only paper. I'll have another one drawn up for you.

BEATRICE: That's very kind of you.

TRUFFALDINO: This never would have happened if Brighella knew how tables are supposed to be set.

BEATRICE: Truffaldino, you're an ass. Be off with you.

TRUFFALDINO: Yes, sir. *(He exits)*

BEATRICE: I hope dinner will be ready soon.

BRIGHELLA: Two courses of eight dishes each will take a while.

BEATRICE: Who needs that much food?

BRIGHELLA: How much do you want?

BEATRICE: Five or six dishes total. Tell Truffaldino to be ready to serve us. (BRIGHELLA *nods and exits*)

PANTALONE: This is too kind of you, sir. I should have had you dine with us instead, but Clarice would have spoiled our appetite. I don't understand why she's so upset again.

BEATRICE: Women's moods are like the weather.

PANTALONE: How's that? Stormy?

BEATRICE: Changeable. *(Aside)* Some more than others.

(TRUFFALDINO *returns*)

TRUFFALDINO: They've got the soup on the table.

BEATRICE: That was fast!

PANTALONE: Brighella's kitchen and staff are all first-rate. *(They enter one of the two dining rooms. A brief pause, then* TRUFFALDINO *comes out again)* Maybe it *is* a first-rate kitchen, but how will I ever find out, dining so frugally? A single dish at a time? I tell you what I think— Master Number One is a bit of a penny-pincher.

(A WAITER *comes out with a dish of food*)

WAITER: Truffaldino, where'd you get to? People eat soup one-two-three. Here's the second course. *(Exits)*

TRUFFALDINO: Looks like boiled lamb. *(He tastes it)* Delicious!

(He starts to take it inside when FLORINDO enters)

FLORINDO: Truffaldino, where are you taking that food?

TRUFFALDINO: I was just going to serve it to you.

FLORINDO: But I wasn't even here!

TRUFFALDINO: I saw you coming.

FLORINDO: What dinner starts with meat? How about soup?

TRUFFALDINO: In Venice, they serve the soup last.

FLORINDO: Nonsense. Take that back and bring me some soup.

TRUFFALDINO: Whatever you say, sir. *(He exits to kitchen)*

FLORINDO: I can't find Beatrice. For all I know, she could be in the very next room. *(He enters the other dining room.* TRUFFALDINO *reappears and takes the lamb to* BEATRICE*'s room.* FLORINDO *calls from offstage)* Truffaldino, what's taking you so long?

*(*TRUFFALDINO *enters antechamber)*

TRUFFALDINO: Coming right away, sir!

(The WAITER *enters with another dish)*

WAITER: Here's the stew.

TRUFFALDINO: Give it to me. There's a gentleman in that room waiting for soup.

WAITER: I'll get him some.

TRUFFALDINO: No, set his table and then bring me the soup.

WAITER: Right away. *(He exits into the kitchen)*

TRUFFALDINO: This stew smells heavenly. *(He tastes it)* It is! (TRUFFALDINO *takes the stew into* BEATRICE*'s room. The waiter brings dining table accoutrements and takes them to* FLORINDO*'s room.* TRUFFALDINO *returns)* Whew —serving two masters simultaneously is tough! By tonight, I'll be five pounds lighter. *(The waiter returns)* Hurry up with the soup!

WAITER: It's coming! *(He runs into the kitchen and comes right back with the soup)* Here it is.

TRUFFALDINO: I'll take it.

WAITER: But—

TRUFFALDINO: Give it to me. *(He takes the soup to* FLORINDO*)*

WAITER: He's out of his mind! He's trying to serve everybody in the whole damn place!

BEATRICE *(off):* Truffaldino!

*(*TRUFFALDINO *reappears)*

WAITER: Your master just called you.

TRUFFALDINO: I heard, I heard! *(He runs to* BEATRICE*'s room)*

WAITER: If he wants to do all of my work, let him. He'd better not expect me to split the tip, though.

FLORINDO *(off):* Truffaldino!

(The WAITER *exits.* TRUFFALDINO *re-enters with an armload of dishes to be washed)*

TRUFFALDINO: Coming, sir! *(Sighs)* Make that ten pounds lighter.

(The WAITER *returns with two dishes of food)*

WAITER: Here we go, meat for one, ravioli for the other. *(With great difficulty, they manage to exchange armloads. The waiter exits to the kitchen)*

TRUFFALDINO: Who gets the ravioli? I lost track. I know what! I'll divide the raviolis between them. *(He does so)* They don't come out even. *(He eats the odd ravioli)* Wonderful! It would be nice if I could manage more than one mouthful at a time . . .

BEATRICE *(off):* Truffaldino!

FLORINDO *(off):* Truffaldino!

TRUFFALDINO: Coming . . . coming!

(He sets one dish down and takes the other to BEATRICE's *room. The* WAITER *returns with food)*

WAITER: Truffaldino!

*(*TRUFFALDINO *runs out, wild-eyed)*

TRUFFALDINO: What—? Oh, it's you! *(Aside)* Thank God! I thought I suddenly had a third master!

WAITER *(indicating the dish he's holding):* I brought the—

TRUFFALDINO: Wait a minute! *(He runs the other plate to* FLORINDO's *room and comes back)* Brought the what?

WAITER: Trifle.

TRUFFALDINO: What?

WAITER: Trifle!

TRUFFALDINO: I am not to be trifled with!

WAITER: This is called trifle. It's English.

TRUFFALDINO: Oh. *(He takes it)* Who gets it?

WAITER: Your master. *(Exits)*

TRUFFALDINO: WHICH MASTER?!

BEATRICE *(off):* Truffaldino!

TRUFFALDINO: I never tasted trifle. *(He tastes it)* Excellent!

FLORINDO *(off):* Truffaldino!

TRUFFALDINO *(tasting some more):* It's really out of this world! *(*BEATRICE *enters and kicks* TRUFFALDINO*)*

BEATRICE: Will you get in here?! *(She exits)*

TRUFFALDINO: I'm there already!

(TRUFFALDINO *follows her out.* FLORINDO *enters*)

FLORINDO: Where the hell is he? Truffaldino?

(TRUFFALDINO *reappears*)

TRUFFALDINO: Here I am, sir.

FLORINDO: Where'd you disappear to?

TRUFFALDINO: I was waiting for them to hand me the next course.

FLORINDO: One more course will be enough food for me. *(Yawns)* I'd better take a short nap after I eat. *(Exits)*

TRUFFALDINO: A nap is good, sir . . . let's see, I'll keep the trifle for myself. What's next? Anything? Waiter!

(The WAITER *enters with another dish)*

WAITER: Just coming.

TRUFFALDINO: What's that?

WAITER: Roast meat.

TRUFFALDINO *(nodding at* BEATRICE's *room):* They're ready for dessert.

WAITER: Coming right up. *(He exits to the kitchen)*

FLORINDO *(calls):* Truffaldino!

TRUFFALDINO: I've got it, I've got it! *(He runs the roast to* FLORINDO. *The waiter returns)*

WAITER: Truffaldino! Dessert! *(*TRUFFALDINO *staggers in)*

TRUFFALDINO: Got it . . . *(They both start to exit)* Don't go yet! *(*TRUF-FALDINO *takes the dessert to* BEATRICE, *then comes back, panting for breath)*

WAITER: They've all been served. What do you need now?

TRUFFALDINO *(panting):* Mhuh . . . me . . .

WAITER: You? What about you?

TRUFFALDINO: My turn to eat. *(The* WAITER *exits)* I've waited on two masters at once. *(Calls)* Bring enough for four!

(Curtain.)

ACT II

Scene One

The town square. SMERALDINA *enters with a letter.*

SMERALDINA: My mistress instructs me to deliver this letter to Signor Rasponi at the inn. Now is that proper? A young woman like me shouldn't be out in public without protection. Furthermore, if she's so head over heels in love with Signor Silvio, why do you suppose she's writing to another man? "La donna è mobile," I suppose. Well, it's bad enough to be here on the street all by myself, but I'm certainly not setting foot inside a tavern! Hey, you! Come here!

(The WAITER *appears)*

WAITER: What do you want?

SMERALDINA: Is Signor Rasponi staying here?

WAITER: Federigo Rasponi? Yeah, he just got through eating.

SMERALDINA: I've got a message for him.

WAITER: So bring it in and give it to him.

SMERALDINA: I don't think it's proper.

WAITER: Well, I can't haul him out here, can I? Besides, he's got company.

SMERALDINA: Who?

WAITER: Signor Pantalone.

SMERALDINA: Oh, then I definitely can't come in.

WAITER: What if I send you his servant, would that do?

SMERALDINA: You mean Truffaldino?

WAITER: That's the one.

SMERALDINA: That's a very good idea.

WAITER *(aside):* There's one for the books. She likes Master Busy Legs, but is too proper to meet him inside, so, instead, she picks broad daylight! *(Exits)*

SMERALDINA: What do I tell the master, if I should run into him? I know . . . I came to get *him*. Mistress Clarice will back me up on that one, if necessary.

*(*TRUFFALDINO *comes out, holding a bottle and glass)*

TRUFFALDINO: Someone looking for me?

SMERALDINA: I am.

TRUFFALDINO: Talk about luck!

SMERALDINA: I'm afraid I interrupted your dinner.

TRUFFALDINO: I was just finishing. Your smile is my dessert.

SMERALDINA *(aside):* I think he likes me, too!

TRUFFALDINO: How may I be of service?

SMERALDINA: My mistress asked me to bring this letter to Signor Rasponi. I don't feel comfortable going inside, so I hope you'll deliver it for me.

TRUFFALDINO: Gladly, and with great joy.

SMERALDINA: Thank you. *(She hands him the letter)*

TRUFFALDINO: Fair exchange . . . I've got one for you, too.

SMERALDINA: A message?

TRUFFALDINO: Yes, from a certain Master Battochio.

SMERALDINA: That name's familiar.

TRUFFALDINO: He's a nice-looking fellow and quite clever.

SMERALDINA: That doesn't sound like anyone I know.

TRUFFALDINO: You do, too, know him. His heart belongs to you.

SMERALDINA: I don't have any such thing in my possession!

TRUFFALDINO: But if I introduced him to you and you liked him—

SMERALDINA: Well, if he struck my fancy, I'd tell him so.

TRUFFALDINO: Good. Wait here.

SMERALDINA: Where are you off to?

TRUFFALDINO: I'm going to get him for you. *(He exits)*

SMERALDINA: Bother! I thought he was talking about himself. (TRUFFALDINO *re-enters, pantomimes his affection and leaves again)* Now what was that supposed to mean?! (TRUFFALDINO *re-enters)*

TRUFFALDINO: Well, what did you think of him?

SMERALDINA: Who?

TRUFFALDINO: The man I was telling you about.

SMERALDINA: He never showed himself.

TRUFFALDINO: Didn't you see anybody?

SMERALDINA: Just you.

TRUFFALDINO: Just me? *Just* me?

SMERALDINA: Are you trying to tell me it's you?

TRUFFALDINO: Of course it's me!

SMERALDINA: Then why didn't you say so?

TRUFFALDINO: I was too . . . well . . . fainthearted.

SMERALDINA *(aside):* He's adorable! *(To him)* I'm a bit shy, too.

TRUFFALDINO: Then we've got something in common.

SMERALDINA: And is that a good thing?

TRUFFALDINO: Married people ought to have something in common.

SMERALDINA: Who brought up marriage?

TRUFFALDINO: Hasn't anyone ever asked you?

SMERALDINA: I *beg* your pardon. Lots of men have declared their intentions, but none of them appeal to me.

TRUFFALDINO: Do I?

SMERALDINA: As a husband? It's not out of the question.

TRUFFALDINO: Just how would I go about asking for your hand?

SMERALDINA: Well, I'm an orphan, so a suitor would have to speak to my mistress or my master.

TRUFFALDINO: And how do you think they'll react?

SMERALDINA: They'll probably say, "If it's what Smeraldina wants, we're satisfied."

TRUFFALDINO: And is it?

SMERALDINA: Is it what?

TRUFFALDINO: What you want?

SMERALDINA: I think so . . . *(He almost kisses her. At the last moment, she hands him the letter instead)* Don't forget to take this to Signor Federigo.

TRUFFALDINO: After I do, we'll talk some more.

SMERALDINA: Possibly.

TRUFFALDINO *(eyeing the letter)*: I hope this isn't bad news or something insulting. The bearer of evil tidings usually gets the worst of it.

SMERALDINA: It's certainly not a love letter—I hope it's not.

TRUFFALDINO: I wish I knew what it said.

SMERALDINA: I'd open it, but how could we close it up again?

TRUFFALDINO: Leave that to me! I've got a foolproof method.

SMERALDINA: How?

TRUFFALDINO: A trick my Grandma taught me. Nobody will ever know. *(He tears the end off the letter)* Here we are. Read it aloud.

SMERALDINA: Me? Why don't you read it?

TRUFFALDINO: I . . . I don't know how.

SMERALDINA: Neither do I!

TRUFFALDINO: Then this was a total waste of time.

SMERALDINA *(taking the letter from him)*: Maybe not. I know what certain letters look like. I recognize the vowels.

TRUFFALDINO: Is that the letter M?

SMERALDINA: I don't think so. It looks like an R.

(PANTALONE and BEATRICE come out of the inn)

PANTALONE: Smeraldina, what brings you here?

SMERALDINA: Oh, sir . . . my mistress wants to speak with you.

BEATRICE: Truffaldino, what's that you two were looking at?

TRUFFALDINO: Uh—a letter.

BEATRICE: A letter? Who's it for?

TRUFFALDINO: Uh—you, sir.

BEATRICE: Me? And you opened it? *(She snatches it from him)*

PANTALONE *(suspicious)*: Signor Federigo, may I ask who sent it?

BEATRICE *(glancing at it)*: It's from your daughter.

PANTALONE: Oho, now she's sending love letters? Who brought it?

SMERALDINA: Truffaldino was about to bring it to his master.

TRUFFALDINO: Thank you very much, miss!

PANTALONE: And who brought it to Truffaldino?

TRUFFALDINO *(looking at SMERALDINA meaningfully)*: Who do you think?

SMERALDINA: That other matter we talked about . . . forget it!

PANTALONE: So you caused this mess, brat! I ought to slap you.

SMERALDINA: You'll have to catch me first! *(She runs off)*

PANTALONE: I'd better not catch you! *(He chases her off)*

BEATRICE *(reading):* Poor Clarice! Silvio's anger is destroying her. I must come forward soon and reveal the truth.

TRUFFALDINO *(aside):* Now's a good time to scram, while he's preoccupied.

BEATRICE: Where do you think you're going, wretch? Do you think it slipped my mind that this is the second letter of mine today that you opened?

TRUFFALDINO: I was kind of hoping it had.

BEATRICE: Well, it hasn't. *(She beats him with a stick)* In future, you'll allow me to open my own mail. *(She goes inside.* TRUFFALDINO *groans)*

TRUFFALDINO: Whatever happened to *firing* unsatisfactory help?

(Enter FLORINDO*)*

FLORINDO: What's all this ruckus? Why are you groaning?

TRUFFALDINO: I got beat up.

FLORINDO: You *what?* Why?

TRUFFALDINO: No big deal. An argument with a stranger.

FLORINDO: That's not the point. You're my servant. If someone lays a hand on you, it's like beating me.

TRUFFALDINO: Not exactly.

FLORINDO: I take it as an insult. Didn't you defend yourself?

TRUFFALDINO: It didn't seem appropriate.

FLORINDO: Not appropriate?! Why, you cowardly puff pastry, such a craven answer deserves a coward's reward! *(He beats him)* Next time, behave like a man! *(Exits)*

TRUFFALDINO: Another fringe benefit of serving two masters! Twice the punishment. *(He groans)* I'd better do something or other to appease my masters. But what? *(Rummaging in his pockets, he finds keys)* Hm. The keys to both of their trunks. That gives me an idea of how I can mollify 'em. *(Calls)* Hey, waiter! *(The* WAITER *comes out)*

WAITER: What do you want now, Truffaldino?

TRUFFALDINO: I'm going to air my master's clothes.

WAITER: Which master?

TRUFFALDINO: Oh, so you've figured it out, eh? Shhh!

WAITER: My lips are sealed. *(Aside)* As long as nobody asks.

TRUFFALDINO: I've got a pair of trunks to move. Will you help me?

WAITER: All right. Come on. (TRUFFALDINO *goes inside)* He seems a decent fellow, but still, he bears watching. Why would he work for two men at a time? What if he means to rob them both? *(Follows him in. A short pause, then they emerge with the two trunks. The* WAITER *exits)*

TRUFFALDINO *(taking out his keys):* Two keys, now which is which? *(He unlocks a trunk)* Guessed right. Now the other. (TRUFFALDINO *unlocks the second trunk and begins to unpack both. Though the contents otherwise differ, each trunk contains a nearly identical man's coat)*

FLORINDO *(off):* Truffaldino!

TRUFFALDINO: Uh-oh! What if he sees the other trunk?

FLORINDO *(off):* Where are you?

TRUFFALDINO *(quickly stuffing things back into the trunks):* Out here, sir! *(He looks at the two matching coats)* Damn! Which of these goes where? *(He shrugs)* If *I* can't tell the difference, neither will they. *(He repacks one of the coats in* BEATRICE'*s trunk.* FLORINDO *enters and sees* TRUFFALDINO *about to repack the other coat)*

FLORINDO: What are you doing out here?

TRUFFALDINO: You told me to air your clothing, remember?

FLORINDO: And this is where you do it?

TRUFFALDINO: As good a place as any.

FLORINDO: I suppose. Who does that other trunk belong to?

TRUFFALDINO: I don't know. It was sitting here when I came out.

FLORINDO: I was just looking for that coat.

TRUFFALDINO: Do you want to put it on?

FLORINDO: What else would I do with it?

TRUFFALDINO: I'll help you on with it, sir.

FLORINDO: Thank you. *(With* TRUFFALDINO'*s aid,* FLORINDO *dons the coat. He puts his hands in his pockets and finds something)* How did this portrait get in my pocket?

TRUFFALDINO *(aside):* Oh, great! I mixed up the coats! *(To* FLORINDO) It's not yours?

FLORINDO: No, but I recognize it.

TRUFFALDINO *(looking at it):* This fellow looks familiar.

FLORINDO: It ought to, dolt, it's me!

TRUFFALDINO: You?! May I? (FLORINDO *hands him the portrait)*

FLORINDO *(aside):* That's the same picture of myself I gave to Beatrice. How did it get back in my pocket?

TRUFFALDINO *(examining portrait):* Now it comes back to me . . .

FLORINDO: What does?

TRUFFALDINO: This belonged to the last master I served. He died suddenly and left me with a handful of odds and ends which I sold, all except this. I guess I stuck it in your pocket by accident.

FLORINDO *(horrified):* When did your master die?

TRUFFALDINO: A week ago.

FLORINDO: What was his name?

TRUFFALDINO: I don't know, sir. He was traveling in disguise.

FLORINDO *(aside):* Oh, God, it must have been Beatrice! *(To* TRUFFALDINO*)* Was your master a young man?

TRUFFALDINO: So young he was clean-shaven.

FLORINDO: And where did he come from?

TRUFFALDINO *(aside):* Is this going to end up with him beating me again? *(To* FLORINDO*)* I'm trying to remember, sir.

FLORINDO: Did he come from Turin?

TRUFFALDINO: Turin? That's it. He came from Turin.

FLORINDO: What killed him?

TRUFFALDINO *(aside):* Every lie that I tell breeds ten others! *(To* FLORINDO*)* He had an accident. *(Aside)* Please, God, don't let him ask for details!

FLORINDO: Where did they bury him?

TRUFFALDINO *(aside):* I should have said "Amen." *(To* FLORINDO*)* I don't know where he's buried, sir. Another servant arranged to have his body sent back to Turin.

FLORINDO: Another servant? Not the one you met this morning?

TRUFFALDINO: Yes, Pasquale.

FLORINDO: Pasquale! Then it's true. There's nothing left for me now but anguish and grief. *(He exits to the inn)*

TRUFFALDINO: My poor master . . . he must be friends with my other master. This is all my fault.

(BEATRICE enters with PANTALONE)

BEATRICE: I'm telling you, there's a mistake in the inventory.

PANTALONE: One of my clerks must've copied it wrong. We'll take another look at my account books.

BEATRICE *(seeing her trunk):* What's this doing out here?

TRUFFALDINO: I was about to air your clothes, sir.

BEATRICE: Out here?! *(Sees other trunk)* Whose is that?

TRUFFALDINO: A gentleman who just arrived.

BEATRICE: Well, open up my trunk. I need my notebook.

TRUFFALDINO: Yes, sir. *(He unlocks her trunk and finds a book)* Is this it, sir?

BEATRICE *(takes it):* What's this? This is not my—*(stops)*

TRUFFALDINO *(aside):* I've done it again!

BEATRICE *(aside):* This is Florindo's book! Look, it's got a pair of letters in it from me.

PANTALONE: Signor Federigo, what's the matter? You look faint.

BEATRICE: I'm all right. *(Aside to* TRUFFALDINO*)* How'd this book get into my trunk?

TRUFFALDINO: Well . . . well . . .

BEATRICE: Don't concoct lies! I want the truth!

TRUFFALDINO: I put it there to keep it safe.

BEATRICE: So it's your book?

TRUFFALDINO: Yes.

BEATRICE: But you can't read.

TRUFFALDINO *(aside):* The same predicament, the same solution. *(To* BE-
ATRICE*)* My last master left this book to me.

BEATRICE: What do you mean, left it to you?

TRUFFALDINO: As in dead. He fell in a canal and drowned.

BEATRICE: What . . . what was his name?

TRUFFALDINO: His name?

BEATRICE: Your last master's name—was it Florindo?

TRUFFALDINO: That was it.

BEATRICE: Florindo Aretusi?

TRUFFALDINO: Yes, sir, that's it. Did you know him?

BEATRICE *(raising her voice):* Know him? I loved him! He's why I ran away
from home in the first place. He's why I dressed up like a man and
came to Venice! Wasn't it bad enough I lost my brother without
Florindo dying, too? *(She runs off hysterically into the inn)*

PANTALONE: I can't believe what I just heard!

TRUFFALDINO: He's a she!

PANTALONE: A woman! I'm thunderstruck!

TRUFFALDINO: I'm not the servant of two masters after all. One of them's a
mistress! *(He exits into the inn)*

PANTALONE: Wait till I tell this to Clarice! (PANTALONE *starts for his house.*
LOMBARDI *enters)*

LOMBARDI *(to himself):* There's that swine, Pantalone. I'd like to thrash
him!

PANTALONE *(effusively):* Ah, Doctor Lombardi, my *dear* old friend, it's so
good to see you!

LOMBARDI: How do you have the nerve to talk to me, sir?

PANTALONE: I've got something important to tell you.

LOMBARDI: That the marriage has taken place? Spare me.

PANTALONE: No. Everything has changed. My daughter will be glad to
marry your son.

LOMBARDI: Isn't that generous of her? Give her to Rasponi!

PANTALONE: Rasponi is not the man I thought he was.

LOMBARDI: Too bad. My son's not interested in damaged goods.

PANTALONE: How dare you, sir! Clarice is an honorable girl!

LOMBARDI: Yes and I know where she gets it from.

PANTALONE: What's that supposed to mean?

LOMBARDI: That you're a conniving old codger.

PANTALONE: You go to the Devil!

LOMBARDI: I'm already looking at him! *(He exits)*

PANTALONE: He put me in such a temper, I didn't even get to tell him that Rasponi is a woman!

(SILVIO *enters*)

SILVIO: There's Clarice's father. I'd like to pierce him like swiss cheese.

PANTALONE: Signor Silvio, if you'll keep your temper, not like that hot-headed father of yours, I'll tell you something you'll be very glad to hear.

SILVIO: Well, go ahead, I'm listening.

PANTALONE: My daughter's wedding to Rasponi fell through.

SILVIO: It did?

PANTALONE: Yes. If you still want her, she's yours.

SILVIO: Sir, you make me happy again! And yet . . .

PANTALONE: And yet what?

SILVIO: It's not honorable for me to accept your daughter, now that she's been with Rasponi.

PANTALONE: She has never "been with" Rasponi!

SILVIO: Well, of course, you'd tell me that, but—

PANTALONE: Damn it, man, Signor Rasponi is not Signor Rasponi!

SILVIO: What are you talking about?

PANTALONE: I'm trying to tell you. Federigo is dead after all.

SILVIO: Then who's this man pretending to be him?

PANTALONE: It's not a man. It's Federigo's sister Beatrice.

SILVIO: What? Dressed up like that?

PANTALONE: That's right. I just found out. I haven't even told my daughter yet.

SILVIO: Can I be there when you do?

PANTALONE: Let's do it immediately . . . son-in-law.

(*They go into* PANTALONE's *house.* FLORINDO *rushes out of the inn, sword in hand. The* WAITER *pursues him*)

WAITER: For the love of God, sir, hold your hand!

FLORINDO: I won't bring disgrace upon your establishment by taking my life within its walls, but have pity on me and don't interfere with my intent!

WAITER (*struggling with him*): This is pure insanity!

FLORINDO: Release me, sir!

WAITER: I mustn't!

(*While they are struggling,* BEATRICE *runs out clutching a dagger.* BRIGHELLA *pursues her*)

BRIGHELLA: Stop! I won't let you throw your life away!

BEATRICE: I have nothing left to live for!

BRIGHELLA *(trying to take her dagger):* Give me that, Beatrice!

FLORINDO *(suddenly sees her):* Beatrice?!

BEATRICE *(suddenly sees him):* Florindo!?

FLORINDO: You're alive!

BEATRICE: You're not dead!

FLORINDO *(dropping his sword):* My darling . . .

BEATRICE *(dropping her dagger):* My beloved . . . *(They rush into each other's arms)*

BRIGHELLA: The crisis seems to be over.

WAITER: Just in case they change their minds, I think I'd better hide these. *(He takes the weapons and exits)*

FLORINDO: Were you really going to kill yourself?

BEATRICE: Yes. I was told that you drowned.

FLORINDO: Where'd you hear that?

BEATRICE: My servant said so.

FLORINDO: Strange, I heard you were dead, too . . .

BEATRICE: Who told you that?

FLORINDO: *My* servant! This portrait convinced me it was true.

BEATRICE: This book accomplished the same for me.

FLORINDO: How'd you get your hands on it? Wait, I see . . . the trunks. Our servants deliberately deceived us.

BEATRICE: I think we'd better have a word with them.

FLORINDO: Yes. Innkeeper, please send our servants out to us.

BRIGHELLA: I only know one of them. I'll ask my staff. *(Exits)*

BEATRICE: Talk about coincidence, both of us staying here.

FLORINDO: Destiny first punished, then rewarded us. But what about your brother?

BEATRICE: Federigo? You know he's dead.

FLORINDO: I'd heard he recovered from his wound and came here.

BEATRICE: That was me. I pretended to be him so I could—

FLORINDO: Find me. I know.

BEATRICE: How?

FLORINDO: My servant mistakenly got hold of a letter addressed to you. I'm afraid I opened it.

BEATRICE: It's all right. I would have done the same thing.

(A very unwilling TRUFFALDINO *is brought on by* BRIGHELLA *and the* WAITER*)*

FLORINDO: Well, here's one of the miscreants.

BEATRICE: Probably the principal villain of the pair.

FLORINDO: Probably. All right, you, get over here!

BEATRICE: Don't be afraid. We won't hurt you.

TRUFFALDINO: I've already had a sample of your mercy.

FLORINDO: Hush!

BRIGHELLA *(to the* WAITER*)*: Do you know their other servant?

WAITER *(with a glance at* TRUFFALDINO*)*: No, sir.

BRIGHELLA: Let's see if we can find him. *(They exit)*

FLORINDO: Now tell us what you and your co-conspirator hoped to gain by switching my book and her portrait.

TRUFFALDINO *(to* BEATRICE*)*: Give me a moment to apologize to this gentleman and I'll explain everything to you.

BEATRICE: Well, go ahead.

TRUFFALDINO *(drawing* FLORINDO *aside)*: It's like this, sir. This lady's servant mixed those things up all by himself.

FLORINDO: You mean Pasquale?

TRUFFALDINO: That's the one! When Pasquale found out what he'd done, he was so afraid his mistress would fire him that he begged me to take the heat for his mistake.

FLORINDO: That's why you made up the story about her dying?

TRUFFALDINO: Exactly! I had no idea it'd give you so much pain.

BEATRICE *(aside)*: This must be the longest apology on record.

FLORINDO: You and Pasquale deserve to be whipped.

TRUFFALDINO: Oh, sir, if you spare him, I'll take double measure.

FLORINDO: Now that's a manly answer!

BEATRICE *(calls)*: Hey! What's all this colloquy about?

FLORINDO: Why, this lad's been telling me—

TRUFFALDINO *(to* FLORINDO*)*: Shh! Please don't mention Pasquale!

FLORINDO: I hope he knows what a good friend he's got in you.

TRUFFALDINO: With your permission, I'll tell the lady this business is all my fault.

FLORINDO: Yes, go ahead.

(TRUFFALDINO *crosses to* BEATRICE)

BEATRICE: It's about time!

TRUFFALDINO *(draws her aside)*: It took some delicate handling.

BEATRICE: What did?

TRUFFALDINO: Ma'am, that gentleman's got a poor doddering fool working for him by the name of Pasquale. He mixed things up all by himself.

BEATRICE: Pasquale did?

TRUFFALDINO: Pasquale did. When he realized what he'd done, he was so afraid he'd be fired that I covered for him with that unfortunate tale about the drowning. I was just telling Signor Florindo it was all my fault.

BEATRICE: But why?

TRUFFALDINO: Pasquale's a dear friend.

BEATRICE: Some friend.

FLORINDO *(aside):* What's taking him so long?

TRUFFALDINO: Please don't mention Pasquale, ma'am.

FLORINDO: Beatrice!

BEATRICE: Yes?

FLORINDO: I've thought it over. Our servants do deserve to be chastised, but considering how happily things have turned out for us, perhaps we ought to spare them.

BEATRICE: Yes, perhaps we should.

TRUFFALDINO *(aside):* Have I actually pulled it off?!

BEATRICE: I must visit Signor Pantalone. Will you join me?

FLORINDO: First I must make myself presentable.

BEATRICE: I'm in a hurry. Why don't you meet me there?

FLORINDO: I'll do that. Where does he live?

BEATRICE *(points):* Right over there. I'm going to my room now to freshen up. *(Beckoning* TRUFFALDINO, *she exits)*

TRUFFALDINO *(to* FLORINDO*):* Since Pasquale isn't here, sir, should I assist Signora Beatrice in his absence?

FLORINDO: Please do! I'm delighted by your thoughtfulness.

TRUFFALDINO *(aside):* I *have* brought it off! *(Exits)*

FLORINDO: What a day! Heartbreak, attempted suicide, blissful reconciliation! This is the stuff of theatre!

*(*BEATRICE *returns, followed by* TRUFFALDINO*)*

BEATRICE: There, that didn't take long. *(To* FLORINDO*)* Why the long face?

FLORINDO: I was hoping you might put on a dress.

BEATRICE: What's wrong with how I look?

FLORINDO: Trousers conceal your womanly charms.

TRUFFALDINO *(aside):* A servant sees this from a different perspective.

BEATRICE: I'm comfortable as is. Meet me at Pantalone's.

TRUFFALDINO *(to her):* Madame, Pasquale's nowhere to be found. Should I stay and help Signor Florindo get dressed?

BEATRICE: That notion pleases me! *(She goes to* PANTALONE*'s)*

TRUFFALDINO *(aside):* Damn, I'm good! *(Sees* SMERALDINA *answer door)* Master, are you going to Pantalone's, too?

FLORINDO: Presently. Why?

TRUFFALDINO: Could I ask you to do me a favor?

FLORINDO: That depends on what it is.

TRUFFALDINO: Well, it's this way. I'm in love.

FLORINDO: You, too?

TRUFFALDINO: It's catching.

FLORINDO: Who is she?

TRUFFALDINO: Signora Clarice's servant. Her name's Smeraldina.

FLORINDO: Does she return your affection?

TRUFFALDINO: She's absolutely wild about me!

FLORINDO: Then I'll talk to Signor Pantalone on your behalf. But can you really afford to get married?

TRUFFALDINO: I'm doing all right . . . but if I need advice, I'll just talk to Pasquale.

FLORINDO: Are you crazy? Don't listen to that jackass!

(Curtain.)

Scene Two

A room in PANTALONE's *house.* CLARICE *is surrounded by* SILVIO, PANTALONE, LOMBARDI *and* SMERALDINA.

CLARICE: I feel like I'm a fortress under attack!

PANTALONE: Young Silvio is genuinely sorry. I've forgiven him.

CLARICE: I haven't.

SILVIO: Forgive me. I acted rashly out of grief. I thought I'd lost you to another. (CLARICE *glares at him, but says nothing*) I thought you were no longer faithful to me. *(She glares harder, but remains silent)*

LOMBARDI: Come, come, lass, my son went mad with jealousy and sorrow. Show some mercy and forgive him.

SMERALDINA: Look at it this way, ma'am. Men want their wives to be virtuous. If they begin to suspect us, with or without proof, they'll boss us around, beat us up or even destroy us. However—

CLARICE: "However?" What can possibly follow *that* catalog?

SMERALDINA: However, if we want to get married, what other choice have we got?

PANTALONE: We can dispense with your help, girl! You make marriage sound worse than going to the doctor's.

LOMBARDI: I beg your pardon, sir!

PANTALONE: It was only a figure of speech.

SILVIO: Clarice, beloved, I know I've earned your anger—*(She nods decisively)*

SMERALDINA: My mistress agrees with you.

PANTALONE: Shush! He doesn't need an interpreter.

SILVIO *(kneeling):* Of all punishments you might have devised for my sins, your refusal to speak to me is the most eloquent. I beg a single word from your ruby lips. *(She whispers a word into his ear. Shocked)* Clarice!

PANTALONE: At least he broke the ice.

SILVIO: How else may I apologize? I'll gladly bleed for you. *(She shakes her head. He touches his breast)* If not these precious drops, then these . . . (SILVIO *begins to cry)*

CLARICE: That's what I was waiting for. When I wept, your eyes stayed dry. Now we're even.

SILVIO: Does this mean you love me again?

CLARICE *(taking his hand):* Oh, Silvio, I never stopped!

LOMBARDI: Bravo!

PANTALONE: They're as good as married!

(BRIGHELLA *enters)*

BRIGHELLA: I hope I'm not intruding?

PANTALONE: Ah, my old friend Brighella. I've been meaning to speak to you . . .

BRIGHELLA: I know I misled you, Pantalone, but I forgot to mention that Signor Federigo and Beatrice were twins. Clad in trousers, I was sure she was he.

PANTALONE: There! I *knew* that was it! So what brings you here?

BRIGHELLA: Signora Beatrice is outside and begs to be admitted.

PANTALONE: By all means, ask her to come in.

(BRIGHELLA *steps to the door and beckons in* BEATRICE)

BEATRICE: Thank you for seeing me. I owe you all apologies.

CLARICE: Never mind the past! Be joyful! *(She embraces her)*

SILVIO: This is intolerable!

CLARICE: She's like a sister to me. Why can't I hug her?

SILVIO: Sorry, I got confused. *(Aside)* Women in pants!

(TRUFFALDINO *enters)*

TRUFFALDINO: Good evening, gentlemen, ladies. Signor Florindo Aretusi wishes to be announced.

BEATRICE *(to* PANTALONE): Florindo is my husband-to-be.

PANTALONE: Then he's welcome in my home.

TRUFFALDINO *(to* SMERALDINA): Well?

SMERALDINA: Well, what?

TRUFFALDINO: Well, do you want me or not?

SMERALDINA: Ohhh . . . I guess so.

TRUFFALDINO: By the way, I love you. *(He exits)*

SMERALDINA *(to* CLARICE): Mistress, I've got a favor to ask you.

CLARICE: There's no better time to ask a favor than now.

SMERALDINA: Signora Beatrice's servant wishes to marry me.

CLARICE: Do you love him?

SMERALDINA: Oh, yes!

CLARICE: Then I'll talk to Beatrice on your behalf.

(Enter FLORINDO *and* TRUFFALDINO*)*

PANTALONE: Well, sir, I presume you're Signor Florindo?

FLORINDO: Yes. Have I the pleasure of addressing Signor Pantalone Dei Bisognosi?

PANTALONE: I'm that gentleman, and this is my daughter Clarice.

FLORINDO: Your humble servant. I understand you're to be wed?

CLARICE: To this gentleman.

FLORINDO: Beatrice and I are also betrothed. I hope you'll do us the honor, sir, of giving the bride away.

PANTALONE: I'm delighted to be asked.

TRUFFALDINO *(to* FLORINDO*)*: Uh . . . sir?

FLORINDO: What? Oh, yes, of course! *(To* PANTALONE*)* I have another boon to beg of you, sir.

PANTALONE: What's that?

FLORINDO: It seems my personal servant is in love with a maid of yours named Smeraldina. He wants to marry her.

SMERALDINA *(aside):* Here's a surprise! First Truffaldino falls for me, and now some servant I haven't even met!

PANTALONE: I have no objection, but it's really up to her.

CLARICE: I'm afraid I've got a problem with it.

FLORINDO: You do, madame?

CLARICE: I was about to ask my father the same favor on behalf of Beatrice's personal servant.

FLORINDO: Oh, in that case, please forget I even asked.

CLARICE: Oh, dear, now I'm sorry I spoke up. You're very generous, sir, but after all, you did speak first.

FLORINDO: I will not promote my man's plea in place of yours.

CLARICE: Then I must withdraw my man's suit, as well.

SMERALDINA *(aside):* From two proposals to none in nothing flat!

TRUFFALDINO *(aside):* Their scruples condemn me and Pasquale to a life of celibacy!

PANTALONE: Well, this isn't really fair to anyone, is it?

SMERALDINA: *I* don't think so.

FLORINDO: I refuse to offer an affront to this gracious lady.

CLARICE: I will not wrong my new friend Florindo.

TRUFFALDINO *(sighing):* There's only one way out of this mess. *(Aloud)* If I may have everyone's attention?

BRIGHELLA: Hark! The nincompoop speaks!

FLORINDO: You mustn't plead your own case, Truffaldino.

TRUFFALDINO: Hear me out, sir. Smeraldina, give me your hand—(SMER-ALDINA *rushes to do so*)

PANTALONE: Not so fast! Nobody gave you permission.

TRUFFALDINO: But didn't you hear Signor Florindo ask for her hand on behalf of his servant?

PANTALONE: Yes, but—

TRUFFALDINO: And didn't your daughter ask the same thing—

PANTALONE: For Signora Beatrice's servant. Yes. So what?

TRUFFALDINO: So I'm both.

PANTALONE: Both what?!

TRUFFALDINO: Both servants.

FLORINDO *(suddenly suspicious):* Signora Beatrice . . .

BEATRICE *(suddenly suspicious):* Signor Florindo . . .

BOTH *(together):* Who's your servant?

BEATRICE: He's standing right there—Truffaldino.

FLORINDO: Aha! Guess who my servant is?

BEATRICE: Truffaldino!

TRUFFALDINO *(bowing to one, then the other):* At your service. At your service.

BEATRICE: I thought your servant's name was Pasquale.

FLORINDO: Pasquale?! I thought he worked for you. *(They round on* TRUF-FALDINO*)*

BEATRICE: You honey-tongued rascal!

FLORINDO: You villainous double-dealer!

TRUFFALDINO: Would you like me to explain?

EVERYONE: YES!!!

TRUFFALDINO: I admit, at first I was beguiled by extra rations and double wages, but the main reason I kept serving two masters at a time is, I wanted to see if I could bring it off . . . and I almost did.

SMERALDINA *(smiling proudly):* But you gave yourself away for me.

TRUFFALDINO: That's the truth. Now remember, I had to work twice as hard—and don't forget that both of you already thrashed me. So considering all that, is there anyone here who thinks I deserve further punishment?

ALL *(excluding* SMERALDINA*):* YES!!!

TRUFFALDINO *(indicating the audience):* How about if we leave it up to them? (SMERALDINA *prompts the audience to applaud. Curtain.)*

THE LYING VALET

by
David Garrick

Long before muggers and train schedules curtailed the playing time of modern legitimate drama, an evening at the theatre was likely to be an event of some duration. If the major offering of the evening was deemed too brief, producers commissioned and presented "afterpieces," many of them farces.

Possibly the most famous "afterpiece" in English drama is Henry Fielding's parodistic "Tom Thumb." Far less familiar is THE LYING VALET, a British "wily servant" comedy by DAVID GARRICK (1717–79), a native of Hereford who accompanied his illustrious teacher, Dr. Samuel Johnson, to London, where Garrick became an occasional playwright and one of England's most popular actors.

CAST OF CHARACTERS

MEN
TIMOTHY SHARP, the lying valet
CHARLES GAYLESS
JUSTICE GUTTLE
BEAU TRIPPIT
DICK
SERVANTS

WOMEN
MELISSA
KITTY PRY
MRS. GADABOUT
MRS. TRIPPIT
PRISSY, Mrs. Gadabout's daughter
A niece of Mrs. Gadabout

ACT I

Scene One

GAYLESS' *lodgings. Enter* GAYLESS *and* SHARP.

SHARP: How, sir! shall you be married tomorrow? Eh, I'm afraid you joke with your poor humble servant.

GAY: I tell thee, Sharp, last night Melissa consented, and fixed tomorrow for the happy day.

SHARP: 'Twas well she did, sir, or it might have been a dreadful one for us in our present condition: all your money spent; your movables sold; your honor almost ruined, and your humble servant almost starved; we could not possibly have stood it two days longer. But if this young lady will marry you and relieve us, o' my conscience, I'll turn friend to the sex, rail no more at matrimony, but curse the whores, and think of a wife myself.

GAY: And yet, Sharp, when I think how I have imposed upon her, I am almost resolved to throw myself at her feet, tell her the real situation of my affairs, ask her pardon, and implore her pity.

SHARP: After marriage, with all my heart, sir; but don't let your conscience and honor so far get the better of your poverty and good sense, as to rely on so great uncertainties as a fine lady's mercy and good nature.

GAY: I know her generous temper, and am almost persuaded to rely upon it: what, because I am poor, shall I abandon my honor?

SHARP: Yes, you must, sir, or abandon me: pray, discharge one of us; for eat I must; and speedily too: and you know very well that that honor of yours will neither introduce you to a great man's table, nor get me credit for a single beefsteak.

GAY: What can I do?

SHARP: Nothing while honor sticks in your throat: so gulp, master, and down with it.

GAY: Prithee leave me to my thoughts.

SHARP: Leave you! No, not in such bad company, I'll assure you! why, you must certainly be a very great philosopher, sir, to moralize and declaim so charmingly, as you do, about honor and conscience, when your doors are beset with bailiffs, and not one single guinea in your pocket to bribe the villains.

GAY: Don't be witty, and give your advice, sirrah!

SHARP: Do you be wise, and take it, sir. But to be serious, you certainly have spent your fortune, and outlived your credit, as your pockets and my belly can testify: your father has disowned you; all your friends forsook you, except myself, who am starving with you. Now, sir, if you marry this young lady, who as yet, thank heaven, knows nothing of your misfortunes, and by that means procure a better fortune than that you squandered away, make a good husband, and turn economist, you still may be happy, may still be Sir William's heir, and the lady too no loser by the bargain; there's reason and argument, sir.

GAY: 'Twas with that prospect I first made love to her; and though my fortune has been ill spent, I have, at least, purchased discretion with it.

SHARP: Pray then convince me of that, sir, and make no more objections to the marriage. You see I am reduced to my waistcoat already; and when necessity has undressed me from top to toe, she must begin with you; and then we shall be forced to keep to the house and die by inches. Look you, sir, if you won't resolve to take my advice, while you have one coat to your back, I must e'en take to my heels while I have strength to run, and something to cover me: so, sir, wishing you much comfort and consolation with your bare conscience, I am your most obedient and half-starved friend and servant. *(Going)*

GAY: Hold, Sharp, you won't leave me.

SHARP: I must eat, sir; by my honor and appetite I must!

GAY: Well then, I am resolved to favor the cheat, and as I shall quite change my former course of life, happy may be the consequences; at least of this I am sure—

SHARP: That you can't be worse than you are at present. *(A knocking without)*

GAY: Who's there?

SHARP: Some of your former good friends, who favored you with money at fifty per cent, and helped you to spend it; and are now become daily mementoes to you of the folly of trusting rogues, following whores, and laughing at my advice.

GAY: Cease your impertinence! to the door! If they are duns, tell 'em my marriage is now certainly fixed, and persuade 'em still to forbear a few days longer, and keep my circumstances a secret for their sakes as well as my own.

SHARP: Oh, never fear it, sir: they still have so much friendship for you, not to desire your ruin to their own disadvantage.

GAY: And do you hear, Sharp, if it should be anybody from Melissa, say I am not at home, lest the bad appearance we make here should make 'em suspect something to our disadvantage.

SHARP: I'll obey you, sir;—but I am afraid they will easily discover the consumptive situation of our affairs by my chopfallen countenance. *(Exit)*

GAY: These very rascals who are now continually dunning and persecuting me were the very persons who led me to my ruin, partook of my prosperity, and professed the greatest friendship.

SHARP *(without):* Upon my word, Mrs. Kitty, my master's not at home.

KITTY *(without):* Look'ee, Sharp, I must and will see him!

GAY: Ha, what do I hear? Melissa's maid! what has brought her here? my poverty has made her my enemy too—she is certainly come with no good intent—no friendship there, without fees—she's coming up stairs. —What must I do?—I'll get into this closet and listen. *(Exit)*

(Enter SHARP *and* KITTY*)*

KITTY: I must know where he is, and will know too, Mr. Impertinence!

SHARP *(aside):* Not of me you won't.—He's not within, I tell you, Mrs. Kitty; I don't know myself: do you think I can conjure?

KITTY: But I know you will lie abominably; therefore don't trifle with me. I come from my mistress Melissa; you know, I suppose, what's to be done tomorrow morning?

SHARP: Ay, and tomorrow night too, girl!

KITTY *(aside):* Not if I can help it.—But come, where is your master? for see him I must.

SHARP: Pray, Mrs. Kitty, what's your opinion of this match between my master and your mistress?

KITTY: Why, I have no opinion of it at all; and yet most of our wants will be relieved by it too: for instance now, your master will get a fortune, that's what I'm afraid he wants; my mistress will get a husband, that's what she has wanted for some time; you will have the pleasure of my conversation, and I an opportunity of breaking your head for your impertinence.

SHARP: Madam, I'm your most humble servant! but I'll tell you what, Mrs. Kitty, I am positively against the match; for, was I a man of my master's fortune—

KITTY: You'd marry if you could and mend it. Ha, ha, ha! Pray, Sharp, where does your master's estate lie!

GAY *(aside):* Oh, the devil! what a question was there!

SHARP: Lie, lie! why it lies—faith, I can't name any particular place, it lies in so many; his effects are divided, some here, some there; his steward hardly knows himself.

KITTY: Scattered, scattered, I suppose. But hark'ee, Sharp, what's become of your furniture? You seem to be a little bare here at present.

GAY *(aside):* What, has she found out that too?

SHARP: Why, you must know, as soon as the wedding was fixed, my master ordered me to remove his goods into a friend's house, to make room for a ball which he designs to give here the day after the marriage.

KITTY: The luckiest thing in the world! for my mistress designs to have a ball and entertainment here tonight before the marriage; and that's my business with your master.

SHARP *(aside):* The devil it is!

KITTY: She'll not have it public; she designs to invite only eight or ten couple of friends.

SHARP: No more?

KITTY: No more: and she ordered me to desire your master not to make a great entertainment.

SHARP: Oh, never fear—

KITTY: Ten or a dozen little nice things, with some fruit, I believe, will be enough in all conscience.

SHARP *(aside):* Oh, curse your conscience!

KITTY: And what do you think I have done of my own head.

SHARP: What?

KITTY: I have invited all my Lord Stately's servants to come and see you, and have a dance in the kitchen: won't your master be surprised!

SHARP: Much so indeed!

KITTY: Well, be quick and find out your master, and make what haste you can with your preparations: you have no time to lose.—Prithee, Sharp, what's the matter with you? I have not seen you for some time, and you seem to look a little thin.

SHARP *(aside):* Oh, my unfortunate face!—I'm in pure good health, thank you, Mrs. Kitty; and I'll assure you, I have a very good stomach, never better in all my life, and I am as full of vigor, hussy! *(Offers to kiss her)*

KITTY: What, with that face! well, bye, bye. *(Going)*—Oh, Sharp, what ill-looking fellows are those, were standing about your door when I came in? They want your master too, I suppose.

SHARP: Hum! yes, they are waiting for him.—They are some of his tenants out of the country that want to pay him some money.

KITTY: Tenants! what, do you let his tenants stand in the street?

SHARP: They choose it; as they seldom come to town, they are willing to see as much of it as they can, when they do; they are raw, ignorant, honest people.

KITTY: Well, I must run home, farewell!—But do you hear? Get something substantial for us in the kitchen—a ham, a turkey, or what you will— we'll be very merry; and, be sure remove the tables and chairs away there too, that we may have room to dance: I can't bear to be confined in my French dances; tal, lal, lal. *(Dancing)* Well, adieu! Without any compliment, I shall die if I don't see you soon. *(Exit* KITTY*)*

SHARP: And without any compliment, I pray heaven you may!

(Enter GAYLESS. *They look for some time sorrowful at each other*)

GAY: O Sharp!

SHARP: O master!

GAY: We are certainly undone!

SHARP: That's no news to me.

GAY: Eight or ten couple of dancers—ten or a dozen little nice dishes, with some fruit—my Lord Stately's servants, ham and turkey!

SHARP: Say no more, the very sound creates an appetite: and I am sure of late I have had no occasion for whetters and provocatives.

GAY: Cursed misfortune! what can we do?

SHARP: Hang ourselves; I see no other remedy; except you have a receipt to give a ball and a supper without meat or music.

GAY: Melissa has certainly heard of my bad circumstances, and has invented this scheme to distress me, and break off the match.

SHARP: I don't believe it, sir; begging your pardon.

GAY: No? why did her maid then make so strict an enquiry into my fortune and affairs?

SHARP: For two very substantial reasons: the first, to satisfy a curiosity, natural to her as a woman; the second, to have the pleasure of my conversation, very natural to her as a woman of taste and understanding.

GAY: Prithee be more serious: is not our all at stake?

SHARP: Yes, sir: and yet that all of ours is of so little consequence, that a man, with a very small share of philosophy may part from it without much pain or uneasiness. However, sir, I'll convince you in half an hour, that Mrs. Melissa knows nothing of your circumstances, and I'll tell you what too, sir, she shan't be here tonight, and yet you shall marry her tomorrow morning.

GAY: How, how, dear Sharp!

SHARP: 'Tis here, here, sir! warm, warm, and delays will cool it; therefore I'll away to her, and do you be as merry as love and poverty will permit you.

Would you succeed, a faithful friend depute,

Whose head can plan, and front can execute.

I am the man, and I hope you neither dispute my friendship or qualification.

GAY: Indeed I don't. Prithee be gone.

SHARP: I fly. *(Exeunt.)*

Scene Two

MELISSA's *lodgings. Enter* MELISSA *and* KITTY.

MEL: You surprise me, Kitty! the master not at home! the man in confusion! no furniture in the house! and ill-looking fellows about the doors! 'Tis all a riddle.

KITTY: But very easy to be explained.

MEL: Prithee explain it then, nor keep me longer in suspense.

KITTY: The affair is this, madam: Mr. Gayless is over head and ears in debt; you are over head and ears in love; you'll marry him tomorrow, the next day, your whole fortune goes to his creditors, and you and your children are to live comfortably upon the remainder.

MEL: I cannot think him base.

KITTY: But I know they are all base—you are very young, and very ignorant of the sex; I am young too, but have more experience: you never was in love before; I have been in love with a hundred, and tried 'em all; and know 'em to be a parcel of barbarous, perjured, deluding, bewitching devils.

MEL: The low wretches you have had to do with may answer the character you give 'em; but Mr. Gayless—

KITTY: Is a man, madam.

MEL: I hope so, Kitty, or I would have nothing to do with him.

KITTY: With all my heart—I have given you my sentiments upon the occasion, and shall leave you to your own inclinations.

MEL: Oh, madam, I am much obliged to you for your great condescension, ha, ha, ha! However, I have so great a regard for your opinion, that had I certain proofs of his villainy—

KITTY: Of his poverty you may have a hundred: I am sure I have had none to the contrary.

MEL *(aside):* Oh, there the shoe pinches.

KITTY: Nay, so far from giving me the usual perquisites of my place, he has not so much as kept me in temper with little endearing civilities; and one might reasonably expect when a man is deficient in one way, that he should make it up in another. *(Knocking without)*

MEL: See who's at the door. *(Exit* KITTY*)*—I must be cautious how I hearken too much to this girl; her bad opinion of Mr. Gayless seems to arise from his disregard of her. *(Enter* SHARP *and* KITTY*)* So, Sharp; have you found your master? will things be ready for the ball and entertainment?

SHARP: To your wishes, madam. I have just now bespoke the music and supper, and wait now for your ladyship's farther commands.

MEL: My compliments to your master, and let him know I and my company will be with him by six; we design to drink tea, and play at cards, before we dance.

KITTY *(aside):* So shall I and my company, Mr. Sharp.

SHARP: Mighty well, madam!

MEL: Prithee, Sharp, what makes you come without your coat? 'Tis too cool to go so airy, sure.

KITTY: Mr. Sharp, madam, is of a very hot constitution, ha, ha, ha!

SHARP: If it had been ever so cool I have had enough to warm me since I came from home, I'm sure; but no matter for that. *(Sighing)*

MEL: What d'ye mean?

SHARP: Pray don't ask me, madam; I beseech you don't: let us change the subject.

KITTY: Insist upon knowing it, madam—*(aside)* my curiosity must be satisfied, or I shall burst.

MEL: I do insist upon knowing—on pain of my displeasure, tell me!

SHARP: If my master should know—I must not tell you, madam, indeed.

MEL: I promise you, upon my honor, he never shall.

SHARP *(indicating* KITTY*)*: But can your ladyship insure secrecy from that quarter?

KITTY: Yes, Mr. Jackanapes, for anything you can say.

MEL: I'll engage for her.

SHARP: Why then, in short, madam—I cannot tell you.

MEL: Don't trifle with me.

SHARP: Then since you will have it, madam,—I lost my coat in defense of your reputation.

MEL: In defense of my reputation!

SHARP: I will assure you, madam, I've suffered very much in defense of it; which is more than I would have done for my own.

MEL: Prithee explain.

SHARP: In short, madam, you was seen, about a month ago, to make a visit to my master alone.

MEL: Alone! my servant was with me.

SHARP: What, Mrs. Kitty? So much the worse; for she was looked upon as my property; and I was brought in guilty as well as you and my master.

KITTY: What, your property, jackanapes!

MEL: What is all this?

SHARP: Why, madam, as I came out but now to make preparations for you and your company tonight, Mrs. Pryabout, the attorney's wife at next door, calls to me: 'Hark'ee fellow!' says she, 'Do you and your modest master know that my husband shall indict your house, at the next parish meeting, for a nuisance?'

MEL: A nuisance!

SHARP: I said so:—'A nuisance! I believe none in the neighborhood live with more decency and regularity than I and my master,' as is really the case. 'Decency and regularity!' cries she, with a sneer,—'why, sirrah, does not my window look into your master's bed chamber? And did not he bring in a certain lady, such a day?'—describing you, madam. 'And did not I see—'

MEL: See! oh scandalous! what?

SHARP: Modesty requires my silence.

MEL: Did not you contradict her?

SHARP: Contradict her! why, I told her I was sure she lied: 'For, zounds!' said I—for I could not help swearing—'I am so well convinced of the lady's and my master's prudence, that, I am sure, had they a mind to amuse themselves they would certainly have drawn the window curtains.'

MEL: What, did you say nothing else? Did not you convince her of her error and impertinence?

SHARP: She swore to such things, that I could do nothing but swear and call names: upon which out bolts her husband upon me, with a fine taper crabwood cudgel in his hand and fell upon me with such violence, that, being half delirious, I made a full confession.

MEL: A full confession! what did you confess?

SHARP: That my master loved fornication; that you had no aversion to it; that Mrs. Kitty was a bawd, and your humble servant a pimp.

KITTY: A bawd! a bawd! do I look like a bawd, madam?

SHARP: And so, madam, in the scuffle, my coat was torn to pieces as well as your reputation.

MEL: And so you joined to make me infamous!

SHARP: For heaven's sake, madam, what could I do? his proofs fell so thick upon me, as witness my head, *(showing his head plastered)* that I would have given up all the maidenheads in the kingdom, rather than have my brains beat to a jelly.

MEL: Very well!—but I'll be revenged!—and did not you tell your master this?

SHARP: Tell him! No, madam; had I told him, his love is so violent for you, that he would certainly have murdered half the attorneys in town by this time.

MEL: Very well! but I'm resolved not to go to your master's tonight.

SHARP *(aside):* Heavens and my impudence be praised.

KITTY: Why not, madam? If you are not guilty, face your accusers.

SHARP *(aside):* Oh, the devil! ruined again!—To be sure, face 'em by all means, madam—they can but be abusive, and break the windows a little:—besides, madam, I have thought of a way to make this affair quite diverting to you—I have a fine blunderbuss charged with half a hundred slugs, and my master has a delicate large Swiss broad sword; and between us, madam, we shall so pepper and slice 'em, that you will die with laughing.

MEL: What, at murder?

KITTY: Don't fear, madam, there will be no murder if Sharp's concerned.

SHARP: Murder, madam! 'Tis self-defense; besides, in these sort of skirmishes, there are never more than two or three killed: for, supposing they bring the whole body of militia upon us, down but with a brace of them, and away fly the rest of the covey.

MEL: Persuade me never so much, I won't go; that's my resolution.

KITTY: Why then, I'll tell you what, madam; since you are resolved not to go to the supper, suppose the supper was to come to you: 'tis great pity such great preparations as Mr. Sharp has made should be thrown away.

SHARP: So it is, as you say, Mistress Kitty. But I can immediatcly run back and unbespeak what I have ordered; 'tis soon done.

MEL: But then what excuse can I send to your master? He'll be very uneasy at my not coming.

SHARP: Oh terribly so!—but I have it—I'll tell him you are very much out of order—that you were suddenly taken with the vapors or qualms; or what you please, madam.

MEL: I'll leave it to you, Sharp, to make my apology; and there's half a guinea for you to help your invention.

SHARP *(aside):* Half a guinea!—'Tis so long since I had anything to do with money, that I scarcely know the current coin of my own country. O Sharp, what talents hast thou! to secure thy master; deceive his mistress; out-lie her chamber-maid; and yet be paid for thy honesty? But my joy will discover me.—Madam, you have eternally fixed Timothy Sharp your most obedient humble servant! *(Aside)* Oh, the delights of impudence and a good understanding! *(Exit)*

KITTY: Ha, ha, ha! was there ever such a lying varlet? with his slugs and his broad swords; his attorneys and broken heads, and nonsense! well, madam, are you satisfied now? do you want more proofs?

MEL: Of your modesty I do: but I find, you are resolved to give me none.

KITTY: Madam?

MEL: I see through your little mean artifice: you are endeavoring to lessen Mr. Gayless in my opinion, because he has not paid you for services he had no occasion for.

KITTY: Pay me, madam! I am sure I have very little occasion to be angry with Mr. Gayless for not paying me, when, I believe, 'tis his general practice.

MEL: 'Tis false! he's a gentleman and a man of honor, and you are—

KITTY *(curtsying):* Not in love, I thank heaven!

MEL: You are a fool.

KITTY: I have been in love; but I am much wiser now.

MEL: Hold your tongue, impertinence!

KITTY *(aside):* That's the severest thing she has said yet.

MEL: Leave me.

KITTY: Oh this love, this love is the devil! *(Exit)*

MEL: We discover our weaknesses to our servants, make them our confidents, put 'em upon an equality with us, and so they become our advisers—Sharp's behavior, though I seemed to disregard it, makes me tremble with apprehensions; and though I have pretended to be angry with Kitty for her advice, I think it of too much consequence to be neglected.

(Enter KITTY*)*

KITTY: May I speak, madam?

MEL: Don't be a fool. What do you want?

KITTY: There is a servant just come out of the country says he belongs to Sir William Gayless, and has got a letter for you from his master, upon very urgent business.

MEL: Sir William Gayless! What can this mean? where is the man?

KITTY: In the little parlor, madam.

MEL: I'll go to him—my heart flutters strangely. *(Exit)*

KITTY: O woman, woman, foolish woman! she'll certainly have this Gayless: nay, were she as well convinced of his poverty as I am, she'd have him. A strong dose of love is worse than one of ratafia; when it once gets into our heads, it trips up our heels, and then good night to discretion. Here is she going to throw away fifteen thousand pounds; upon what? faith, little better than nothing—he's a man, and that's all —and heaven knows mere man is but small consolation.

Be this advice pursued by each fond maid,

Ne'er slight the substance for an empty shade:

Rich, weighty sparks alone should please and charm ye:

For should spouse cool, his gold will always warm ye.

(Curtain.)

ACT II

GAYLESS' *lodgings. Enter* GAYLESS *and* SHARP.

GAY: Prithee be serious, Sharp. Hast thou really succeeded?

SHARP: To our wishes, sir. In short, I have managed the business with such skill and dexterity, that neither your circumstances nor my veracity are suspected.

GAY: But how hast thou excused me from the ball and entertainment?

SHARP: Beyond expectation, sir. But in that particular I was obliged to have recourse to truth, and declare the real situation of your affairs. I told her we had so long disused ourselves to dressing either dinners or suppers, that I was afraid we should be but awkward in our preparations. In short, sir—at that instant a cursed gnawing seized my stomach, that I could not help telling her that both you and myself seldom make a good meal now-a-days once in a quarter of a year.

GAY: Hell and confusion, have you betrayed me, villain? Did you not tell me this moment, she did not in the least suspect my circumstances?

SHARP: No more she did, sir, till I told her.

GAY: Very well; and was this your skill and dexterity?

SHARP: I was going to tell you; but you won't hear reason; my melancholy face and piteous narration had such an effect upon her generous bowels, that she freely forgives all that's past.

GAY: Does she, Sharp?

SHARP: Yes; and desires never to see your face again; and, as a farther consideration for so doing, she has sent you half a guinea. *(Shows the money)*

GAY: What do you mean?

SHARP: To spend it, spend it, sir; and regale.

GAY: Villain, you have undone me!

SHARP: What, by bringing you money, when you are not worth a farthing in the whole world? Well, well, then to make you happy again, I'll keep it myself, and wish somebody would take it in their head to load me with such misfortunes. *(Puts away the money)*

GAY: Do you laugh at me, rascal!

SHARP: Who deserves more to be laughed at! ha, ha, ha! Never for the future, sir, dispute the success of my negotiations, when even you, who know me so well, can't help swallowing my hook. Why, sir, I could have played with you backwards and forwards at the end of my line, till I had put your senses into such a fermentation, that you should not have known in an hour's time, whether you was a fish or a man.

GAY: Why, what is all this you have been telling me?

SHARP: A downright lie from beginning to end.

GAY: And have you really excused me to her?

SHARP: No, sir; but I have got this half guinea to make her excuses to you; and, instead of a confederacy between you and me to deceive her, she thinks she has brought me over to put the deceit upon you.

GAY: Thou excellent fellow!

SHARP: Don't lose time, but slip out of the house immediately; the back way, I believe, will be the safest for you, and to her as fast as you can; pretend vast surprise and concern, that her indisposition has debarred you the pleasure of her company here tonight: you need know no more, away!

GAY: But what shall we do, Sharp? here's her maid again.

SHARP: The devil she is—I wish I could poison her; for I'm sure, while she lives, I can never prosper.

(Enter KITTY*)*

KITTY: Your door was open, so I did not stand upon ceremony.

GAY: I am sorry to hear your mistress is taken so suddenly.

KITTY: Vapors, vapors only, sir, a few matrimonial omens, that's all; but I suppose Mr. Sharp has made her excuses.

GAY: And tells me I can't have the pleasure of her company, tonight. I had made a small preparation; but 'tis no matter: Sharp shall go to the rest of the company; and let 'em know 'tis put off.

KITTY: Not for the world, sir; my mistress was sensible you must have provided for her, and the rest of the company; so is she resolved, though she can't, the other ladies and gentlemen shall partake of your entertainment; she's very good-natured.

SHARP: I had better run, and let 'em know 'tis deferred. *(Going)*

KITTY *(stopping him):* I have been with 'em already, and told 'em my mistress insists upon their coming, and they have all promised to be here; so, pray, don't be under any apprehensions, that your preparations will be thrown away.

GAY: But as I can't have her company, Mrs. Kitty, 'twill be a greater pleasure to me, and a greater compliment to her, to defer our mirth; besides I can't enjoy anything at present, and she not partake of it.

KITTY: Oh, no, to be sure; but what can I do? My mistress will have it so, and Mrs. Gadabout and the rest of the company will be here in a few minutes; there are two or three coachfuls of 'em.

SHARP *(aside):* Then my master must be ruined in spite of my parts.

GAY *(aside to* SHARP): 'Tis all over, Sharp.

SHARP: I know it, sir.

GAY: I shall go distracted; what shall I do?

SHARP: Why, sir, as our rooms are a little out of furniture at present, take 'em into the captain's that lodges here, and set 'em down to cards; if he should come in the meantime, I'll excuse you to him.

KITTY *(aside):* I have disconcerted their affairs, I find; I'll have some sport with 'em.—Pray, Mr. Gayless, don't order too many things; they only make you a friendly visit; the more ceremony, you know, the less welcome. Pray, sir, let me entreat you not to be profuse. If I can be of service, pray command me; my mistress has sent me on purpose; while Mr. Sharp is doing the business without doors, I may be employed within; *(to* SHARP*)* if you'll lend me the keys of your side-board I'll dispose of your plate to the best advantage. *(Knocking)*

SHARP: Thank you, Mrs. Kitty; but it is disposed of already. *(Knocking at the door)*

KITTY: Bless me, the company's come! I'll go to the door and conduct 'em into your presence. *(Exit)*

SHARP: If you'd conduct 'em into a horse pond, and wait of 'em there yourself, we should be more obliged to you.

GAY: I can never support this!

SHARP: Rouse your spirits and put on an air of gaiety, and I don't despair of bringing you off yet.

GAY: Your words have done it effectually.

(Enter MRS. GADABOUT, *her daughter and niece,* MR. GUTTLE, MR. TRIPPIT *and* MRS. TRIPPIT*)*

GAD: Ah, my dear, Mr. Gayless! *(Kisses him)*

GAY: My dear widow! *(Kisses her)*

GAD: We are come to give you joy, Mr. Gayless.

SHARP *(aside):* You never was more mistaken in your life.

GAD: I have brought some company here, I believe, is not so well known to you, and I protest I have been all about the town to get the little I have —Prissy, my dear—Mr. Gayless, my daughter.

GAY: And as handsome as her mother; you must have a husband shortly, my dear.

PRIS: I'll assure you I don't despair, sir.

GAD: My niece, too.

GAY: I know by her eyes she belongs to you, widow.

GAD: Mr. Guttle, sir, Mr. Gayless; Mr. Gayless, Justice Guttle.

GAY *(aside):* Oh, destruction! one of the quorum of magistrates.

GUT: Hem, though I had not the honor of any personal knowledge of you, yet at the instigation of Mrs. Gadabout I have, without any previous acquaintance with you, throwed aside all ceremony to let you know that I joy to hear the solemnization of your nuptials is so near at hand.

GAY: Sir, though I cannot answer you with the same elocution, however, sir, I thank you with the same sincerity.

GAD: Mr. and Mrs. Trippit, sir, the properest lady in the world for your purpose, for she'll dance for four and twenty hours together.

TRIP: My dear Charles, I am very angry with you, faith; so near marriage and not let me know, 'twas barbarous; you thought, I suppose, I should rally you upon it; but dear Mrs. Trippit here has long ago eradicated all my anti-matrimonial principles.

MRS. TRIP: I eradicate! fie, Mr. Trippit, don't be so obscene.

KITTY: Pray, ladies, walk into the next room; Mr. Sharp can't lay his cloth till you are set down to cards.

GAD: One thing I had quite forgot; Mr. Gayless, my nephew who you never saw will be in town from France presently, so I left word to send him here immediately to make one.

GAY: You do me honor, madam.

SHARP: Do the ladies choose cards or the supper first?

GAY *(aside):* Supper! what does the fellow mean?

GUT: Oh, the supper by all means, for I have eat nothing to signify since dinner.

SHARP *(aside):* Nor I, since last Monday was a fortnight.

GAY: Pray, ladies, walk into the next room: Sharp, get things ready for supper, and call the music.

SHARP: Well said, master.

GAY: Without ceremony, ladies. *(Exeunt ladies and* GAYLESS*)*

KITTY *(aside):* I'll to my mistress, and let her know everything is ready for her appearance. *(Exit)*

GUT: Pray Mr. What's-your-name, don't be long with supper; but hark'ee, what can I do in the meantime? Suppose you get me a pipe and some good wine; I'll try to divert myself that way till supper's ready.

SHARP: Or suppose, sir, you was to take a nap till then, there's a very easy couch in that closet.

GUT: The best thing in the world. I'll take your advice, but be sure to wake me when supper is ready. *(Exit)*

SHARP: Pray heav'n you may not wake till then—what a fine situation my master is in at present! I have promised him my assistance, but his affairs are in so desperate a way, that I am afraid 'tis out of all my skill to recover 'em. Well, fools have fortune, says an old proverb, and a very true one it is, for my master and I are two of the most unfortunate mortals in the creation.

(Enter GAYLESS*)*

GAY: Well, Sharp, I have set 'em down to cards, and now what have you to propose?

SHARP: I have one scheme left which in all probability may succeed. The good citizen, overloaded with his last meal, is taking a nap in that closet, in order to get him an appetite for yours. Suppose, sir, we should make him treat us.

GAY: I don't understand you.

SHARP: I'll pick his pocket, and provide us a supper with the booty.

GAY: Monstrous! for without considering the villainy of it, the danger of waking him makes it impracticable!

SHARP: If he wakes, I'll smother him, and lay his death to indigestion—a very common death among the justices.

GAY: Prithee be serious, we have no time to lose; can you invent nothing to drive 'em out of the house?

SHARP: I can fire it.

GAY: Shame and confusion so perplex me, I cannot give myself a moment's thought.

SHARP: I have it; did not Mrs. Gadabout say her nephew would be here?

GAY: She did.

SHARP: Say no more, but in to your company; if I don't send 'em out of the house for the night, I'll at least frighten their stomachs away; and if this stratagem fails, I'll relinquish politics, and think my understanding no better than my neighbors'.

GAY: How shall I reward thee, Sharp?

SHARP: By your silence and obedience; away to your company, sir. *(Exit)* Now, dear madam Fortune, for once, open your eyes, and behold a poor unfortunate man of parts addressing you; now is your time to convince your foes you are not that blind whimsical whore less they take you for; but let 'em see by your assisting me, that men of sense, as well as fools, are sometimes entitled to your favor and protection.—So much for prayer, now for a great noise and a lie. *(Goes aside and cries out)* Help, help, master; help, gentlemen, ladies; murder, fire, brimstone; help, help, help!

(Enter MR. GAYLESS, MR. TRIPPET, *and the ladies, with cards in their hands, and* SHARP *enters running, and meets 'em)*

GAY: What's the matter?

SHARP: Matter, sir! if you don't run this minute with that gentleman, this lady's nephew will be murdered; I am sure 'twas he; he was set upon the corner of the street, by four; he has killed two, and if you don't make haste, he'll be either murdered or took to prison.

GAD: For heaven's sake, gentlemen, run to his assistance. *(Aside)* How I tremble for Melissa; this frolic of hers may be fatal.

GAY: Draw, sir, and follow me. *(Exeunt GAYLESS and GADABOUT)*

TRIP: Not I; I don't care to run myself into needless quarrels; I have suffered too much formerly by flying into passions; besides I have pawned my honor to Mrs. Trippit, never to draw my sword again; and in her present condition, to break my word might have fatal consequences.

SHARP: Pray, sir, don't excuse yourself, the young gentleman may be murdered by this time.

TRIP: Then my assistance will be of no service to him; however—I'll go to oblige you, and look on at a distance.

MRS. TRIP: I shall certainly faint, Mr. Trippit, if you draw.

(Enter GUTTLE, disordered, as from sleep)

GUT: What noise and confusion is this?

SHARP: Sir, there's a man murdered in the street.

GUT: Is that all—zounds, I was afraid you had throwed the supper down— a plague of your noise—I shan't recover my stomach this half hour.

(Enter GAYLESS and GADABOUT, with MELISSA in boy's clothes, dressed in the French manner)

GAD: Well, but my dear Jemmy, you are not hurt, sure?

MEL: A little with riding post only.

GAD: Mr. Sharp alarmed us all with an account of your being set upon by four men; that you had killed two, and was attacking the other when he came away, and when we met you at the door, we were running to your rescue.

MEL: I had a small encounter with half a dozen villains; but finding me resolute, they were wise enough to take to their heels; I believe I scratched some of 'em. *(Laying her hand to her sword)*

SHARP *(aside):* His vanity has saved my credit. I have a thought come into my head may prove to our advantage, provided monsieur's ignorance bears any proportion to his impudence.

GAD: Now my fright's over, let me introduce you, my dear, to Mr. Gayless; sir, this is my nephew.

GAY *(saluting her):* Sir, I shall be proud of your friendship.

MEL: I don't doubt but we shall be better acquainted in a little time.

GUT: Pray, sir, what news in France?

MEL: Faith, sir, very little that I know of in the political way; I had no time to spend among the politicians. I was—

GAY: Among the ladies, I suppose.

MEL: Too much, indeed. Faith, I have not philosophy enough to resist their solicitations; *(To* GAYLESS *aside)* you take me.

GAY *(aside to* SHARP): Yes, to be a most incorrigible fop; 'sdeath, this puppy's impertinence is an addition to my misery.

MEL *(aside to* GADABOUT): Poor Gayless, to what shifts is he reduced? I cannot bear to see him much longer in this condition; I shall discover myself.

GAD: Not before the end of the play; besides, the more his pain now, the greater his pleasure when relieved from it.

TRIP: Shall we return to our cards? I have a superb hand here, and must insist you play it out.

LADIES: With all my heart.

MEL: *Allons donc.*

(As the company goes out, SHARP *pulls* MELISSA *by the sleeve)*

SHARP: Sir, sir, shall I beg leave to speak with you? Pray, did you find a bank-note in your way hither?

MEL: What, between here and Dover do you mean?

SHARP: No, sir, within twenty or thirty yards of this house.

MEL: You are drunk, fellow.

SHARP: I am undone, sir; but not drunk, I'll assure you.

MEL: What is all this?

SHARP: I'll tell you, sir: a little while ago my master sent me out to change a note of twenty pounds; but I, unfortunately hearing a noise in the street of, 'damme, sir,' and clashing of swords, and 'rascal,' and 'murder'; I runs up to the place, and saw four men upon one; and having heard you was a mettlesome young gentleman, I immediately concluded it must be you; so ran back to call my master, and when I went to look for the note to change it, I found it gone, either stole or lost; and if I don't get the money immediately, I shall certainly be turned out of my place, and lose my character.

MEL *(aside):* I shall laugh in his face.—Oh, I'll speak to your master about it, and he will forgive you at my intercession.

SHARP: Ah, sir! you don't know my master.

MEL: I'm very little acquainted with him; but I have heard he's a very good-natured man.

SHARP: I have heard so too, but I have felt it otherwise; he has so much good nature, that, if I could compound for one broken head a day, I should think myself very well off.

MEL: Are you serious, friend?

SHARP: Look'ee, sir, I take you for a man of honor; there is something in your face that is generous, open, and masculine; you don't look like a

foppish, effeminate tell-tale; so I'll venture to trust you.—See here, sir
—*(Shows his head)* these are the effects of my master's good nature.

MEL *(aside):* Matchless impudence!—Why do you live with him then after
such usage?

SHARP: He's worth a great deal of money, and when he's drunk, which is
commonly once a day he's very free, and will give me anything; but I
design to leave him when he's married, for all that.

MEL: Is he going to be married then?

SHARP: Tomorrow, sir, and between you and I, he'll meet with his match,
both for humor and something else, too.

MEL: What, she drinks, too?

SHARP: Damnably, sir; but mum.—You must know this entertainment was
designed for madam tonight; but she got so very gay after dinner, that
she could not walk out of her own house; so her maid, who was half
gone, too, came here with an excuse, that Mrs. Melissa had got the
vapors, and so she had indeed violently; here, here, sir. *(Pointing to his
head)*

MEL *(aside):* This is scarcely to be borne.—Melissa! I have heard of her;
they say she's very whimsical.

SHARP: A very woman, and please your honor, and between you and I,
none of the mildest or wisest of her sex—but to return, sir, to the
twenty pounds.

MEL: I am surprised you who have got so much money in his service,
should be at a loss for twenty pounds, to save your bones at this junc-
ture.

SHARP: I have put all my money out at interest; I never keep above five
pounds by me; and if your honor would lend me the other fifteen, and
take my note for it. *(Knocking)*

MEL: Somebody's at the door.

SHARP: I can give very good security. *(Knocking)*

MEL: Don't let the people wait, Mr.—

SHARP: Ten pounds will do. *(Knocking)*

MEL: *Allez-vous-cu!*

SHARP: Five, sir. *(Knocking)*

MEL: *Je ne puis pas.*

SHARP *(aside):* 'Je ne puis pas.' I find we shan't understand one another, I
do but lose time; and, if I had any thought, I might have known young
fops return from their travels generally with as little money as improve-
ment. *(Exit)*

MEL: Ha, ha, ha, what lies doth this fellow invent, and what rogueries does
he commit for his master's service? There never sure was a more
faithful servant to his master, or a greater rogue to the rest of mankind;

but here he comes again; the plot thickens; I'll in and observe Gayless. *(Exit)*

(Enter SHARP *before several persons with dishes in their hands, and a Cook, drunk)*

SHARP *(aside):* Fortune, I thank thee: the most lucky accident!—This way, gentlemen, this way.

COOK: I am afraid I have mistook the house. Is this Mr. Treatwell's?

SHARP: The same, the same: what, don't you know me?

COOK: Know you!—Are you sure there was a supper bespoke here?

SHARP: Yes: upon my honor, Mr. Cook, the company is in the next room, and must have gone without, had not you brought it. I'll draw in a table. I see you have brought a cloth with you; but you need not have done that, for we have a very good stock of linen—*(Aside)* at the pawnbroker's. *(Exit, and returns immediately, drawing in a table)* Come, come my boys, be quick, the company began to be very uneasy; but I knew my old friend Lick-spit here would not fail us.

COOK: Lick-spit! I am no friend of yours; so I desire less familiarity: Lick-spit, too!

(Enter GAYLESS, *and stares)*

GAY: What is all this?

SHARP *(aside to* GAYLESS*):* Sir, if the sight of the supper is offensive, I can easily have it removed.

GAY: Prithee explain thyself, Sharp.

SHARP: Some of our neighbors, I suppose, have bespoke this supper; but the cook has drank away his memory, forgot the house, and brought it here; however, sir, if you dislike it, I'll tell him of his mistake, and send him about his business.

GAY: Hold, hold, necessity obliges me against my inclination to favor the cheat, and feast at my neighbor's expense.

COOK: Hark you, friend, is that your master?

SHARP: Ay, and the best master in the world.

COOK: I'll speak to him then.—Sir, I have according to your commands, dressed as genteel a supper as my art and your price would admit of.

SHARP *(aside to* GAYLESS*):* Good again, sir, 'tis paid for.

GAY: I don't in the least question your abilities, Mr. Cook, and I am obliged to you for your care.

COOK: Sir, you are a gentleman—and if you would but look over the bill and approve it, *(Pulls out a bill)* you will over and above return the obligation.

SHARP *(aside):* Oh, the devil!

GAY *(looking on a bill):* Very well, I'll send my man to pay you tomorrow.

COOK: I'll spare him that trouble, and take it with me, sir—I never work but for ready money.

GAY: Hah?

SHARP *(aside):* Then you won't have our custom.—My master is busy now, friend; do you think he won't pay you?

COOK: No matter what I think; either my meat or my money.

SHARP: 'Twill be very ill-convenient for him to pay you tonight.

COOK: Then I'm afraid it will be ill-convenient to pay me tomorrow, so d'ye hear—

(Enter MELISSA*)*

GAY: Prithee be advised! 'sdeath, I shall be discovered! *(Takes the* COOK *aside)*

MEL *(to* SHARP*):* What's the matter?

SHARP: The cook has not quite answered my master's expectations about the supper, sir, and he's a little angry at him, that's all.

MEL: Come, come, Mr. Gayless, don't be uneasy; a bachelor cannot be supposed to have things in the utmost regularity; we don't expect it.

COOK: But I do expect it, and will have it.

MEL: What does that drunken fool say?

COOK: That I will have my money, and I won't stay till tomorrow—and, and—

SHARP *(runs and stops his mouth):* Hold, hold, what are you doing? are you mad?

MEL: What do you stop the man's breath for?

SHARP: Sir, he was going to call you names.—Don't be abusive, cook; the gentleman is a man of honor, and said nothing to you; pray be pacified; you are in liquor.

COOK: I will have my—

SHARP *(holding, still):* Why, I tell you, fool, you mistake the gentleman; he is a friend of my master's, and has not said a word to you—Pray, good sir, go into the next room; the fellow's drunk, and takes you for another.—You'll repent this when you are sober, friend. —Pray, sir, don't stay to hear his impertinence.

GAY: Pray, sir, walk in—he's below your anger.

MEL: Damn the rascal! What does he mean by affronting me! Let the scoundrel go; I'll polish his brutality, I warrant you: here's the best reformer of manners in the universe. *(Draws his sword)* Let him go, I say.

SHARP: So, so you have done finely, now.—Get away as fast as you can:

he's the most courageous mettlesome man in all England. Why, if his passion was up he could eat you.—Make your escape, you fool!

COOK: I won't. Eat me! he'll find me damned hard of digestion though—

SHARP: Prithee come here; let me speak with you.

(They walk aside. Enter KITTY*)*

KITTY: Gad's me, is supper on the table already? Sir, pray defer it for a few moments; my mistress is much better, and will be here immediately.

GAY: Will she indeed! bless me—I did not expect—but however—Sharp?

KITTY *(aside to* MELISSA*)*: What success, madam?

MEL: As we could wish, girl—but he is in such pain and perplexity I can't hold it out much longer.

KITTY: Ay, that not holding out is the ruin of half our sex.

SHARP: I have pacified the cook, and if you can but borrow twenty pieces of that young prig, all may go well yet; you may succeed though I could not: remember what I told you—about it straight, sir—

GAY *(to* MELISSA*)*: Sir, sir, I beg to speak a word with you; my servant, sir, tells me he has had the misfortune, sir, to lose a note of mine of twenty pounds, which I sent him to receive—and the bankers' shops being shut up, and having very little cash by me, I should be much obliged to you if you would favor me with twenty pieces till tomorrow.

MEL: Oh, sir, with all my heart *(Taking out her purse),* and as I have a small favor to beg of you, sir, the obligation will be mutual.

GAY: How may I oblige you, sir?

MEL: You are to be married, I hear, to Melissa.

GAY: Tomorrow, sir.

MEL: Then you'll oblige me, sir, by never seeing her again.

GAY: Do you call this a small favor, sir!

MEL: A mere trifle, sir—breaking of contracts, suing for divorces, committing adultery, and such like, are all reckoned trifles nowadays; and smart young fellows, like you and myself, Gayless, should never be out of fashion.

GAY: But pray, sir, how are you concerned in this affair!

MEL: Oh, sir, you must know I have a very great regard for Melissa, and, indeed, she for me; and, by the by, I have a most despicable opinion of you; for *entre nous,* I take you, Charles, to be a very great scoundrel.

GAY: Sir!

MEL: Nay, don't look fierce, sir! and give yourself airs—damme, sir, I shall be through your body else in the snapping of a finger.

GAY: I'll be as quick as you, villain! *(Draws and makes at* MELISSA*)*

KITTY: Hold, hold, murder! you'll kill my mistress—the young gentleman, I mean.

GAY: Ah! her mistress! *(Drops his sword)*

SHARP: How! Melissa! nay, then drive away cart. All's over now.

(Enter all the company laughing)

GAD: What, Mr. Gayless, engaging with Melissa before your time. Ah, ah, ah!

KITTY *(to* SHARP*)*: Your humble servant, good Mr. Politician.—This is, gentlemen and ladies, the most celebrated and ingenious Timothy Sharp, schemer general, and redoubted squire to the most renowned and fortunate adventurer Charles Gayless, knight of the woeful countenance: ha, ha, ha! Oh, that dismal face and more dismal head of yours. *(Strikes* SHARP *upon the head)*

SHARP: 'Tis cruel in you to disturb a man in his last agonies.

MEL: Now, Mr. Gayless!—what, not a word! you are sensible I can be no stranger to your misfortunes, and I might reasonably expect an excuse for your ill treatment of me.

GAY: No, madam, silence is my only refuge; for to endeavor to vindicate my crimes would show a greater want of virtue than even the commission of 'em.

MEL: Oh, Gayless! 'twas poor to impose upon a woman, and one that loved you, too.

GAY: Oh, most unpardonable; but my necessities—

SHARP: And mine, madam, were not to be matched, I'm sure, o' this side starving.

MEL *(aside):* His tears have softened me at once.—Your necessities, Mr. Gayless, with such real contrition, are too powerful motives not to affect the breast already prejudiced in your favor—you have suffered too much already for your extravagance; and as I take part in your sufferings, 'tis easing myself to relieve you: know, therefore, all that's past I freely forgive.

GAY: You cannot mean it, sure: I am lost in wonder.

MEL: Prepare yourself for more wonder—you have another friend in masquerade here: Mr. Cook, pray throw aside your drunkenness, and make your sober appearance—don't you know that face, sir?

COOK: Ay, master, what, have you forgot your friend Dick, as you used to call me?

GAY: More wonder indeed! don't you live with my father?

MEL: Just after your hopeful servant there had left me, comes this man from Sir William with a letter to me; upon which (being by that wholly convinced of your necessitous condition) I invented, by the help of Kitty and Mrs. Gadabout, this little plot, in which your friend Dick there has acted miracles, resolving to tease you a little, that you might have a greater relish for a happy turn in your affairs. Now, sir, read that letter, and complete your joy.

GAY *(reads):* 'Madam, I am father to the unfortunate young man, who, I hear by a friend of mine (that by my desire, has been a continual spy upon him) is making his addresses to you: if he is so happy as to make himself agreeable to you (whose character I am charmed with) I shall own him with joy for my son, and forget his former follies. I am,

Madam,

Your most humble servant,

William Gayless.

P.S. I will be soon in town myself to congratulate his reformation and marriage.'

O Melissa, this is too much; thus let me show my thanks and gratitude, *(Kneeling; she raises him)* for here 'tis only due.

SHARP: A reprieve! a reprieve! a reprieve!

KITTY *(to GAYLESS):* I have been, sir, a most bitter enemy to you; but since you are likely to be a little more conversant with cash than you have been, I am now, with the greatest sincerity, your most obedient friend and humble servant. And I hope, sir, all former enmity will be forgotten.

GAY: Oh, Mrs. Pry, I have been too much indulged with forgiveness myself not to forgive lesser offenses in other people.

SHARP: Well then, madam, since my master has vouchsafed pardon to your handmaid Kitty, I hope you'll not deny it to his footman Timothy.

MEL: Pardon! for what?

SHARP: Only for telling you about ten thousand lies, madam, and, among the rest, insinuating that your ladyship would—

MEL: I understand you; and can forgive any thing, Sharp, that was designed for the service of your master; and if Pry and you will follow our example, I'll give her a small fortune as a reward for both your fidelities.

SHARP: I fancy, madam, 'twould be better to half the small fortune between us, and keep us both single: for as we shall live in the same house, in all probability we may taste the comforts of matrimony, and not be troubled with its inconveniences; what say you, Kitty?

KITTY: Do you hear, Sharp, before you talk of the comforts of matrimony, taste the comforts of a good dinner, and recover your flesh a little; do, puppy.

SHARP: The devil backs her, that's certain; and I am no match for her at any weapon.

MEL: And now, Mr. Gayless, to show I have not provided for you by halves, let the music prepare themselves, and, with the approbation of the company, we'll have a dance.

ALL: By all means, a dance.

GUT: By all means a dance—after supper, though—

SHARP: Oh, pray, sir, have supper first, or, I'm sure, I shan't live till the dance is finished.

GAY: Behold, Melissa, as sincere a convert as ever truth and beauty made. The wild impetuous sallies of my youth are now blown over, and a most pleasing calm of perfect happiness succeeds.

Thus Ætna's flames the verdant earth consume,
But milder heat makes drooping nature bloom:
So virtuous love affords us springing joy,
Whilst vicious passions, as they burn, destroy.

(Curtain.)

THE STRANGE GENTLEMAN

A Comic Burletta in Two Acts

by
Charles Dickens

An authentic doorslammer by the great English novelist CHARLES DICKENS (1812–70) is not as surprising as it first may seem. Dickens loved the stage. He wrote about the theatre, acted on more than one occasion, entertained as a magician, composed and produced several plays and ultimately wrecked his health touring England and America in solo readings from his own books.

THE STRANGE GENTLEMAN, first produced on September 29, 1836, at the St. James's Theatre, London, was Dickens's first play. It ran some seventy performances and was deemed an artistic and commercial success.

CAST OF CHARACTERS

MR. OWEN OVERTON, Mayor of a small town on the road to
Gretna, and useful at the St. James's Arms
JOHN JOHNSON, detained at the St. James's Arms
THE STRANGE GENTLEMAN, just arrived at the St. James's Arms
CHARLES TOMKINS, incognito at the St. James's Arms
TOM SPARKS, a one-eyed 'Boots' at the St. James's Arms

JOHN ⎫
TOM ⎬ Waiters at the
WILL ⎭ St. James's Arms

JULIA DOBBS, looking for a husband at the St. James's Arms
FANNY WILSON, with an appointment at the St. James's Arms
MARY WILSON, her sister, awkwardly situated at the
St. James's Arms
MRS. NOAKES, the Landlady at the St. James's Arms
CHAMBERMAID, at the St. James's Arms

Scene—a small town on the road to Gretna
Time—part of a day and night

ACT I

Scene One

A room at the St. James's Arms; door in center, with a bolt on it. A table with cover and two chairs. Enter MRS. NOAKES.

MRS. NOAKES: Bless us, what a coachful! Four inside—twelve out; and the guard blowing the key-bugle in the fore-boot, for fear the informers should see that they have got one over the number. Post-chaise and a gig besides. We shall be filled to the very attics. Now, look alive, there —bustle about. *(Enter* FIRST WAITER, *running)* Now, John.

FIRST WAITER: Single lady, inside the stage, wants a private room, ma'am.

MRS. NOAKES: Much luggage?

FIRST WAITER: Four trunks, two bonnet-boxes, six brown-paper parcels and a basket.

MRS. NOAKES: Give her a private room, directly. No. 1, on the first floor.

FIRST WAITER: Yes, ma'am.

(Exit FIRST WAITER, *running. Enter* SECOND WAITER, *running)*

MRS. NOAKES: Now, Tom.

SECOND WAITER: Two young ladies and one gentleman in a post-chaise want a private sitting room d'rectly, ma'am.

MRS. NOAKES: Brother and sisters, Tom?

SECOND WAITER: Ladies are something alike, ma'am. Gentleman like neither of 'em.

MRS. NOAKES: Husband and wife and wife's sister, perhaps. Eh, Tom?

SECOND WAITER: Can't be husband and wife, ma'am, because I saw the gentleman kiss one of the ladies.

MRS. NOAKES: Kissing one of the ladies! Put them in the small sitting room behind the bar, Tom, that I may have an eye on them through the little window, and see that nothing improper goes forward.

SECOND WAITER: Yes, ma'am. *(Going)*

MRS. NOAKES: And Tom!

SECOND WAITER: Yes, ma'am.

MRS. NOAKES: Tell Cook to put together all the bones and pieces that were left on the plates at the great dinner yesterday, and make some nice soup to feed the stagecoach passengers with.

SECOND WAITER: Very well, ma'am.

(Exit SECOND WAITER. *Enter* THIRD WAITER, *running)*

MRS. NOAKES: Now, Will.

THIRD WAITER: A strange gentleman in a gig, ma'am, wants a private sitting room.

MRS. NOAKES: Much luggage, Will?

THIRD WAITER: One portmanteau and a greatcoat.

MRS. NOAKES: Oh! nonsense!—Tell him to go into the commercial room.

THIRD WAITER: I told him so, ma'am, but the Strange Gentleman says he *will* have a private apartment and that it's as much as his life is worth to sit in a public room.

MRS. NOAKES: As much as his life is worth?

THIRD WAITER: Yes, ma'am. Gentleman says he doesn't care if it's a dark closet; but a private room of some kind he must and will have.

MRS. NOAKES: Very odd. Did you ever see him before, Will?

THIRD WAITER: No, ma'am; he's quite a stranger here. He's a wonderful man to talk, ma'am—keeps on like a steam engine. Here he is, ma'am.

STRANGE GENTLEMAN (*without*): Now don't tell me, because that's all gammon and nonsense; and gammoned I never was, and never will be, by any waiter that ever drew the breath of life, or a cork. And just have the goodness to leave my portmanteau alone, because I can carry it very well myself; and show me a private room without further delay; for a private room I must and will have.—Damme, do you think I'm going to be murdered!—(*Enter the three* WAITERS, *the* STRANGE GENTLEMAN *following, carrying his portmanteau and greatcoat*) There—this room will do capitally well. Quite the thing—just the fit. How are you, ma'am? I suppose you are the landlady of this place? Just order those very attentive young fellows out, will you, and I'll order dinner.

MRS. NOAKES (*to* WAITERS): You may leave the room.

STRANGE GENTLEMAN: Hear that?—You may leave the room. Make yourselves scarce. Evaporate—disappear—come. (*Exeunt* WAITERS) That's right. And now, madam, while we're talking over this important matter of dinner, I'll just secure us effectually against further intrusion. (*Bolts the door*)

MRS. NOAKES: Lor, sir! Bolting the door, and *me* in the room!

STRANGE GENTLEMAN: Don't be afraid—I won't hurt you. I have no designs against you, my dear ma'am: but *I must be private.* (*Sits on the portmanteau*)

MRS. NOAKES: Well, sir—I have no objection to break through our rules for once; but it is not our way, when we're full, to give private rooms to solitary gentlemen who come in a gig and bring only one portmanteau. You're quite a stranger *here,* sir. If I'm not mistaken, it's your first appearance in this house.

STRANGE GENTLEMAN: You're right, ma'am. It *is* my first, my very first—but not my last, I can tell you.

MRS. NOAKES: No?

STRANGE GENTLEMAN: No. *(Looking round him)* I like the look of this place. Snug and comfortable—neat and lively. You'll very often find me at the St. James's Arms, I can tell you, ma'am.

MRS. NOAKES *(aside):* A civil gentleman. Are you a stranger in this town, sir?

STRANGE GENTLEMAN: Stranger! Bless you, no. I have been here for many years past, in the season.

MRS. NOAKES: Indeed!

STRANGE GENTLEMAN: Oh, yes. Put up at the Royal Hotel regularly for a long time, but I was obliged to leave it at last.

MRS. NOAKES: I have heard a good many complaints of it.

STRANGE GENTLEMAN: O! terrible! such a noisy house.

MRS. NOAKES: Ah!

STRANGE GENTLEMAN: Shocking! Din, din, din—Drum, drum, drum, all night. Nothing but noise, glare and nonsense. I bore it a long time for old acquaintance sake; but what do you think they did at last, ma'am?

MRS. NOAKES: I can't guess.

STRANGE GENTLEMAN: Turned the fine Old Assembly Room into a stable and took to keeping horses. I tried that, too, but I found I couldn't stand it; so I came away, ma'am, and—and—here I am. *(Rises)*

MRS. NOAKES: And I'll be bound to say, sir, that you will have no cause to complain of the exchange.

STRANGE GENTLEMAN: I'm sure not, ma'am; I know it—I feel it, already.

MRS. NOAKES: About dinner, sir; what would you like to take?

STRANGE GENTLEMAN: Let me see; will you be good enough to suggest something, ma'am?

MRS. NOAKES: Why, a broiled fowl and mushrooms is a very nice dish.

STRANGE GENTLEMAN: You are right, ma'am; a broiled fowl and mushrooms form a very delightful and harmless amusement, either for one or two persons. Broiled fowl and mushrooms let it be, ma'am.

MRS. NOAKES: In about an hour, I suppose, sir?

STRANGE GENTLEMAN: For the second time, ma'am, you have anticipated my feelings.

MRS. NOAKES: You'll want a bed tonight, I suppose, sir; perhaps you'd like to see it? Step this way, sir, and—

STRANGE GENTLEMAN: No, no, never mind. *(Aside)* This is a plot to get me out of the room. She's bribed by somebody who wants to identify me. I must be careful; I am exposed to nothing but artifice and stratagem. Never mind, ma'am, never mind.

MRS. NOAKES: If you'll give me your portmanteau, sir, the Boots will carry it into the next room for you.

STRANGE GENTLEMAN *(aside):* Here's diabolical ingenuity; she thinks it's got the name upon it. *(To her)* I'm very much obliged to the Boots for his disinterested attention, ma'am, but with your kind permission this port-manteau will remain just exactly where it is; consequently, ma'am, *(With great warmth)* if the aforesaid Boots wishes to succeed in remov-ing this portmanteau, he must previously remove *me*, ma'am, *me;* and it will take a *pair* of very stout Boots to do that, ma'am, I promise you.

MRS. NOAKES: Dear me, sir, you needn't fear for your portmanteau in this house; I dare say nobody wants it.

STRANGE GENTLEMAN: I hope not, ma'am, because in that case nobody will be disappointed. *(Aside)* How she fixes her old eyes on me!

MRS. NOAKES *(aside):* I never saw such an extraordinary person in all my life. What can he be? *(Looks at him very hard and exits)*

STRANGE GENTLEMAN: She's gone at last! Now let me commune with my own dreadful thoughts and reflect on the best means of escaping from my horrible position. *(Takes a letter from his pocket)* Here's an illegal death warrant; a pressing invitation to be slaughtered; a polite request just to step out and be killed, thrust into my hand by some disguised assassin in a dirty black calico jacket the very instant I got out of the gig at the door. I know the hand; there's a ferocious recklessness in the cross to this 'T' and a baleful malignity in the dot of that 'I' which warns me that it comes from my desperate rival. *(Opens it and reads)* "Mr. Horatio Tinkles"—that's him—"presents his compliments to his en-emy"—that's me—"and requests the pleasure of his company tomor-row morning under the clump of trees on Corpse Common,"—Corpse Common!—"to which any of the town's people will direct him and where he hopes to have the satisfaction of giving him his gruel."—Giving him his gruel! Ironical cutthroat!—"His punctuality will be es-teemed a personal favor, as it will save Mr. Tinkles the trouble and inconvenience of calling with a horsewhip in his pocket. Mr. Tinkles has ordered breakfast at the Royal for *one*. It is paid for. The individual who returns alive can eat it. Pistols—half-past five—precisely."—Bloodthirsty miscreant! *The* individual who returns alive! I have seen him hit the painted man at the shooting gallery regularly every time in his center shirt plait, except when he varied the entertainments by lodging the ball playfully in his left eye. Breakfast! I shall want nothing beyond the gruel. What's to be done? Escape! I can't escape; conceal-ment's of no use, he knows I am here. He has dodged me all the way from London and will dodge me all the way to the residence of Miss Emily Brown whom my respected but swine-headed parents have picked out for my future wife. A pretty figure I should cut before the old people, whom I have never beheld more than once in my life and Miss Emily Brown, whom I have never seen at all, if I went down there, pursued by this Salamander who, I suppose, is her accepted lover! What is to be done? I can't go back again; Father would be furious.

What can be done? Nothing! *(Sinks into a chair)* I must undergo this fiery ordeal and submit to be packed up and carried back to my weeping parents like an unfortunate buck with a flat piece of lead in my head and a brief epitaph on my breast. "Killed on Wednesday morning." No, I won't. *(Starting up and walking about)* I won't submit to it; I'll accept the challenge, but first I'll write an anonymous letter to the local authorities, giving them information of this intended duel and desiring them to place me under immediate restraint. That's feasible; on further consideration, it's capital. My character will be saved—I shall be bound over—he'll be bound over—I shall resume my journey —reach the house—marry the girl—pocket the fortune and laugh at him. No time to be lost; it shall be done forthwith. *(Goes to table and writes)* There; the challenge accepted with a bold defiance that'll look very brave when it comes to be printed. Now for the other. *(Writes)* "To the Mayor—Sir—A Strange Gentleman at the St. James's Arms, whose name is unknown to the writer of this communication, is bent upon committing a rash and sanguinary act at an early hour tomorrow morning. As you value human life, secure the amiable youth without delay. Think, I implore you, sir, think what would be the feelings of those to whom he is nearest and dearest, if any mischance befall the interesting young man. Do not neglect this solemn warning; the number of his room is seventeen." There—*(Folding it up)*. Now if I can find any one who will deliver it secretly.

(TOM SPARKS, *with a pair of boots in his hand, peeps in at the door*)

TOM: Are these here your'n?

STRANGE GENTLEMAN: No.

TOM: Oh! *(Going back)*

STRANGE GENTLEMAN: Hallo! Stop, are you the Boots?

TOM *(still at the door):* I'm the head o' that branch o' the establishment. There's another man under me as brushes the dirt off and puts the blacking on. The fancy work's my department; I do the polishing, nothing else.

STRANGE GENTLEMAN: You are the upper Boots, then?

TOM: Yes, I'm the reg'lar; t' other one's only the deputy; top boots and half boots, I calls us.

STRANGE GENTLEMAN: You're a sharp fellow.

TOM: Ah! I'd better cut then. *(Going)*

STRANGE GENTLEMAN: Don't hurry, Boots—don't hurry; I want you. *(Rises, and comes forward)*

TOM *(coming forward):* Well!

STRANGE GENTLEMAN: Can—can—you be secret, Boots?

TOM: That depends entirely on accompanying circumstances;—see the point?

STRANGE GENTLEMAN: I think I comprehend your meaning, Boots. You insinuate that you could be secret *(Putting his hand in his pocket)* if you had—five shillings for instance—isn't that it, Boots?

TOM: That's the line o' argument I should take up; but that an't exactly my meaning.

STRANGE GENTLEMAN: No!

TOM: No. A secret's a thing as is always a-rising to one's lips. It requires an astonishing weight to keep one on 'em down.

STRANGE GENTLEMAN: Ah!

TOM: Yes; I don't think I could keep one snug—reg'lar snug, you know—

STRANGE GENTLEMAN: Yes, regularly snug, of course.

TOM:—If it had a less weight a-top on it, than ten shillins.

STRANGE GENTLEMAN: You don't think three half-crowns would do it?

TOM: It might, I won't say it wouldn't, but I couldn't warrant it.

STRANGE GENTLEMAN: You could the other!

TOM: Yes.

STRANGE GENTLEMAN: Then there it is. *(Gives him four half-crowns)* You see these letters?

TOM: Yes, I can manage that without my spectacles.

STRANGE GENTLEMAN: Well; that's to be left at the Royal Hotel. This, *this,* is an anonymous one; and I want it to be delivered at the Mayor's house, without his knowing from whom it came or seeing who delivered it.

TOM *(taking the letters):* I say—you're a rum 'un, you are.

STRANGE GENTLEMAN: Think so! Ha, ha! So are you.

TOM: Ay, but you're a rummer one than me.

STRANGE GENTLEMAN: No, no, that's your modesty.

TOM: No it an't. I say, how vell you did them last haystacks. How do you contrive that ere now, if it's a fair question. Is it done with a pipe or do you use them Lucifer boxes?

STRANGE GENTLEMAN: Pipe—Lucifer boxes—haystacks! Why, what do you mean?

TOM *(looking cautiously round):* I know your name, old 'un.

STRANGE GENTLEMAN: You know my name! *(Aside)* Now how the devil has he got hold of that, I wonder!

TOM: Yes, I know it. It begins with an "S."

STRANGE GENTLEMAN: Begins with an "S"!

TOM: And ends with a "G." *(Winking)* We've all heard talk of *Swing* down here.

STRANGE GENTLEMAN: Heard talk of Swing! Here's a situation! Damme,

d'ye think I'm a walking carbois of vitriol and burn everything I touch?
—Will you go upon the errand you're paid for?

TOM: Oh, I'm going—I'm going. It's nothing to me, you know; I don't care.
I'll only just give these boots to the deputy, to take them to whoever
they belong to, and then I'll pitch this here letter in at the Mayor's
office window, in no time.

STRANGE GENTLEMAN: Will you be off?

TOM: Oh, I'm going, I'm going. Close, you knows, close! *(Exit* TOM)

STRANGE GENTLEMAN: In five minutes more the letter will be delivered; in
another half hour, if the Mayor does his duty, I shall be in custody and
secure from the vengeance of this infuriated monster. I wonder
whether they'll take me away? Egad! I may as well be provided with a
clean shirt and a nightcap in case. Let's see, she said the next room was
my bedroom, and as I have accepted the challenge, I may venture so far
now. *(Shouldering the portmanteau)* What a capital notion it is; there'll
be all the correspondence in large letters in the county paper and my
name figuring away in roman capitals with a long story, how I was such
a desperate dragon and so bent upon fighting that it took four constables to carry me to the Mayor and one boy to carry my hat. It's a capital
plan—must be done—the only way I have of escaping unpursued from
this place, unless I could put myself in the General Post and direct
myself to a friend in town. And then it's a chance whether they'd take
me in, being so much over weight.

(Exit STRANGE GENTLEMAN, *with portmanteau.* MRS. NOAKES, *peeps in at door,
then enters)*

MRS. NOAKES: This is the room, ladies, but the gentleman has stepped out
somewhere, he won't be long, I dare say. Pray come in, Miss.

(Enter MARY *and* FANNY WILSON)

MARY: This is the Strange Gentleman's apartment, is it?

MRS. NOAKES: Yes, Miss; shall I see if I can find him, ladies, and tell him
you are here?

MARY: No; we should prefer waiting till he returns, if you please.

MRS. NOAKES: Very well, ma'am. He'll be back directly, I dare say, for it's
very near his dinner time. *(Exit* MRS. NOAKES)

MARY: Come, Fanny, dear; don't give way to these feelings of depression.
Take pattern by me—I feel the absurdity of our situation acutely; but
you see that I keep up, nevertheless.

FANNY: It is easy for you to do so. *Your* situation is neither so embarrassing
nor so painful a one as mine.

MARY: Well, my dear, it *may* not be, certainly; but the circumstances which
render it less so are, I own, somewhat incomprehensible to me. My

harebrained, madcap swain, John Johnson, implores me to leave my guardian's house and accompany him on an expedition to Gretna Green. I, with immense reluctance and after considerable pressing—

FANNY: Yield a very willing consent.

MARY: Well, we won't quarrel about terms; at all events I *do* consent. He bears me off and when we get exactly halfway discovers that his money is all gone and that we must stop at this Inn, until he can procure a remittance from London by post. I think, my dear, you'll own that *this* is rather an embarrassing position.

FANNY: Compare it with mine. Taking advantage of your flight, I send express to *my* admirer, Charles Tomkins, to say that I have accompanied you; first, because I should have been miserable if left behind with a peevish old man alone; secondly, because I thought it proper that your sister should accompany you——

MARY: And, thirdly, because you knew that he would immediately comply with this indirect assent to his entreaties of three months' duration and follow you without delay on the same errand. Eh, my dear?

FANNY: It by no means follows that such was my intention or that I knew he would pursue such a course, but supposing he *has* done so; supposing this Strange Gentleman should be himself——

MARY: *Supposing!*—Why, you know it is. You told him not to disclose his name, on any account; and the *Strange Gentleman* is not a very common traveling name, I should imagine; besides the hasty note, in which he said he should join you here.

FANNY: Well, granted that it is he. In what a situation am I placed. You tell me, for the first time, that *my* violent intended must on no account be beheld by *your* violent intended, just now, because of some old quarrel between them of long standing, which has never been adjusted to this day. What an appearance this will have! How am I to explain it or relate your present situation? I should sink into the earth with shame and confusion.

MARY: Leave it to me. It arises from my heedlessness. I will take it all upon myself and see him alone. But tell me, my dear—as you got up this love affair with so much secrecy and expedition during the four months you spent at Aunt Martha's, I have never yet seen Mr. Tomkins, you know. Is he so very handsome?

FANNY: See him and judge for yourself.

MARY: Well, I will; and you may retire, till I have paved the way for your appearance. But just assist me first, dear, in making a little noise to attract his attention, if he really be in the next room, or I may wait here all day. *(They engage in a duet, at end of which exit* FANNY. *Enter* STRANGE GENTLEMAN)

STRANGE GENTLEMAN: There; now with a clean shirt in one pocket and a nightcap in the other, I'm ready to be carried magnanimously to my dungeon in the cause of love.

MARY *(aside):* He says, he's ready to be carried magnanimously to a dungeon in the cause of love. I thought it was Mr. Tomkins! Hem!

STRANGE GENTLEMAN *(seeing her):* Hallo! Who's this! Not a disguised peace officer in petticoats. Beg your pardon, ma'am. *(Advancing towards her)* What—did—you——

MARY: Oh, sir; I feel the delicacy of my situation.

STRANGE GENTLEMAN *(aside):* Feels the delicacy of her situation; Lord bless us, what's the matter! Permit me to offer you a seat, ma'am, if you're in a delicate situation. *(He places chairs; they sit)*

MARY: You are very good, sir. You are surprised to see me here, sir?

STRANGE GENTLEMAN: No, no, at least not very; rather, perhaps—rather. *(Aside)* Never was more astonished in all my life!

MARY *(aside):* His politeness, and the extraordinary tale I have to tell him, overpower me. I must summon up courage. Hem!

STRANGE GENTLEMAN: Hem!

MARY: Sir!

STRANGE GENTLEMEN: Ma'am!

MARY: You have arrived at this house in pursuit of a young lady, if I mistake not?

STRANGE GENTLEMAN: You are quite right, ma'am. *(Aside)* Mysterious female!

MARY: If you *are* the gentleman I'm in search of, you wrote a hasty note a short time since, stating that you would be found here this afternoon.

STRANGE GENTLEMAN *(drawing back his chair):* I—I—wrote a note, ma'am!

MARY: You need keep nothing secret from me, sir. I know all.

STRANGE GENTLEMAN *(aside):* That villain, Boots, has betrayed me! Know all, ma'am?

MARY: Everything.

STRANGE GENTLEMAN *(aside):* It must be so. She's a constable's wife.

MARY: You *are* the writer of that letter, sir? I think I am not mistaken.

STRANGE GENTLEMAN: You are not, ma'am; I confess I did write it. What was I to do, ma'am? Consider the situation in which I was placed.

MARY: In your situation, you had, as it appears to me, only one course to pursue.

STRANGE GENTLEMAN: You mean the course I adopted?

MARY: Undoubtedly.

STRANGE GENTLEMAN: I am very happy to hear you say so, though of course I should like it to be kept a secret.

MARY: Oh, of course.

STRANGE GENTLEMAN *(drawing his chair close to her and speaking very softly):* Will you allow me to ask you, whether the constables are downstairs?

MARY *(surprised):* The constables!

STRANGE GENTLEMAN: Because if I am to be apprehended, I should like to have it over. I am quite ready, if it must be done.

MARY: No legal interference has been attempted. There is nothing to prevent your continuing your journey tonight.

STRANGE GENTLEMAN: But will not the other party follow?

MARY *(looking down):* The other party, I am compelled to inform you, is detained here by—by want of funds.

STRANGE GENTLEMAN *(starting up):* Detained here by want of funds! Hurrah! Hurrah! I have caged him at last. I'm revenged for all his blustering and bullying. This is a glorious triumph, ha, ha, ha! I have nailed him—nailed him to the spot!

MARY *(rising indignantly):* This exulting over a fallen foe, sir, is mean and pitiful. In my presence, too, it is an additional insult.

STRANGE GENTLEMAN: Insult! I wouldn't insult you for the world, after the joyful intelligence you have brought me—I could hug you in my arms! —One kiss, my little constable's deputy. *(Seizing her)*

MARY *(struggling with him):* Help! help!

(Enter JOHN JOHNSON)

JOHN: What the devil do I see! *(Seizes STRANGE GENTLEMAN by the collar)*

MARY: John and Mr. Tomkins met together! They'll kill each other. Here, help! help! *(Exit MARY, running)*

JOHN *(shaking him):* What do you mean by that, scoundrel?

STRANGE GENTLEMAN: Come, none of your nonsense—there's no harm done.

JOHN: No harm done. How dare you offer to salute that lady?

STRANGE GENTLEMAN: What did you send her here for?

JOHN: *I* send her here!

STRANGE GENTLEMAN: Yes, *you;* you gave her instructions, I suppose. *(Aside)* Her husband, the constable, evidently.

JOHN: That lady, Sir, is attached to me.

STRANGE GENTLEMAN: Well, I know she is; and a very useful little person she must be, to be attached to anybody—it's a pity she can't be legally sworn in.

JOHN: *Legally* sworn in! Sir, that is an insolent reflection upon the temporary embarrassment which prevents our taking the marriage vows. How dare you to insinuate——

STRANGE GENTLEMAN: Pooh! pooh!—don't talk about daring to insinuate; it doesn't become a man in your station of life——

JOHN: My station of life!

STRANGE GENTLEMAN: But as you have managed this matter very quietly and say you're in temporary embarrassment—here—here's five shillings for you. *(Offers it)*

JOHN: Five shillings! *(Raises his cane)*

STRANGE GENTLEMAN *(flourishing a chair):* Keep off, sir!

(Enter MARY, TOM SPARKS *and two* WAITERS*)*

MARY: Separate them or there'll be murder! (TOM *clasps* STRANGE GEN-TLEMAN *round the waist—the* WAITERS *seize* JOHN JOHNSON)

TOM: Come, none o' that 'ere, Mr. S. We don't let private rooms for such games as these.—If you want to try it on wery partickler, we don't mind making a ring for you in the yard, but you mustn't do it here.

JOHN: Let me get at him. Let me go; waiters—Mary, don't hold me. I insist on your letting me go.

STRANGE GENTLEMAN: Hold him fast.—Call yourself a *peace* officer, you prizefighter!

JOHN *(struggling):* Let me go, I say!

STRANGE GENTLEMAN: Hold him fast! Hold him fast!

*(*TOM *takes* STRANGE GENTLEMAN *off right.* WAITERS *take* JOHN *off left,* MARY *following.)*

Scene Two

Another room in the inn. Enter JULIA DOBBS *and* OVERTON.

JULIA: You seem surprised, Overton.

OVERTON: Surprised, Miss Dobbs! Well I may be when, after seeing noth-ing of you for three years and more, you come down here without any previous notice, for the express purpose of running away—positively running away, with a young man. I am astonished, Miss Dobbs!

JULIA: You would have had better reason to be astonished if I had come down here with any notion of positively running away with an old one, Overton.

OVERTON: Old or young, it would matter little to me, if you had not conceived the preposterous idea of entangling me—*me,* an attorney, and mayor of the town, in so ridiculous a scheme. Miss Dobbs, I can't do it. I really cannot consent to mix myself up with such an affair.

JULIA: Very well, Overton, very well. You recollect that in the lifetime of that poor old dear, Mr. Woolley, who——

OVERTON:—Who would have married you, if he hadn't died; and who, as it was, left you his property, free from all encumbrances, the encumbrance of himself as a husband, not being among the least.

JULIA: Well, you may recollect that in the poor old dear's lifetime, sundry advances of money were made to you, at my persuasion, which still remain unpaid. Oblige me by forwarding them to my agent in the course of the week and I free you from any interference in this little matter. *(Going)*

OVERTON: Stay, Miss Dobbs, stay. As you say, we *are* old acquaintances and there certainly *were* some small sums of money which—which——

JULIA: Which certainly *are* still outstanding.

OVERTON: Just so, just so; and which, perhaps, you would be likely to forget, if you had a husband—eh, Miss Dobbs, eh?

JULIA: I have little doubt that I should. If I gained one through your assistance, indeed—I can safely say I should forget all about them.

OVERTON: My dear Miss Dobbs, we perfectly understand each other.— Pray proceed.

JULIA: Well—dear Lord Peter——

OVERTON: That's the young man you're going to run away with, I presume?

JULIA: That's the young *nobleman* who's going to run away with me, Mr. Overton.

OVERTON: Yes, just so.—I beg your pardon—pray go on.

JULIA: Dear Lord Peter is young and wild, and the fact is, his friends do not consider him very sagacious or strong-minded. To prevent their interference, our marriage is to be a secret one. In fact, he is stopping now at a friend's hunting seat in the neighborhood; he is to join me here; and we are to be married at Gretna.

OVERTON: Just so. A matter, as it seems to me, which you can conclude without my interference.

JULIA: Wait an instant. To avoid suspicion, and prevent our being recognized and followed, I settled with him that you should give out in this house that he was a lunatic and that I—his aunt—was going to convey him in a chaise tonight to a private asylum at Berwick. I have ordered the chaise at half-past one in the morning. You can see him and make our final arrangements. It will avert all suspicion if I have no communication with him, till we start. You can say to the people of the house that the sight of me makes him furious.

OVERTON: Where shall I find him?—Is he here?

JULIA: You know best.

OVERTON: I!

JULIA: I desired him, immediately on his arrival, to write you some mysterious nonsense, acquainting you with the number of his room.

OVERTON *(producing a letter):* Dear me, he has arrived, Miss Dobbs.

JULIA: No!

OVERTON: Yes—see here—a most mysterious and extraordinary composition which was thrown in at my office window this morning and which I could make neither head nor tail of. Is that his handwriting? *(Giving her the letter)*

JULIA *(taking letter):* I never saw it more than once, but I know he writes very large and straggling. *(Looks at letter)* Ha, ha, ha! This is capital, isn't it?

OVERTON: Excellent!—Ha, ha, ha!—So mysterious

JULIA: Ha, ha, ha! So very good. "Rash act."

OVERTON: Yes. Ha, ha!

JULIA: "Interesting young man."

OVERTON: Yes. Very good.

JULIA: "Amiable youth!"

OVERTON: Capital!

JULIA: "Solemn warning!"

OVERTON: Yes. That's best of all. *(They both laugh)*

JULIA: Number seventeen, he says. See him at once, that's a good creature. *(Returning the letter)*

OVERTON *(taking letter):* I will. *(He rings a bell. Enter* WAITER*)* Who is there in number seventeen, waiter?

WAITER: Number seventeen, sir?—Oh!—the Strange Gentleman, sir.

OVERTON: Show me the room. *(Exit* WAITER*. Looking at* JULIA *and pointing to the letter)* "The Strange Gentleman."—Ha, ha, ha! Very good—very good indeed—Excellent notion! *(They both laugh and exit.)*

Scene Three

Same as the first. A small table with wine, dessert and lights on it, two chairs.
STRANGE GENTLEMAN *discovered seated at table.*

STRANGE GENTLEMAN: "The other party is detained here, by want of funds." Ha, ha, ha! I can finish my wine at my leisure, order my gig when I please and drive on to Brown's in perfect security. I'll drink the other party's good health and long may he be detained here. *(Fills a glass)* Ha, ha, ha! The other party; and long may he—*(A knock)* Hallo! I hope *this* isn't the other party. Talk of the—*(A knock)* Well—*(Setting down his glass)*—this is the most extraordinary private room that was ever invented. I am continually disturbed by unaccountable knockings. *(A gentle tap)* There's another; that was a gentle rap—a persuasive tap—like a friend's forefinger on one's coat sleeve. It *can't* be Tinkles with the gruel. —Come in.

OVERTON *(peeping in at door):* Are you alone, my lord?

STRANGE GENTLEMAN *(amazed):* Eh!

OVERTON: Are you alone, my lord?

STRANGE GENTLEMAN: My lord!

OVERTON *(stepping in and closing the door):* You are right, sir, we cannot be too cautious, for we do not know who may be within hearing. You are very right, sir.

STRANGE GENTLEMAN *(rising from table and coming forward):* It strikes me, sir, that you are very wrong.

OVERTON: Very good, very good; I like this caution; it shows me you are wide awake.

STRANGE GENTLEMAN: Wide awake!—damme, I begin to think I am fast asleep and have been for the last two hours.

OVERTON *(whispering):* I—am—the mayor.

STRANGE GENTLEMAN *(in the same tone):* Oh!

OVERTON: This is your letter? *(Shows it;* STRANGE GENTLEMAN *nods assent solemnly)* It will be necessary for you to leave here tonight at half-past one o'clock in a post-chaise and four; and the higher you bribe the postboys to drive at their utmost speed, the better.

STRANGE GENTLEMAN: You don't say so?

OVERTON: I do indeed. You are not safe from pursuit here.

STRANGE GENTLEMAN: Bless my soul, can such dreadful things happen in a civilized community, Mr. Mayor?

OVERTON: It certainly does at first sight appear rather a hard case that people cannot marry whom they please without being hunted down in this way.

STRANGE GENTLEMAN: To be sure. To be hunted down and killed as if one was game, you know.

OVERTON: Certainly; and you *an't* game, you know.

STRANGE GENTLEMAN: Of course not. But can't you prevent it? Can't you save me by the interposition of your power?

OVERTON: My power can do nothing in such a case.

STRANGE GENTLEMAN: Can't it, though?

OVERTON: Nothing whatever.

STRANGE GENTLEMAN: I never heard of such dreadful revenge, never! Mr. Mayor, I am a victim, I am the unhappy victim of parental obstinacy.

OVERTON: Oh, no; don't say that. You may escape yet.

STRANGE GENTLEMAN *(grasping his hand):* Do you think I may? Do you think I may, Mr. Mayor?

OVERTON: Certainly! certainly! I have little doubt of it, if you manage properly.

STRANGE GENTLEMAN: I thought I *was* managing properly. I understood the other party was detained here, by want of funds.

OVERTON: Want of funds!—There's no want of funds in that quarter, I can tell you.

STRANGE GENTLEMAN: An't there, though?

OVERTON: Bless you, no. Three thousand a year!—But who told you there was a want of funds?

STRANGE GENTLEMAN: Why, she did.

OVERTON: *She!* You *have* seen her then? She told me you had not.

STRANGE GENTLEMAN: Nonsense; don't believe her. She was in this very room half an hour ago.

OVERTON: Then I must have misunderstood her and you must have misunderstood her, too—But to return to business. Don't you think it would keep up appearances if I had you put under some restraint?

STRANGE GENTLEMAN: I think it would. I am very much obliged to you. *(Aside)* This regard for my character in an utter stranger, and in a Mayor, too, is quite affecting.

OVERTON: I'll send somebody up to mount guard over you.

STRANGE GENTLEMAN: Thank 'ee, my dear friend, thank 'ee.

OVERTON: And if you make a little resistance, when we take you upstairs to your bedroom or away in the chaise, it will be keeping up the character, you know.

STRANGE GENTLEMAN: To be sure. So it will. I'll do it.

OVERTON: Very well, then. I shall see your lordship again by and by.—For the present, my lord, good evening. *(Going)*

STRANGE GENTLEMAN: Lord!—Lordship!—Mr. Mayor!

OVERTON: Eh?—Oh!—I see. *(Comes forward)* Practicing the lunatic, my lord. Ah, very good—very vacant look indeed— Admirable, my lord, admirable!—I say, my lord—*(pointing to letter)*—"Amiable youth!"—"Interesting young man."—"Strange Gentleman."—Eh? Ha, ha, ha! Knowing trick indeed, my lord, very! *(Exit* OVERTON*)*

STRANGE GENTLEMAN: That mayor is either in the very last stage of mystified intoxication or in the most hopeless state of incurable insanity. I have no doubt of it. A little touched here *(Tapping his forehead)* Never mind, he is sufficiently sane to understand my business at all events. *(Goes to table and takes a glass)* Poor fellow!—I'll drink his health and speedy recovery. *(A knock)* It is a most extraordinary thing now that, every time I propose a toast to myself, some confounded fellow raps at that door, as if he were receiving it with the utmost enthusiasm. Private room!—I might as well be sitting behind the little shutter of a Two-penny Post Office, where all the letters put in were to be postpaid. *(A knock)* Perhaps it's the guard! I shall feel a great deal safer if it is. Come in.

(He has brought a chair forward and sits. Enter TOM SPARKS, *very slowly, with an enormous stick. He closes the door and, after looking at the* STRANGE GENTLEMAN *very steadily, brings a chair and sits opposite him)*

STRANGE GENTLEMAN: Are you sent by the mayor of this place, to mount guard over me?

TOM: Yes, yes. It's all right.

STRANGE GENTLEMAN *(aside):* It's all right—I'm safe. *(To* TOM, *with affected indignation)* Now mind, I have been insulted by receiving this challenge and I want to fight the man who gave it me. I protest against being kept here. I denounce this treatment as an outrage.

TOM: Ay, ay. Anything you please—poor creature; don't put yourself in a passion. It'll only make you worse. *(Whistles)*

STRANGE GENTLEMAN: This is most extraordinary behavior. I don't understand it. What d'ye mean by behaving in this manner? *(Rising)*

TOM *(aside):* He's a-getting wiolent. I must frighten him with a steady look. I say, young fellow, do you see this here eye? *(Staring at him and pointing at his own eye)*

STRANGE GENTLEMAN *(aside):* Do I see his eye!—What can he mean by glaring upon me, with that large round optic!—Ha! a terrible light flashes upon me. He thought I was "Swing" this morning. It was an insane delusion. That eye is an insane eye.—He's a madman!

TOM: Madman! Damme, I think he is a madman with a wengeance.

STRANGE GENTLEMAN: He acknowledges it. He is sensible of his misfortune! Go away—leave the room instantly and tell them to send somebody else. Go away!

TOM: Oh, you unhappy lunatic!

STRANGE GENTLEMAN: What a dreadful situation!—I shall be attacked, strangled, smothered and mangled by a madman! Where's the bell?

TOM *(advancing and brandishing his stick):* Leave that 'ere bell alone— leave that 'ere bell alone—and come here!

STRANGE GENTLEMAN: Certainly, Mr. Boots, certainly. He's going to strangle me. *(Going towards table)* Let me pour you out a glass of wine, Mr. Boots—pray do! *(Aside)* If he said "Yes," I'd throw the decanter at his temple.

TOM: None o' your nonsense. Sit down there. *(Forces him into a chair)* I'll sit here. *(Opposite him)* Look me full in the face and I won't hurt you. Move hand, foot or eye and you'll never want to move either of 'em again.

STRANGE GENTLEMAN: I'm paralyzed with terror.

TOM: Ha! *(Raising his stick in a threatening attitude)*

STRANGE GENTLEMAN: I'm dumb, Mr. Boots—dumb, sir.

(They sit gazing intently on each other, TOM *with the stick raised, as the Act Drop slowly descends. End of Act I.)*

ACT II

Scene One

The same as Act I, Scene Three. TOM SPARKS *discovered in the same attitude watching the* STRANGE GENTLEMAN, *who has fallen asleep with his head over the back of his chair.*

TOM: He's asleep; poor unhappy wretch! How very mad he looks with his mouth wide open and his eyes shut! (STRANGE GENTLEMAN *snores)* Ah! there's a wacant snore; no meaning in it at all. I cou'd ha' told he was out of his senses from the very tone of it. *(He snores again)* That's a wery insane snore. I should say he was melancholy mad from the sound of it. *(Enter* OVERTON, MRS. NOAKES, *a* CHAMBERMAID *and two* WAITERS; MRS. NOAKES *with a warming pan, the* MAID *with a light.* STRANGE GENTLEMAN *starts up, greatly exhausted.* TOM *starts up)* Hallo!—Hallo! keep quiet, young fellow. Keep quiet!

STRANGE GENTLEMAN: Out of the way, you savage maniac. Mr. Mayor *(Crossing to him)*, the person you sent to keep guard over me is a madman, sir. What do you mean by shutting me up with a madman?— what do you mean, sir, I ask?

OVERTON *(aside to* STRANGE GENTLEMAN): Bravo! bravo! very good indeed— excellent!

STRANGE GENTLEMAN: Excellent, sir!—It's horrible!—The bare recollection of what I have endured makes me shudder, down to my very toenails.

MRS. NOAKES: Poor dear!—Mad people always think other people mad.

STRANGE GENTLEMAN: Poor dear! Ma'am! What the devil do you mean by "Poor dear"? How dare you have a madman here, ma'am, to assault and terrify the visitors to your establishment?

MRS. NOAKES: Ah! terrify indeed! I'll never have another, to please anybody, you may depend upon that, Mr. Overton. *(To* STRANGE GENTLEMAN) There, there. Don't exert yourself, there's a dear.

STRANGE GENTLEMAN: Exert myself!—Damme! it's a mercy I have any life left to exert myself with. It's a special miracle, ma'am, that my existence has not long ago fallen a sacrifice to that sanguinary monster in the leather smalls.

OVERTON (*aside to* STRANGE GENTLEMAN): I never saw any passion more real in my life. Keep it up, it's an admirable joke.

STRANGE GENTLEMAN: Joke!—joke!—Peril a precious life and call it a joke, you, a man with a sleek head and a broad-brimmed hat, who ought to know better, calling it a joke. Are you mad too, sir, are you mad? (*Confronting* OVERTON)

TOM (*very loud):* Keep your hands off. Would you murder the wery mayor, himself, you mis-rable being?

STRANGE GENTLEMAN: Mr. Mayor, I call upon you to issue your warrant for the instant confinement of that one-eyed Orson in some place of security.

OVERTON (*aside, advancing a little):* He reminds me that he had better be removed to his bedroom. He is right. Waiters, carry the gentleman upstairs. Boots, you will continue to watch him in his bedroom.

STRANGE GENTLEMAN: *He* continue!—What, am I to be boxed up again with this infuriated animal and killed off when he has done playing with me? —I won't go—I won't go—help there, help!

(*The* WAITERS *cross behind him. Enter* JOHN JOHNSON *hastily*)

JOHN (*coming forward):* What on earth is the meaning of this dreadful outcry which disturbs the whole house?

MRS. NOAKES: Don't be alarmed, sir, I beg.—They're only going to carry an unfortunate gentleman, as is out of his senses, to his bedroom.

STRANGE GENTLEMAN (*to* JOHN): Constable—constable—do your duty—apprehend these persons—every one of them. Do you hear, officer, do you hear?—(*The* WAITERS *seize him by the arms*)—Here—here—you see this. You've seen the assault committed. Take them into custody—off with them.

MRS. NOAKES: Poor creature!—He thinks you are a constable, sir.

JOHN: Unfortunate man! It is the second time today that he has been the victim of this strange delusion.

STRANGE GENTLEMAN (*breaking from* WAITERS *and going to* JOHN): Unfortunate man!—What, do *you* think I am mad?

JOHN: Poor fellow! His hopeless condition is pitiable indeed. (*Goes up*)

STRANGE GENTLEMAN: They're all mad!—Every one of 'em!

MRS. NOAKES: Come now, come to bed—there's a dear young man, do.

STRANGE GENTLEMAN: Who are you, you shameless old ghost, standing there before company, with a large warming pan and asking me to come to bed?—Are *you* mad?

MRS. NOAKES: Oh! he's getting shocking now. Take him away.—Take him away.

OVERTON: Ah, you had better remove him to his bedroom at once.

(The WAITERS *take him up by the feet and shoulders)*

STRANGE GENTLEMAN: Mind, if I survive this, I'll bring an action of false imprisonment against every one of you. Mark my words—especially against that villainous old mayor. Mind, I'll do it! *(They bear him off, struggling and talking—the others crowding round, and assisting)*

OVERTON *(following)*: How well he does it!

(Enter a WAITER, *showing in* CHARLES TOMKINS *in a traveling coat)*

WAITER: This room is disengaged now, sir. There *was* a gentleman in it, but he has just left it.

CHARLES: Very well, this will do. I may want a bed here tonight, perhaps, waiter.

WAITER: Yes, sir. Shall I take your card to the bar, sir?

CHARLES: My card! No, never mind.

WAITER: No name, sir?

CHARLES: No—it doesn't matter.

WAITER *(aside, as going out): Another* Strange Gentleman!

CHARLES: Ah!—*(Takes off coat)*—The sun and dust on this long ride have been almost suffocating. I wonder whether Fanny has arrived? If she has—the sooner we start forward on our journey further North the better. Let me see; she would be accompanied by her sister, she said in her note—and they would both be on the lookout for me. Then the best thing I can do is to ask no questions, for the present at all events, and to be on the lookout for them. *(Looking towards door)* Why here she comes, walking slowly down the long passage, straight towards this room—she can't have seen me yet. Poor girl, how melancholy she looks! I'll keep in the background for an instant and give her a joyful surprise.

(Enter FANNY*)*

FANNY: Was ever unhappy girl placed in so dreadful a situation!—Friendless and almost alone in a strange place—my dear, dear Charles a victim to an attack of mental derangement, and I unable to avow my interest in him or express my anxious sympathy and solicitude for his sufferings! I cannot bear this dreadful torture of agonizing suspense. I must and will see him, let the cost be what it may. *(Going)*

CHARLES *(coming forward)*: Hist! Fanny!

FANNY *(starting and repressing a scream)*: Ch—Charles—here in this room!

CHARLES: Bodily present, my dear, in this very room. My darling Fanny, let me strain you to my bosom. *(Advancing)*

FANNY *(shrinking back):* N—n—no, dearest Charles, no, not now. *(Aside)* How flushed he is!

CHARLES: No! Fanny, this cold reception is a very different one to what I looked forward to meeting with from you.

FANNY *(advancing and offering the tip of her finger):* N—n—no—not cold, Charles; not cold. I do not mean it to be so, indeed.—How is your head, now, dear?

CHARLES: How is my head! After days and weeks of suspense and anxiety, when half our dangerous journey is gained and I meet you here to bear you whither you can be made mine for life, you greet me with the tip of your longest finger and inquire after my head—Fanny, what can you mean?

FANNY: You—you have startled me rather, Charles—I thought you had gone to bed.

CHARLES: Gone to bed!—Why, I have but this moment arrived.

FANNY *(aside):* Poor, poor Charles!

CHARLES: Miss Wilson, what am I to——

FANNY: No, no; pray, pray, do not suffer yourself to be excited——

CHARLES: Suffer myself to be excited!—Can I possibly avoid it? can I do aught but wonder at this extraordinary and sudden change in your whole demeanor?—Excited! But five minutes since, I arrived here, brimful of the hope and expectation which had buoyed up my spirits during my long journey. I find you cold, reserved, and embarrassed—everything but what I expected to find you—and then you tell me not to be excited.

FANNY *(aside):* He is wandering again. The fever is evidently upon him.

CHARLES: This altered manner and ill-disguised confusion all convince me of what you would fain conceal. Miss Wilson, you repent of your former determination, and love another!

FANNY: Poor fellow!

CHARLES: Poor fellow!—What, am I pitied?

FANNY: Oh, Charles, do not give way to this. Consider how much depends upon your being composed.

CHARLES: I see how much depends upon my being composed, ma'am—well, very well—A husband depends upon it, ma'am. Your new lover is in this house and if he overhears my reproaches he will become suspicious of the woman who has jilted *another* and may jilt *him.* That's it, madam—a great deal depends, as you say, upon my being composed. A great deal, ma'am.

FANNY: Alas! these are indeed the ravings of frenzy!

CHARLES: Upon my word, ma'am, you must form a very modest estimate of your own power, if you imagine that disappointment has impaired my senses. Ha, ha, ha!—I am delighted. I am delighted to have escaped you, ma'am. I am glad, ma'am—damn'd glad! *(Kicks a chair over)*

FANNY *(aside):* I must call for assistance. He grows more incoherent and furious every instant.

CHARLES: I leave you, ma'am.—I am unwilling to interrupt the tender *tête-à-tête* with the other gentleman to which you are, no doubt, anxiously looking forward. To you I have no more to say. To *him* I must beg to offer a few rather unexpected congratulations on his approaching marriage. *(Exit CHARLES hastily)*

FANNY: Alas! it is but too true. His senses have entirely left him. *(Exit.)*

Scene Two

A gallery in the inn, leading to the bedrooms. Four doors in the flat, and one at each of the upper entrances, numbered from 20 to 25. A pair of boots at the door of 23. Enter CHAMBERMAID *with two lights; and* CHARLES TOMKINS.

MAID: This is your room, sir, No. 21. *(Opening the door)*

CHARLES: Very well. Call me at seven in the morning.

MAID: Yes, sir. *(Gives him a light and exits)*

CHARLES: And at nine, if I can previously obtain a few words of explanation with this unknown rival, I will just return to the place from whence I came in the same coach that brought me down here. I wonder who he is and where he sleeps. *(Looking round)* I have a lurking suspicion of those boots. *(Pointing to No. 23)* They are an ill-looking, underhanded sort of pair and an undefinable instinct tells me that they have clothed the feet of the rascal I am in search of. Besides myself, the owner of those ugly articles is the only person who has yet come up to bed. I will keep my eyes open for half an hour or so; and my ears, too.

(Exit CHARLES *into No. 21. Enter* MRS. NOAKES *with two lights, followed by* MARY *and* FANNY*)*

MRS. NOAKES: Take care of the last step, ladies. This way, ma'am, if you please. No. 20 is your room, ladies: nice large double-bedded room with coals and a rushlight.

FANNY *(aside to* MARY*):* I must ask which is his room. I cannot rest unless I know he has at length sunk into the slumber he so much needs. *(Crosses to* MRS. NOAKES*)* Which is the room in which the Strange Gentleman sleeps?

MRS. NOAKES: No. 23, ma'am. There's his boots outside the door. Don't be frightened of him, ladies. He's very quiet now and our Boots is a-watching him.

FANNY: Oh, no—we are not afraid of him. *(Aside)* Poor Charles!

MRS. NOAKES *(going to door No. 20):* This way, if you please; you'll find everything very comfortable and there's a bell-rope at the head of the bed, if you want anything in the morning. Good night, ladies.

(As MARY *and* FANNY *pass* MRS. NOAKES, FANNY *takes a light. Exeunt* FANNY *and* MARY *into No. 20)*

MRS. NOAKES *(tapping at No. 23):* Tom—Tom—

TOM *(coming forward from No. 23):* Is that you, missis?

MRS. NOAKES: Yes.—How's the Strange Gentleman, Tom?

TOM: He was wery boisterous half an hour ago, but I punched his head a little and now he's uncommon comfortable. He's fallen asleep, but his snores is still wery incoherent.

MRS. NOAKES: Mind you take care of him, Tom. They'll take him away in half an hour's time. It's very nearly one o'clock now.

TOM: I'll pay ev'ry possible attention to him. If he offers to call out, I shall whop him again. *(Exit* TOM *into No. 23)*

MRS. NOAKES *(looking off):* This way, ma'am, if you please. Up these stairs.

(Enter JULIA DOBBS *with a light)*

JULIA: Which did you say was the room in which I could arrange my dress for traveling?

MRS. NOAKES: No. 22, ma'am; the next room to your nephew's. Poor dear— he's fallen asleep, ma'am, and I dare say you'll be able to take him away very quietly by and by.

JULIA *(aside):* Not so quietly as you imagine, if he plays his part half as well as Overton reports he does. *(To* MRS. NOAKES) Thank you.—For the present, good night. *(Exit* JULIA *into No. 22)*

MRS. NOAKES: Wish you good night, ma'am. There.—Now I think I may go downstairs again and see if Mr. Overton wants any more negus. Why who's this? *(Looking off)* Oh, I forgot—No. 24 an't a-bed yet.—It's him. *(Enter* JOHN JOHNSON *with a light)* No. 24, sir, if you please.

JOHN: Yes, yes, I know. The same room I slept in last night.

MRS. NOAKES: Yes, sir.—Wish you good night, sir. *(Exit* MRS. NOAKES)

JOHN: Good night, ma'am. The same room I slept in last night, indeed, and the same room I may sleep in tomorrow night and the next night and the night after that and just as many more nights as I can get credit here, unless this remittance arrives. I could raise the money to prose-cute my journey without difficulty were I on the spot; but my con-founded thoughtless liberality to the post-boys has left me absolutely penniless. Well, we shall see what tomorrow brings forth.

(He goes into No. 24, but immediately returns and places his boots outside his room door, leaving it ajar. CHARLES *peeps from No. 21 and puts out his boots)*

CHARLES: There's another pair of boots. Now I wonder which of these two fellows is the man. I can't help thinking it's No. 23.—Hallo!

(He goes in and closes his door. The door of No. 20 opens; FANNY *comes out with a light in a night shade. No. 23 opens. She retires into No. 20. Enter* TOM SPARKS, *with a stable lantern from No. 23)*

TOM *(closing the door gently):* Fast asleep still. I may as vell go my rounds and glean for the deputy. *(Pulls out a piece of chalk from his pocket and takes up boots from No. 23)* Twenty-three. It's difficult to tell what a fellow is ven he han't got his senses, but I think this here twenty-three's a timorious faint-hearted genus. *(Examines the boots)* You want new soleing, No. 23. *(Goes to No. 24, takes up boots and looks at them)* Hallo! here's a *bust:* and there's been a piece put on in the corner.—I must let my missis know. The bill's always doubtful ven there's any mending. *(Goes to No. 21, takes up boots)* French calf Vellingtons.—All's right here. These here French calves always comes it strong—light vines and all that 'ere. *(Looking round)* Werry happy to see there an't no high-lows—they never drinks nothing but gin-and-vater. Them and the cloth boots is the vurst customers an inn has.—The cloth boots is always obstemious, only drinks sherry vine and vater and never eats no suppers. *(He chalks the No. of the room on each pair of boots as he takes them up)* Lucky for you, my French calves, that you an't done with the patent polish or you'd ha' been witrioled in no time. I don't like to put oil o' witriol on a well-made pair of boots; but ven they're rubbed vith that 'ere polish, it must be done or the profession's ruined.

(Exit TOM *with boots. Enter* FANNY *from No. 20, with light as before)*

FANNY: I tremble at the idea of going into his room, but surely at a moment like this, when he is left to be attended by rude and uninterested strangers, the strict rules of propriety which regulate our ordinary proceedings may be dispensed with. I will but satisfy myself that he sleeps and has those comforts which his melancholy situation demands and return immediately.

(She goes to No. 23 and knocks. CHARLES TOMKINS *peeps from No. 21)*

CHARLES: I'll swear I heard a knock—A woman! Fanny Wilson—and at that door at this hour of the night! (FANNY *comes forward)* Why, what an ass I must have been ever to have loved that girl. It *is* No. 23, though. I'll throttle him presently. The next room-door open—I'll watch there.

(He crosses to No. 24 and goes in. FANNY *returns to No. 23 and knocks—the door opens and the* STRANGE GENTLEMAN *appears, nightcap on his head and a light in his hand.* FANNY *screams and runs back into No. 20)*

STRANGE GENTLEMAN *(coming forward):* Well, of all the wonderful and extraordinary houses that ever did exist, this particular tenement is the most extraordinary. I've got rid of the madman at last—and it's almost time for that vile old mayor to remove me. But where?—I'm lost, bewildered, confused and actually begin to think I am mad. Half these things I've seen today must be visions of fancy—they never could have really happened. No, no, I'm clearly mad!—I've not the least doubt of it now. I've caught it from that horrid Boots. He has inoculated the whole establishment. We're all mad together. *(Looking off)* Lights coming upstairs!—Some more lunatics.

(Exit STRANGE GENTLEMAN *in No. 23. Enter* OVERTON *with a cloak,* MRS. NOAKES, TOM SPARKS *with lantern and three* WAITERS *with lights. The* WAITERS *range themselves along the wall)*

OVERTON: Remain there till I call for your assistance. *(Goes up to No. 23 and knocks. Enter* STRANGE GENTLEMAN *from No. 23)* Now, the chaise is ready.—Muffle yourself up in this cloak. *(Puts it on the* STRANGE GENTLEMAN. *They come forward)*

STRANGE GENTLEMAN: Yes.

OVERTON: Make a little noise when we take you away, you know.

STRANGE GENTLEMAN: Yes—yes—I say, what a queer room this is of mine. Somebody has been tapping at the wall for the last half hour, like a whole forest of woodpeckers.

OVERTON: Don't you know who that was?

STRANGE GENTLEMAN: No.

OVERTON: The other party.

STRANGE GENTLEMAN *(alarmed):* The other party!

OVERTON: To be sure.—The other party is going with you.

STRANGE GENTLEMAN: Going with me!—In the same chaise!

OVERTON: Of course.—Hush! *(Goes to No. 22. Knocks. Enter* JULIA DOBBS *from No. 22, wrapped up in a large cloak)* Look here! *(Bringing her forward)*

STRANGE GENTLEMAN *(starting):* I won't go—I won't go. This is a plot—a conspiracy. I won't go, I tell you. I shall be assassinated.—I shall be murdered!

*(*FANNY *and* MARY *appear at No. 20,* JOHNSON *and* TOMKINS *at 24)*

JOHN *(at the door):* I told you he was mad.

CHARLES *(at the door):* I see—I see—poor fellow!

JULIA *(crossing to* STRANGE GENTLEMAN *and taking his arm):* Come, dear, come.

MRS. NOAKES: Yes, do go, there's a good soul. Go with your affectionate aunt.

STRANGE GENTLEMAN *(breaking from her):* My affectionate aunt!

TOM: He don't deserve no affection. I niver see such an un-fectionate fellow to his relations.

STRANGE GENTLEMAN: Take that wretch away and smother him between two feather beds. Take him away and make a sandwich of him directly.

JULIA *(to* OVERTON*):* What voice was that?—It was not Lord Peter's. *(Throwing off her cloak)*

OVERTON: Nonsense—nonsense. Look at him. *(Pulls cloak off* STRANGE GENTLEMAN*)*

STRANGE GENTLEMAN *(turning round):* A woman!

JULIA: A stranger!

OVERTON: A stranger! What, an't he your husband that is to—your mad nephew, I mean?

JULIA: No!

ALL: No!

STRANGE GENTLEMAN: No!—no, I'll be damned if I am. I an't anybody's nephew—My aunt's dead, and I never had an uncle.

MRS. NOAKES: And an't he mad, ma'am?

JULIA: No.

STRANGE GENTLEMAN: Oh, I'm *not* mad. I was mistaken just now.

OVERTON: And isn't he going away with you?

JULIA: No.

MARY *(coming forward):* And isn't his name Tomkins?

STRANGE GENTLEMAN *(very loud):* No!

(All these questions and answers should be very rapid. JOHNSON *and* TOMKINS *advance to the ladies and they all retire up)*

MRS. NOAKES: What *is* his name? *(Producing a letter)* It an't Mr. Walker Trott, is it? *(She advances a little towards him)*

STRANGE GENTLEMAN: Something so remarkably like it, ma'am, that, with your permission, I'll open that epistle. *(Taking letter. All go up, but* JULIA *and* STRANGE GENTLEMAN, *who opens letter)* Tinkle's hand. *(Reads)* "The challenge was a *ruse.* By this time I shall have been united at Gretna Green to the charming Emily Brown."—Then, through a horror of duels, I have lost a wife!

JULIA *(with her handkerchief to her eyes):* And through Lord Peter's negligence, I have lost a husband!

STRANGE GENTLEMAN: Eh! *(Regards her a moment, then beckons* OVERTON, *who comes forward)* I say, didn't you say something about three thousand a year this morning?

OVERTON: I did.

STRANGE GENTLEMAN: You alluded to that party? *(Nodding towards* JULIA*)*

OVERTON: I did.

STRANGE GENTLEMAN: Hem! *(Puts* OVERTON *back)* Permit me, ma'am *(going to her),* to sympathize most respectfully with your deep distress.

JULIA: Oh, sir! your kindness penetrates to my very heart.

STRANGE GENTLEMAN *(aside):* Penetrates to her heart!—It's taking the right direction.—If I understand your sorrowing murmur, ma'am, you contemplated taking a destined husband away with you, in the chaise at the door?

JULIA: Oh! sir, spare my feelings—I did. The horses were ordered and paid for; and everything was ready. *(Weeps)*

STRANGE GENTLEMAN *(aside):* She weeps. Expensive thing, posting, ma'am.

JULIA: Very, sir.

STRANGE GENTLEMAN: Eighteen-pence a mile, ma'am, not including the boys.

JULIA: Yes, sir.

STRANGE GENTLEMAN: *You've* lost a husband, ma'am—*I* have lost a wife. Marriages are made above—I'm quite certain ours is booked. Pity to have all this expense for nothing—let's go together.

JULIA *(drying her eyes):* The suddenness of this proposal, sir——

STRANGE GENTLEMAN: Requires a sudden answer, ma'am. You don't say no —you mean yes. Permit me to—*(Kisses her).* All right! Old one *(To* OVERTON), I've done it. Mrs. Noakes, don't countermand the chaise. We're off directly.

CHARLES *(who with* FANNY *comes down center):* So are we.

JOHN *(who with* MARY *comes down center):* So are we, thanks to a negotiated loan, and an explanation as hasty as the quarrel that gave rise to it.

STRANGE GENTLEMAN: Three post-chaises and four, on to Gretna, directly. I say—we'll stop here as we come back?

JOHN *and* CHARLES: Certainly.

STRANGE GENTLEMAN: But before I go, as I fear I have given a great deal of trouble here tonight—permit me to inquire whether you will view my mistakes and perils with an indulgent eye and consent to receive *"The Strange Gentleman"* again tomorrow.

(Curtain.)

HASTE TO THE WEDDING

Based on An Italian Straw Hat
by Eugène Labiche & Marc-Michel

by W. S. Gilbert

"An Italian Straw Hat" ("Le Chapeau de Paille d'Italie") by Eugène Labiche and Marc-Michel is one of France's enduring comic gems. It premiered in Paris in 1851, was the basis of a charming René Clair silent film and migrated to England, where the great comic poet and librettist W. S. GILBERT (1836–1911) freely adapted it, retitling his version "The Wedding March."

In 1892, during the unfortunate breach between Gilbert and Arthur Sullivan, the principal G & S comedian George Grossmith collaborated with Gilbert on a musical version of "The Wedding March," which opened September 27 that year at London's Criterion Theatre under the new title, HASTE TO THE WEDDING.

CAST OF CHARACTERS

WOODPECKER TAPPING, a bridegroom
MR. MAGUIRE, a market gardener
UNCLE BOPADDY
COUSIN FOODLE
THE DUKE OF TURNIPTOPSHIRE, an emotional peer
MAJOR-GENERAL BUNTHUNDER
CRIPPS, a milliner's bookkeeper
WILKINSON, a policeman
BARNS, a family retainer
JACKSON, a valet
THE MARCHIONESS OF MARKET HARBOROUGH,
an emotional peeress
LADY POPTON
MARIA, a bride
BELLA CRACKENTHORPE, a milliner
PATTY PARKER, a lady's maid
Wedding guests and members of the upper aristocracy

ACT I

Room in MR. WOODPECKER TAPPING's *house. Doors at center, right and left.*
JACKSON *discovered dusting chairs. Enter* PATTY *on tiptoe.*

PATTY: Is it all right, Mr. Jackson?

JACKSON: All is right, Patty. *(Kisses her)*

PAT: Now none of that, if you please. Your master, Mr. Woodpecker Tapping, is to be married today, and you told me I might come and see the wedding presents. Where are they?

JACK: In the next room—you shall see them presently.

PAT: But how comes it that the wedding takes place from the bridegroom's house, and why are all the wedding presents sent there?

JACK: Because the bride, Miss Maria Maguire, lives at Pettytwiddlllm, in a remote corner of Wales—and as Mr. Tapping can't get leave to go down to a remote corner of Wales, a remote corner of Wales has to come to him.

DUET—JACKSON *and* PATTY

JACK: Today at eleven,
                Young Woodpecker Tapping
         Will enter the heaven
                Of matrimonee—
         To 'Ria Maguire
                That beauty entrapping
         Woodpecker Esquire
                United will be.
(Dancing) And the bells they will jingle,
                The wine it will bubble,
         As Woodpecker, single
                Turned Woodpecker double,
         Reforming his ways, which are rather too free,
         Walks into the heaven of matrimonee!

PAT: Young Woodpecker Tapping
                (Professed lady-killer)
         Is rarely caught napping
                By widow or maid,
         But her fascinations—
                Her gold and her siller—
         All considerations
                Have thrown in the shade.

(Dancing) So the bells they will jingle,
                     The wine it will bubble,
              As Woodpecker, single,
                     Turned Woodpecker double,
              Reforming his ways, which are rather too free,
              Walks into the heaven of matrimonee.

(Enter UNCLE BOPADDY, *who catches them dancing. They stop abruptly when they see him. He is very deaf, and carries a bandbox)*

BOPADDY: Don't mind me—it's only Uncle Bopaddy—nobody minds Uncle Bopaddy! Anybody come yet?

JACK *(with great show of deference):* Not yet, you ridiculous old ragbag! Not yet, you concentrated essence of disreputable senility.

PAT: *(aside to* JACKSON): Hush! hush! you'll make the old gentleman angry.

JACK: Oh, no—he's as deaf as a post—he can't hear. *(Shouting to him)* You can't hear, can you? *(To* PATTY) I always talk to him like that; it amuses me very much. *(To* BOPADDY, *who is much struck with* PATTY) Don't you think that at your age you might find something better to do than to go about chucking young girls under the chin, you disreputable old vagabond?

BO: Yes, yes—you are perfectly right. I told him so myself; but, bless you, you might as well talk to a post! *(To* PATTY) Here, my dear, take this *(Giving her parcel).* It's a little present for the bride—now, don't crush it, there's a nice little gal!

PAT: All right, old sixpennorth of halfpence!

BO *(much amused):* Yes—you're quite right. I often do so myself. Ha, ha! *(Exit* PATTY *with parcel)* What a nice little gal! Very nice little gal! Don't know that I ever saw a nicer little gal!

JACK: Go along, you wicked old pantaloon, you ought to be ashamed of yourself, at your age! *(Gives him a chair)* There, sit down and hold your wicked old tongue! *(Exit* JACKSON)

BO *(sitting):* Thankee kindly. Remarkably civil, well-spoken young man, to be sure! Don't know that I ever met a nicer-spoken young man.

(Enter WOODPECKER TAPPING)

WOOD: Well, here's a pretty piece of business.

BO: My nephew—my dear nephew. *(Shaking his hand)* Where's the wedding party—have they arrived?

WOOD: They're coming—in eight cabs. But listen to my adventure. I was riding in Hyde Park just now, and I accidentally dropped my whip——

BO (*shaking his hand*): My boy, those sentiments do honor to your head and your heart.

WOOD: What sentiments? Oh, I forgot—he's deaf. No matter. Well, I dismounted and picked it up, and then discovered that the noble animal had bolted, and was at that moment half a mile away.

BO: But I go farther than that. I go so far as to say that a good husband makes a good wife.

WOOD: Here's an old donkey!

BO: Thank you, my boy, I am—I always was.

WOOD: Well, after a long run I came up with my spirited grey, and found him in the act of devouring a Leghorn hat belonging to a young and lovely lady who was indulging in an affectionate *tête-à-tête* with a military gentleman who may or may not have been her betrothed. I jumped on my horse—apologized to the lady, threw her a sovereign (or it might have been a shilling—I'm sure I don't know), and this is all the change I got out of it. (*Showing the remains of a straw hat*)

BO: Dear me, that's a very nice straw—a very nice straw! I don't know that I ever saw a nicer straw! Ha! now that's very curious.

WOOD: Eh?

BO: Nothing. It's curious—it's a coincidence. It's just like the one I've given Maria for a wedding present. Hah! At what time is the wedding?

WOOD: Eleven. (*Shows him on fingers*)

BO: Eh?

WOOD (*shouting*): Eleven!

BO: You must speak a great deal louder—I can't hear.

WOOD (*whispering*): Eleven.

BO: Oh! eleven. Why didn't you say so at first? (*Looking at watch*) Half-past ten—just time for a glass of sherry. I saw it on the sideboard as I came up—you'll find me at the sideboard as you go down. (*Exit BOPADDY*)

WOOD: So in one hour I shall be a married man! Married to the daughter of a human porcupine—one of the most ill-tempered, crotchety, exacting old market-gardeners in Great Britain! Maria is a charming girl—she has only one drawback—a cousin, Alfred Foodle, who was brought up with her. He kisses her. It's permitted in some families. It's permitted in hers. I don't quite see why—he's as big as I am. The best of it is, *I'm* not allowed to. Of course it's all right, because they were brought up together. At the same time, I wish he wouldn't.

SONG—WOODPECKER

Maria is simple and chaste—
  She's pretty and tender and modest—
But on one or two matters of taste
  Her views are distinctly the oddest.
Her virtue is something sublime—
  No kissing—on that there's a stopper—
When I try, she says, "All in good time—
  At present it's highly improper."
    Such virtue heroic I call,
      To complain were the act of a noodle—
    She's allowed to kiss no one at all
      But her cousin—her cousin: young Foodle;
Now a maiden could never offend
  By embracing her father or brother;
But I never could quite comprehend
  Why cousins should kiss one another.
Of course it's an innocent whim—
  Beneath it no mischief lies hidden.
But why is that given to him
  Which to me is so strictly forbidden?
    It's as innocent as it can be;
      He's a kind of performing French poodle.
    But why withhold kisses from me
      Which are freely accorded to Foodle?

(Enter CAPTAIN BAPP *and* LEONORA*)*

WOOD: Who's this?

BAPP: This is the scoundrel's house, and *(Seeing* WOODPECKER*)* this is the scoundrel!

WOOD: Confusion! It's the lady of the Leghorn hat and her military admirer!

LEO: Dear Captain Bapp, be careful!

BAPP: Leonora, leave this to me. *(To* WOODPECKER*)* Well, sir, suppose you offer this lady a seat! (WOODPECKER *gives* LEONORA *a chair, and is about to take another)* Don't sit down yourself, sir! How dare you attempt to sit down in this lady's presence? Now, sir, to business. You have grossly insulted this lady.

WOOD: How?

BAPP: In the first place, you devoured this lady's hat.

WOOD: Pardon me—my horse devoured her hat.

BAPP: A quibble, sir; you are responsible for his action. You devoured this lady's hat; and you then have the audacity to throw her this contemptible coin as compensation! *(Showing* WOODPECKER *a shilling)*

WOOD *(aside):* It *was* a shilling! I thought it was. *(Aloud)* Sir, it was a mistake—allow me to rectify it. *(Gives him a sovereign)*

BAPP: Fire and fury! What's this?

WOOD: That is a sovereign—or pound—for the hat.

BAPP: Insult upon insult! We have not come here for compensation.

WOOD: Then, what the deuce have you come for?

BAPP: In the first place, an apology.

LEO: No, no; I forgive him! Come away—it's not necessary.

BAPP: Leonora, *will* you leave this to me? Well, sir, the apology.

WOOD: Well, sir, I apologize.

BAPP: Unreservedly?

WOOD: Unreservedly. Now, what is the moral of all this, Leonora?

LEO: Sir!

BAPP: By the God of War——!

WOOD: I call you Leonora because I don't know your other name. The moral of this is—if you will walk out in Hyde Park with surreptitious captains in the Army——

LEO: Sir, you are in error. This gentleman is my cousin. We were brought up together.

WOOD: Oh, I see; he's your Foodle.

BAPP: This lady's *what,* sir?

WOOD: Her Foodle. I say you're her Foodle. You don't know what I mean; but you may depend upon it you are. I wish you'd go.

BAPP: Oh, but I haven't done yet. This hat, sir, is a present from the lady's husband.

WOOD: What! There's a husband, is there? Oh, Leonora, I should have expected this from Bapp, but I'm surprised at *you.*

LEO: My husband is the most jealous man in the world and, if I go home without it, he'll kill me. There's only one thing to be done—you must get another exactly like it.

WOOD: With pleasure—tomorrow.

BAPP: Tomorrow! And what's to become of the lady in the meantime?

LEO: Oh, I'll remain here. *(Sits)*

WOOD: Here!—in my house? On my wedding day? Impossible!

MAG *(without):* Woodpecker!

WOOD: The wedding party have arrived, and do *not* suppose that that is a bull of Bashan. No—it is my father-in-law elect! *(Shouts)* Coming! *(To* LEONORA*)* Stop—I see a way of doing it. I'll invent an excuse to call at a milliner's on the way to the Registrar's, and tell her to send one here.

MAG (*without*): Woodpecker!

WOOD: Coming! (*To* BAPP) Will that do?

BAPP (*to* LEONORA): Will that do?

LEO (*to* BAPP): That will do.

BAPP (*to* WOODPECKER): That will do.

MAGUIRE (*furiously*): Woodpecker!

WOOD: He's coming up—he mustn't find you here. Go in there—quick! (*Places* BAPP *in room at right and* LEONORA *in room at left*) Just in time!

(*Music, "Haste to the Wedding." Enter the wedding party, composed of semi-grotesque old-fashioned and countrified couples. They dance round the stage.* MARIA, *in bridal dress, dances on with* FOODLE, *a loutish simpleton;* BOPADDY *follows, and finally* MAGUIRE *in a towering rage*)

CHORUS—EPITHALAMIUM

Ring, ye joybells, long and loudly,
Happy hearts together tied—
Bridegroom's heart is swelling proudly
As he takes his blushing bride!

MAG (*furiously*): It's off! It's off!

WOOD: What's off?

MAG: The wedding! I won't have it!

SONG—MAGUIRE

You've kept us all waiting outside!
Such insults I never foresaw:
You've insulted your beautiful bride—
You've insulted your father-in-law!
You've insulted our excellent guests—
You've pooh-poohed the connubial knot—
You've insulted the flymen
Who'd drive you to Hymen—
By George, you've insulted the lot!

ALL: Yes, yes, yes,
By George you've insulted the lot!

MAG: It's off! Her affection's misplaced!
It's off! such a man I disown!
It's off! take your arm from her waist!
It's off! let the lady alone!
And your beautiful bride, who belongs

To a father who never ignores
Insults by the dozen,
Shall marry her cousin—
Here, Foodle, be happy—she's yours!

ALL: Yes, yes, yes,
Here, Foodle, be happy—she's yours!

(MARIA *goes weeping to* FOODLE, *who embraces her*)

CHORUS

Ring, ye joybells, long and loudly,
Happy hearts together tied—
Bridegroom's breast is swelling proudly
As he takes his blushing bride!

WOOD: St! st! st! Suppose I apologize.

MAG: Then it's on again.

WOOD: Then I apologize.

MAG *(joyfully):* It's on again! *(To* FOODLE, *who is embracing* MARIA) Foodle, my boy, it's on again!

FOOD *(releasing her):* Oh, Maria! (MARIA *reverts to* WOODPECKER)

CHORUS

Ring, ye joybells, long and loudly,
Happy hearts together tied—
Bridegroom's breast is swelling proudly
As he takes his blushing bride!

MARIA *(screaming):* Oh!

MAG: What's the matter!

MARIA: Oh, something's pricking me!

WOOD: A pin? Allow me. *(Proceeds to remove it)*

MAG *(stopping him):* How dare you, sir!

MARIA: How dare you!

ALL: For shame!

MAG: Foodles, remove the pin! (FOODLE *crosses to* MARIA *and removes the pin from* MARIA's *back, kisses it and pricks his lips accidentally)* They were brought up together. *(Addressing* WOODPECKER, *who is furious)* Now then, are we all ready? Then away we go!

(Music commences "Haste to the Wedding," the guests are dancing off)

WOOD: Stop! *(Music and guests stop short—aside)* I must find some excuse to stop at a milliner's—what shall I say? I can't tell them I've got to stop and buy a hat for one lady on my way to be married to another!

MAG *(who, like the others, has been standing on one leg in the exact attitude in which he was stopped):* Nearly finished your soliloquy, Woodpecker?

WOOD *(aside):* Ha, I know! *(Aloud)* Hullo! It's very awkward—I've lost the license!

MAG: What!

ALL: Lost the license!

MAG: It's off! Another instance of insulting neglect! It's off! Foodle shall have her! *(Hands her to* FOODLE)

FOOD *(embracing her):* Maria!

CHORUS

Ring, ye joybells—

WOOD: Stop! Don't be absurd—it's very easily rectified. We must call at Doctor's Commons on the way to the church, and get another. You can remain below on the cabs while I apply for it. *(Aside)* They're all country people, and don't know the difference between Doctor's Commons and a milliner's shop! *(Aloud)* Will that do?

MAG: It's on again! *(To* FOODLE, *who is embracing* MARIA) Foodle, my boy, it's on again!

CHORUS

Ring, ye joybells—

MAG: Will you stop that? Foodle, take the bride—pair off and away we go!

(Music "Haste to the Wedding." All dance off, WOODPECKER *last)*

WOOD: If ever I marry again, it shall be into a family without a Foodle! *(Exit, after the others.)*

Scene Two

A milliner's showroom. Some bonnets and two common milliners' dolls' heads on table up left. High desk with ledger right. Wide opening center, with doors. Enter BELLA CRACKENTHORPE.

BELLA *(calling off):* Now, make haste, young ladies—attend to your work and don't chatter. Upon my life I've been very fortunate! I only purchased this business four months ago, and I've quite a large connection already! Ah! it's not everywhere that civility and punctuality, combined with the latest Paris fashions, are to be obtained at a moderate advance on store prices.

BALLAD—BELLA

> By dreams of ample profits lured,
> And overflowing till,
> By easy payments I secured
> Stock, fixtures, and good will.
> But fixtures are but means to end,
> Good will's a term misplaced,
> Unless with them you deftly blend
> Politeness and Good Taste.
>   Without you, money paid is waste,
>   So hail, Politeness and Good Taste!
>
> Without your calm unpurchased aid,
> Work hardly as one may,
> The finest business in the trade
> Falls off and fades away.
> The stock depreciates in tone,
> The good will dwindles fast,
> The humble fixtures, they alone
> Are faithful to the last!
>   Ye fixtures, though but means to ends,
>   You do your best, my humble friends!

(Enter WOODPECKER *in breathless haste)*

WOOD: I want a hat of finest straw,
     At once—a handsome one.
   Trimmed with an armadillo's claw,
     Three truffles and a bun,
   Two thingummies of peacock blue,
     A what's-its-name on each,
   A snuff-box and a cockatoo,
     Two mackerel and a peach.
     If you have such a thing in stock,
     I'll buy it—*(looking at watch)* half-past ten o'clock!

BELLA *(recognizing him):* Ah, heavens! 'Tis Woodpecker! Oh judge and
juries!

WOOD *(aghast):* 'Tis Bella Crackenthorpe, by all the furies!
   (aloud):   You've nothing like it in your shop?
           No consequence; good morning!

BELLA *(holding his coattails):*   Stop!
Ah, false one! (WOODPECKER *much depressed*)

BALLAD—BELLA

You offer to take me, one fine day
   To the Naval Exhibition;
You borrow the money from me to pay
   The price of our admission.
The rain pours down on my brand new dress,
   And boots of thin prunella.
Do you stand me a hansom? Oh dear, no!
You stand me under a portico,
Like a shabby young fellow, and off you go
   To borrow a friend's umbrella!

The rain goes on, and the days they grow—
   To months accumulating;
And patiently under that portico
   They find me waiting—waiting.
To her allegiance staunch and true
   Stands your deserted Bella.
At length six weary months have passed;
The weather, no longer overcast,
Clears up—and you return at last
   Without that friend's umbrella!

WOOD: I forgot the umbrella. I'll go and fetch it. *(Going)*

BELLA *(stops him):* Not if I know it!

WOOD *(aside):* Confound it! And the wedding party at the door, in eight
cabs!

BELLA: To think that this contemptible creature actually promised to
marry me!

WOOD: Marry you? Why, of course I did! Marry you? Certainly I will!

BELLA: You will?

WOOD: Why, of course! What do you take me for?

BELLA: And you didn't desert me in order to run after somebody else?

WOOD: Ha, ha! As if I'd dream of anybody else!

BELLA: Oh, what a relief! Oh, Woodpecker! *(In his arms)*

WOOD: Now, then; I want a Leghorn hat trimmed with a parrot's head, an armadillo's claw, two mackerel, one peach, three truffles, and a bun.

BELLA *(jealous):* Oh, for some young lady, I suppose?

WOOD: For some young lady! That's very likely; come, you know me better than that. No; it's for a Captain in the Guards, who wants it as a birthday present for—for his Colonel.

BELLA: Well, by an odd coincidence, I believe I happen to have the very thing; and you shall have it on one condition: that we dine together at Simpson's this afternoon——

WOOD *(aside):* Very likely!

BELLA: And that you take me to the Adelphi Theatre this evening!

WOOD: Capital! excellent idea! I was just saying to myself as I came in, "What in the world shall I do with myself this evening?" and the Adelphi Theatre is the very thing. Now, then, where's the hat?

BELLA: In the next room. Come along, and don't let me catch you making eyes at the young ladies! *(Exit BELLA)*

WOOD *(in despair):* Here's all the wedding party coming upstairs!

(Music, "Haste to the Wedding." Enter MAGUIRE, MARIA, FOODLE, BOPADDY and the wedding party, two and two, dancing round the stage. The guests range themselves on the left of the scene)

MAG: So here we are in Doctor's Commons! *(To WOODPECKER)* I think you told us this was Doctor's Commons?

WOOD: Yes, yes—but why in the world have you left your cabs?

MAG: Never mind that—have you got the licence?

WOOD: No—the—the Registrar has not arrived yet; that is, he's busy. Go back to your cabs and I'll go and fetch him. Oh, dim! dim! dim! *(Exit hurriedly after BELLA)*

MAG: It's all right—it *is* Doctor's Commons. My friends, let us behave ourselves, we are in Doctor's Commons. Let those who have gloves put them on. I—I am much agitated: and you, my child?

MARIA: Papa, the pin is still there!

MAG: Walk about, my child, and it will work down. *(Goes to desk)* Here is the entry-book. We shall all have to sign our names in it.

MARIA: Papa, what are they going to do to me?

MAG: Nothing, my child. The Registrar will say to you, "Do your parents consent to this marriage?" and you'll reply, "I am." *(Looking off)* Oh, the Registrar is coming. *(To FOODLE, who has only got one glove on)* Put on your other glove, will you?

FOODLE: I can't—I've lost it!

MAG: Then put your hand in your pocket. (FOODLE *puts the gloved hand in his pocket*) Not that one, stupid! the other one! (FOODLE *does so*) Now, then, prepare to receive the Registrar!

(Enter CRIPPS, *out of breath and wet through)*

AIR—CRIPPS and CHORUS

CRIPPS: Gracious, how I have been running,
                         Backwards, forwards, in the rain—
                 Impecunious clients dunning;
                         All my trouble, too, in vain!

CHORUS: Bow to the Registrar!
                         He can the license grant—
                         He is the man we want—
                 Bow to the Registrar! *(All bow to* CRIPPS)

CRIPPS: Sitting in wet things is odious,
                         Rheumatiz my nature loathes;
                 So, behind this desk commodious,
                         I'll at once change all my clothes!

CHORUS: This is the Registrar!
                         He can the license grant—
                         He is the man we want—
                 Bow to the Registrar!

(In the meantime, CRIPPS *has dived under the desk and is concealed from view)*

RECITATIVE

MAG: Why, where's he gone? He's disappeared from view!
                         Hallo, you sir! Hallo! *(Craning over desk)*

CRIPPS *(showing his head only):* Good day to you!

MAG: This is my daughter, sir.

CRIPPS: One moment, pray,

MAG: These are her bridesmaids—this her bridal day!

CRIPPS *(aside):* No doubt a wedding party, come to make some
                         purchases!

MAG: Our names, perhaps, you'll take?

*(*CRIPPS, *who has taken off his coat, puts it on again and prepares to take their names)*

MAG: My name is Anthony Hurricane Egg,
                 Bartholomew Capperboy Property Skegg—
                 I haven't done yet—Conolly Maguire—

CRIPPS: But really—

MAG: I haven't quite finished—Esquire!

CHORUS *(rising from their seats, and dancing up to the Registrar and back again):*
                 His name is Anthony Hurricane Egg, &c.

(All sit down suddenly)

CRIPPS *(speaking):* Sir, the Christian names are immaterial.

MAG: Oh! *(Sings)*
           Oh, I was born at Pettybun
              On a Saturday—on a Saturday—

CRIPPS *(speaking):* Your place of birth is also immaterial.

MAG: Oh! *(Sings)*
           In eighteen hundred twenty-one,
              On the fourth of May—on the fourth of May—

CRIPPS *(angrily):* My dear sir, I don't want your biography—you have told me quite enough!

MAG: Very good. *(To* BOPADDY*)* Now it's your turn. *(Loudly)* Now it's your turn. *(In a whisper)* Now it's your turn.

BO: Oh!—my turn *(Advancing with dignity)*. Sir *(To* CRIPPS*)*, before I consent to become a witness in this matter——

ALL *(bursting into chorus):* On a Saturday—on a Saturday!

BO: I should like to express my views as to the qualifications of a witness——

ALL *(as before):* On the fourth of May—on the fourth of May!

CRIPPS: What is he talking about?

BO: In the first place he should be of full age. I am. In the second, he should be a Briton by birth. I am. In the third—

ALL: Oh, he was born at Pettybun,
           On the fourth of May—on the fourth of May,
        In eighteen hundred twenty-one,
           On a Saturday—on a Saturday!

(All sit suddenly)

FOOD *(looking off right):* Oh, uncle, uncle! look here!

(During the dialogue that follows BOPADDY *has been much fascinated with the two milliners' dolls' heads, flirting first with one, then with the other, as if unable to make up his mind which of them he prefers)*

MAG: What! my son-in-law elect kissing a young woman! It's off! It's off! Foodle, my daughter is yours!

FOOD: Maria! *(Putting his arms round her)*

(Enter WOODPECKER *from right)*

WOOD: Why in the world haven't you gone back to your cabs?

MAG: Sir, it's off! It's off!

WOOD: Very good.

MAG: You ought to be ashamed of yourself!

WOOD: I am. What have I done?

MAG: You dare to ask that when I saw you through that door with a young woman in your arms!

WOOD *(aside):* He saw me! *(Aloud)* I admit it, sir!

MARIA *(crying):* He owns to it!

ALL *(crying):* He owns to it!

FOOD: My darling! *(Embracing* MARIA*)*

WOOD: Will you stop that hugging?

FOOD: She's my cousin—we were brought up together.

MAG: It's quite allowable—she's his cousin.

WOOD: His cousin? Oh, then, the lady I was embracing is *my* cousin!

ALL: Oh indeed—that's quite another matter!

MAG: It's on again! Foodle, my boy, it's on again!

FOOD *(relinquishing* MARIA*)*: Old teetotum!

MAG: Introduce me to your cousin—I'll invite her to the wedding.

WOOD *(aside):* Bella at Maria's wedding! *(Aloud)* It's of no use—she can't come—she's in mourning.

MAG: What, in a pink dress?

WOOD: Yes—it's for her husband.

MAG *(convinced, to* CRIPPS*)*: Oh. Well, we're quite ready, sir, when you are. *(All sit in a row opposite desk)*

WOOD: What are they doing?

CRIPPS: I really must make a complete change. I'll go into the next room— there's no one there. *(Going towards door with his dry clothes under his arm)*

MAG: Where are you going?

CRIPPS: I shall catch my death of cold if I don't—I really can't help it—you must excuse me. *(Exit)*

MAG: My friends, let us follow the Registrar!

(Music. They all dance after CRIPPS *in couples,* BOPADDY *last, with one of the dolls' heads, kissing his hand to the other)*

WOOD: Where the deuce are they all going?

(Enter BELLA*)*

BELLA: Here's your specimen. *(Giving remains of hat)* I'm very sorry, but I can't match it.

WOOD: What!

BELLA: If you like to wait three weeks I can get you one from Florence.

WOOD: Three weeks!

BELLA: I only know of one like it in London.

WOOD: I'll buy it—mind, I'll buy it.

BELLA: Impossible! I sold it a week ago to——

WOOD: To whom?

BELLA: To the Marchioness of Market Harborough! *(Exit* BELLA*)*

WOOD: This is pleasant! A Marchioness! I can't call on a Marchioness and ask her how much she wants for her hat!

(Enter CRIPPS, *with his dry clothes under his arm, pursued by the wedding party dancing as before,* BOPADDY *last, with the doll's head. They exeunt after* CRIPPS. *Music forte while they are on—pianissimo when they are off)*

WOOD: Hi! Mr. Maguire, where are you going? *(Is about to follow)*

(Enter JACKSON*)*

JACKSON: Sir, I've just come from home.

WOOD: Well, is the Captain there still?

JACK: Yes, he's there, but he ain't still. The lady has fainted, and can't leave the house.

WOOD: Wrap her up in a blanket and send her home at once! *(Exit* JACKSON*)* I must have this hat at any rate. *(Refers to Blue Book)* The Marchioness of Market Harborough—Carlton Gardens. I'll get married first, and then I'll call on her. But what shall I do with the wedding party? I know. I'll shut 'em up in the Duke of York's Column. I'll say to the keeper, "I engage this Column for twenty-four hours—let no one out." *(Exit)*

(Enter CRIPPS, *with his dry clothes, very breathless)*

CRIPPS: Why the deuce do the people follow me everywhere? It's impossible for me to change my clothes!

(Enter all the wedding party as before. Music forte. CRIPPS *runs round stage and off, followed by wedding party,* BOPADDY *last, with the doll's head. He is much exhausted with running. Curtain.)*

ACT II

A handsomely furnished front and back drawing room in Carlton Gardens.
The two rooms separated by handsome double curtains which are closed
during the early part of the Act. A sumptuous luncheon is laid on the table in
back room but concealed from audience by curtains. Doors right and left.
Window upstage left. Small table right with vase and bouquet. Grand piano
left of center. Enter BARNS, *an old family retainer.*

BARNS *(announcing):* The Duke of Turniptopshire!

(Enter DUKE. *Exit* BARNS)

DUKE: Admirable! Magnificent! What gorgeous decorations! What refined
taste! What have we here? *(Looks through curtains)* A most luxurious
cold collation! Seven-and-sixpence a head, if it cost a penny! I wonder
if *(Looking around him)* there's no one coming—I wonder if I might
venture to take just one tartlet! I will—

(Takes a tartlet from table and eats it. Enter the MARCHIONESS OF MARKET
HARBOROUGH)

MARCH: Well, Duke.

DUKE: Marchioness *(Embarrassed, with his mouthful)*—I—I—delighted to
see you.

MARCH *(more in sorrow than in anger):* Ah, Duke, Duke—you've been
picking the luncheon again! Now that's too bad!

DUKE: I'm sorry—very, very sorry. Forgive me, it was thoughtless—criminal if you will, but I was ever a wayward child, accustomed to have his
every whim gratified, and now, in middle age, I find it difficult to shake
off the shackles that custom and education have riveted on me. *(In*
tears)

MARCH *(in tears):* You were my late husband's early friend!

DUKE *(with an effort):* And now, my dear Marchioness, whom do you
expect at your concert this morning? Tell me all—do not fear—you can
trust me implicitly!

MARCH: I feel I can! Well, then, there's Lord and Lady Popton, the Duke
and Duchess of Deal, Colonel Coketown, the Dowager Duchess of
Worthing, Lord and Lady Pentwhistle, and the Archbishop of Bayswater.

DUKE *(aside):* All dem snobs! *(Aloud)* And who sings?

MARCH: The most delightful creature in the world—no other than the
distinguished falsetto, Nisnardi, who arrived only a week ago from

Bologna, and who has already turned all the crowned heads of Europe! He can go up to G!

DUKE: Gad bless me, what a gift!

MARCH: You have no idea how deliciously eccentric he is.

DUKE: Well, you know, a man who can touch an upper G is not like us common fellers: he's a genius—a genius.

MARCH: Exactly. I asked him to sing two songs this afternoon, and sent him a cheque for 3000 guineas; here is his reply: *(Reads),* "Madam, you ask me to sing two songs. I will sing three; you offer me 3000 guineas— it is not enough——"

DUKE: Dem foreigner!

MARCH: "It is not enough; my terms are—a flower from your bouquet!"

DUKE: A what?

MARCH: "A flower from your bouquet!" Is it not romantic?

DUKE: It's a poem—a "ballade!" Pardon this weakness! *(Wiping his eyes)*

MARCH: Dear, dear Duke! *(Wiping her eyes)* You know the Princess Polpetti—with the pretty feet?

DUKE: I know her pretty feet.

MARCH: What do you think were his terms for singing at her concert?

DUKE: I don't know. He seems fond of flowers—perhaps a pot of mignonette?

MARCH: Nothing of the kind—one of her old slippers!

DUKE *(in tears):* Don't—demme, I can't stand it—I can't, indeed!

MARCH: What tenderness—what sympathy! *(Pressing his hand)* You were my late husband's early friend! *(Noise and carriage heard)* Here are my guests, and I've been crying! I mustn't be seen in this state! Duke, oblige me by receiving them—I'll be down in one minute. *(Exit* MARCHIONESS*)*

DUKE *(taking out snuffbox, opens it as if about to take snuff, produces powder-puff, and powders his face to remove traces of tears):* Why am I cursed with this tremulous sensitiveness? Why are my heartstrings the sport and toy of every wave of sympathetic secondhand sentiment? Ah! ye small tradesmen and other Members of Parliament, who think rump steak and talk bottled beer, I would give ten years of my life to experience, for one brief day, the joy of being a commonplace man!

SONG——DUKE

Oh butcher, oh baker, oh candlestick-maker,
   Oh vendors of bacca and snuff—
And you, licensed vittler, and public-house skittler,
   And all who sell sticky sweet stuff—

Ye barbers, and Messrs. the Bond Street hairdressers
   (Some shave you, and others do not)—
Ye greasy porkpie-men—ye secondhand flymen—
   All people who envy my lot *(Taking up tambourine),*
      Let each of you lift up his voice—
      With tabor and cymbal rejoice
      That you're not, by some horrible fluke,
      A highly-strung sensitive Duke!
         An over-devotional,
         Super-emotional,
         Hyper-chimerical,
         Extra-hysterical,
         Wildly-aesthetical,
         Madly phrenetical,
      Highly-strung sensitive Duke!

You men of small dealings, of course you've your feelings—
   There's no doubt at all about that—
When a dentist exacting your tooth is extracting,
   You howl like an aristocrat.
But an orphan cock-sparrow, who thrills to the marrow
   A Duke who is doubly refined
Would never turn paler a petty retailer
   Or stagger a middle-class mind!
      So each of you lift up your voice—
      With cymbal and tabor rejoice, &c.

(Dances to tambourine accompaniment. Enter BARNS)

BARNS: Your Grace, a gentleman is below who desires to speak with her
   ladyship.
DUKE *(seizing him by the throat, with startling energy):* His name—his name!
   Do not deceive me, varlet, or I'll throttle you!
BARNS: I have known your Grace, man and boy, these eighteen months,
   and I have never told you a lie yet. The gentleman declines to give his
   name, but he says that he wrote to her ladyship this morning.
DUKE: It is he—the falsetto—the supreme Nisnardi! Show him up, and
   treat him with the utmost courtesy. He can touch an upper G!
BARNS: An upper G! Gad bless me, what a gift!

(Exit in amazement. Enter WOODPECKER *timidly)*

WOOD *(mistaking the* DUKE *for a servant):* I say—Chawles, come here, my man. Half-a-crown for you. *(Gives him money)* Now then, just give this note to her ladyship *(gives him a note),* there's a good fellow.

DUKE *(pocketing the coin):* In one moment; the Marchioness will be here directly. In the meantime, permit me to introduce myself—the Duke of Turniptopshire!

WOOD: The what!

DUKE: The Duke——

WOOD: Go on, you're joking!

DUKE: Not at all—observe—*(Twirls round and postures)* Are you convinced?

WOOD: I am! *(Aside)* And I took him for a flunkey! I've given a live Duke half-a-crown—and I'm going to ask a live Marchioness how much she wants for her hat! I shall never be able to do it!

DUKE *(aside):* He speaks English very well, but he's clearly an Italian, he has such a rummy waistcoat. I'll draw him out a bit. *(Aloud)* Princess— pretty feet—old slippers—ah, you dog!

WOOD *(puzzled):* Pretty feet?

DUKE: Yes, pretty feet—pretty little tootsicums! I've heard all about it, you see.

WOOD *(aside):* The upper circles appear to have a method of expressing themselves which is entirely and absolutely their own. *(Aloud)* Could I see the Marchioness?

DUKE: Yes, I'll send word to her. Ha! ha! *(With deep meaning)* Songs—old slippers—flower from a bouquet—three thousand guineas! My dear sir, you're delicious—you're simply delicious! *(Exit DUKE)*

WOOD: It's quite clear to me that I shall never be equal to the intellectual pressure of aristocratic conversation. So I'm married at last—really and truly married. On leaving Bella's, we started for the church—Maria and I were made one—and now if I can only get the hat from the Marchioness, everything will end happily. *(Looking out of window)* There's the wedding party—in eight cabs—waiting patiently until I come down. I told them—ha! ha!—that this was the Piccadilly Hotel, and that I would go up and make arrangements for the wedding breakfast! And they believe it! I hear the Marchioness. I hope she got my note.

(Enter MARCHIONESS. She approaches him melodramatically)

MARCH: Stop—don't move! Let me gaze upon you until I have drunk you in. Oh! thank you. (WOODPECKER, *much astonished exhibits symptoms of nervousness—buttoning his coat, putting on his hat and taking it off again)* Ah, you are cold—cold—cold! You are unaccustomed to the rigor of our detestable climate.

WOOD: As you say, it's a beast of a climate——

MARCH: Ah, sir, I can offer you an hospitable welcome and an appreciative company, but I cannot—alas! I *cannot* offer you an Italian sky!

WOOD: Pray don't name it—it's not of the least consequence. *(Aside)* I never shall understand the aristocracy!

MARCH: Ah, Bella Italia! It's a lovely country!

WOOD: It is a dooced lovely country! Oh, I beg pardon!

MARCH: What a wealth of Southern emphasis! What Italian fervor of expression!

WOOD: I—I did myself the honor of writing a note to your ladyship——

MARCH: A most delightful note, and one that I shall always carry about me as long as I live.

WOOD: Thank you. *(Aside)* She's very polite. *(Aloud)* In that note I ventured to ask you to grant me a slight favor.

MARCH: Oh, of course—how extremely dull of me! Well, you shall have what you want.

WOOD: Really?

MARCH: Really—though you're a bold bad man! *(Turns to bouquet)*

WOOD: At last, at last the hat is mine! I wonder how much she wants for it. Shall I beat her down? No, no, you can't beat down a marchioness! She shall have her price.

MARCH *(giving him a flower):* There is the flower you asked for—bold bad man!

WOOD: A flower? There's some mistake—I want an article of attire.

MARCH: An article of attire?

WOOD: Yes; didn't you get my note?

MARCH: Yes, here it is. *(Taking note from her bosom)* "My terms are—a flower from your bouquet—Nisnardi."

WOOD: Nisnardi? What's that?

MARCH: Hush, eccentric creature—my guests are arriving.

(Enter BARNS*)*

BARNS *(announcing):* Lord and Lady Popton, Colonel Coketown, the Marquis of Barnsbury, Lady Pentwistle, the Archbishop of Bayswater, and the Duke and Duchess of Deal.

(Exits by the door. Enter LORD *and* LADY POPTON, COLONEL COKETOWN, *and other guests)*

MARCH: My dear Duke—my dear Lady Popton—allow me to present to you the incomparable Nisnardi!

(All bow reverentially to WOODPECKER*)*

LADY P *(crossing to him):* And are you really Nisnardi?

WOOD *(aside):* I must brazen it out. *(Aloud)* I am.

LADY P: Incomparable falsettist!

WOOD *(aside):* Good heavens, I'm a singer—a falsettist! Why, I'm a bad baritone!

LADY P: And are you really about to favor us with a specimen of your marvellous talent?

MARCH: Signor Nisnardi is most kindly going to sing three songs.

ALL: { How delightful! / Charming! / What a treat!

WOOD *(aside):* I must get out of this fix at once. *(Aloud)* Marchioness, I have a most extraordinary and—I am afraid you will say—unreasonable request to make.

MARCH: Oh, name it!

WOOD: But it's a secret!

MARCH: Oh, I'm sure our friends will excuse us.

(Guests bow, and exeunt)

WOOD: Marchioness, I am the slave of impulse!

MARCH: I know you are.

WOOD: Eh? Oh! Well, it's a most remarkable thing, but when a whim enters my head, I lose my voice until it is gratified. A whim has just entered my head, and listen! *(Grunt)*

MARCH: Heavens, what is to be done?

DUET—WOODPECKER *and* MARCHIONESS

WOOD: The slave of impulse I,
              Born 'neath the azure sky,
                  Of beautiful Firenze.
              With fierce desires I brim.
              When I conceive a whim,
                  That whim becomes a frenzy.
              A wish ungratified,
              Wounds my Italian pride,
                  Like stab of sharp stilette.
              My blood is turned to gall;
              I cannot sing—I squall,
              And, this is worst of all—
                  Away goes my falsetto,
                  My exquisite falsetto!

MARCH *(aside):*

Oh, heavens! should it befall,
My guests it will appal,
If, when assembled all—
  Away goes his falsetto!
    His exquisite falsetto!

WOOD:

My blood is turned to gall,
I cannot sing, I squall,
And, this is worst of all—
  Away goes my falsetto,
    My exquisite falsetto!

MARCH:

    Lord of the Upper G,
    By peers of high degree
        Assiduously courted;
    Falsettist all divine,
    No heaven-sent whim of thine
        Ought ever to be thwarted.
    Society should strain
    Each nerve to spare thee pain,
        Whatever's on the *tapis;*
    The impulse I admire
    That's born of Southern fire:
    I know what you require—
        Here—take it, and be happy!

(Takes off her shoe and gives it to him)

MARCH *(hopping):*

The impulse I admire
That's born of Southern fire:
I know what you require—
  So take it, and be happy!

WOODPECKER *(puzzled):*

Although I much desire
A part of your attire,
That's not what I require—
  That will not make me happy!

WOOD: But this is not what I want.
MARCH *(hopping):* You said it was an article of my attire.
WOOD: Yes—but—it's the other end!
MARCH: The other end? *(Still hopping)*
WOOD: You wear a straw hat.
MARCH: I was—I mean I do—
WOOD: It is for that straw hat that I have conceived this indescribable longing! Is it not a mad idea?
MARCH: Mad? Not a bit—most reasonable. I understand perfectly—you want it as a *pendant* to the slipper.
WOOD *(aside):* The aristocratic mind seems to go about in slippers!

MARCH: You shall have it at once, oh divine creature! *(Exit* MARCHIONESS, *hopping off)*

WOOD: In two minutes the hat will be mine, and then I must be off before they have time to discover the imposture. I'll tell Maguire that they've no private room to spare at the Piccadilly Hotel. I wonder how the old boy is by this time. *(Goes to window)* There are the cabs—eight of them! Ha! ha! I can almost hear him growl!

(Enter MAGUIRE *through curtains, rather tipsy, with a bottle of champagne in one hand and a glass in the other.* WOODPECKER *is leaning out of the window)*

RECITATIVE

MAGUIRE: Now, Woodpecker! until you come, my dear sir,
We cannot budge a peg!
WOOD: Why, what the dickens are you doing here, sir?
Explain yourself, I beg!

SONG—MAGUIRE

Why, we're all making merry
On port and on sherry.
It's liberal, very—
At price you don't sti-hickle!
When you spoke of our fooding,
Thinks I, he's allooding
To chops and a pooding,
Bread, cheese, and a pi-hickle—
All very good things though they certainly be.
But that's not the *menoo* at the Piccadillee.
Why, bless us, there's dishes
Of fowls and of fishes—
Of all that's delishes—
There's muckle and mi-hickle!
There's puddings and ices,
And jambong in slices—
And other devices
Our palates to ti-tickle!
Fine Frenchified fixings—delicious they be—
But they do the thing well at the Piccadillee.

CHORUS *(within):*

> There's puddings and ices,
> And jambong in slices—
> And other devices
>   Our palates to tickle!
> Fine Frenchified fixings—delicious they be—
> But they do the thing well at the Piccadillee.

WOOD: Here's a pleasant state of things! We shall be kicked out—given into custody—a honeymoon in Holloway Jail!

(Enter MARCHIONESS *still hopping)*

MARCH: Well, have they brought you the hat?

WOOD *(trying to hide* MAGUIRE): Not yet, my lady. If you would kindly ask them to hurry a little——

MARCH *(seeing* MAGUIRE): Who is this nobleman?

WOOD: That nobleman? Oh, this nobleman is a nobleman who always accompanies me—everywhere!

MARCH: Your accompanist? Indeed, a good accompanist is invaluable. And you, sir, are also Italian?

MAGUIRE *(also hopping sympathetically):* I? Oh, I come from Pettytwiddlllm.

WOOD *(hastily):* Pettytwiddlllm, a romantic village on the Abruzzi. His name is Magghia: he was formerly a brigand, but he's reclaimed. He's quite harmless.

MARCH: A reclaimed brigand? How supremely interesting. Then, if everything is ready, my guests shall come in—they're dying to hear you. *(To* MAGUIRE) Will you oblige me with your arm?

MAGUIRE *(gives his arm to* MARCHIONESS): More guests! What a wedding this is, to be sure! *(Exeunt, both hopping)*

WOOD: I'm going mad—I feel it! My reason totters on its throne!

(Enter PATTY *with bandbox)*

PATTY: Here's the straw hat!

WOOD: The straw hat! Hurrah! Saved—saved! Take this sixpence—and be happy. *(Opens bandbox and takes out a black straw hat)* A black straw! Positively a black straw! Come here, miss, there's some mistake. I want a Leghorn hat, trimmed with a parrot's head, an armadillo's claw, two mackerel, one peach, three truffles, and a bun!

PATTY: Oh! my lady gave that one to her niece, Mrs. Major-General Bunthunder.

WOOD: All the ground to go over again! Where does she live?

PATTY: 12 Park Street, Grosvenor Square!

WOOD: Right! Vanish! *(Exit* PATTY*)* My course is clear—I must be off, and leave my father-in-law and the wedding party to square matters with the Marchioness.

(Exits rapidly. Re-enter MARCHIONESS *and* MAGUIRE *with the* MARCHIONESS*'s guests)*

MARCH: Now if you will kindly take your places, the concert will begin. Why, where is Signor Nisnardi!

(Enter DUKE, *leading* WOODPECKER *by the ear)*

DUKE: He was actually bolting! I napped him just as he was getting into eight cabs.

WOOD: No—no, you are mistaken! I had forgotten my tuning-fork, and I was going to fetch it! *(Aside)* Oh dim! dim! dim!

ALL *(applauding):* Bravo! bravo!

WOOD *(aside):* This is most awkward! I'm a bad baritone! What in the world shall I sing them?

*(*MAGUIRE *sits at piano and strikes a few discords.* WOODPECKER *begins on a ridiculously high note)*

BOPADDY *(behind curtains):* Ladies and gentlemen!

ALL: Eh? *(Movement of surprise)*

BO: As the oldest friend of Maria Tapping, I beg to propose the health of the bride!

(Exclamations from MARCHIONESS *and her guests)*

WEDDING GUESTS *(behind curtains):* Hurrah! hurrah! hurrah!

CHORUS OF WEDDING GUESTS

Hurrah for the bride with a right good will—
 Hurrah! hurrah! hurrah!
For the bridegroom bold who pays the bill—
 Hurrah! hurrah! hurrah!
For his father-in-law give three times three,
And three for her cousin—young Foodle he—
And three for this capital companee—
 Hurrah! hurrah! hurrah!

*(*BARNS *rushes on and draws aside the curtains, discovering the wedding party at luncheon.* BOPADDY *on a chair with one foot on the table, with doll's head*

*in one hand and glass of wine in the other. Music changes to "Haste to the
Wedding." Party all rise and come down dancing two and two. They cross the
stage, dancing off.* BOPADDY *last with doll's head,* WOODPECKER *having disappeared as soon as the curtains opened.* MARCHIONESS *faints in* DUKE*'s arms.
General consternation among her guests. Curtain.*)

ACT III

Scene One

Dressing room in MAJOR-GENERAL BUNTHUNDER*'s House. Door right and left.
Large screen right, with double hinges to fold both ways. The* MAJOR-GENERAL
*is discovered within the screen in full uniform, taking a footbath; a blanket
conceals his legs. His boots are on the floor left of screen. A hot-water can
stands near them. His trousers hang on the screen.*

SONG—BUNTHUNDER

Though called upon I've never been
    To court a warrior's tomb,
Or to defend my Sovereign Queen
    In battle's dread boom—boom!
Resistless I, when I am stirred
    To doughty deeds of wrath,
So on myself I have conferred
    The Order of the Bath!
You trace my humor's devious path?
    You see my meaning through?
(Impressively)   The knightly Order of *the Bath*—
(Disappointed)   I don't believe you do!

Let me explain—you're in the dark—
    The "Bath" a high degree
Conferred no warriors of mark,
    But *not* conferred on me.
From "Bath" we easily derive
    This *footbath*—common delf—
And *that's* the compliment that I've
    Conferred upon myself.
(Explaining)   This bath—of crockery or delf—
    A play on meanings twain.
(Mortified)   I'm sorry: I forgot myself—
    It sha'n't occur again.

BUN: It's a most extraordinary thing that my wife should not have returned
—I can't understand it at all. My wife said to me this morning, at a
quarter to nine o'clock, "Bunthunder, I'm going out to buy a pint of
Barcelona nuts," and it's now twenty minutes past five in the afternoon,
and she has not yet returned. By dint of worrying myself about her I've
got a splitting headache, and for a splitting headache there's nothing
like putting one's feet in hot water. Where can she be? *(Rising)* Oh,
Leonora, Leonora, if I thought you were deceiving me, there is no
vengeance that would be too dire! *(Knock at street door)* There she is—
there she is at last! she's coming upstairs. *(Resuming his seat. Knock at
room door)* Come in, come in! I'm taking a footbath, but come in.

(Enter WOODPECKER*)*

DUET—WOODPECKER and BUNTHUNDER

WOOD: Your pardon, sir. Am I addressing
                        The Major-General Bunthunder,
                            I greatly wonder?
                        In search of him I roam.
BUN: I am, as you are rightly guessing,
                        That most unhappy warrior—
                            No man sorrier—
                        But I am not at home.
WOOD *(suspiciously):* You're not at home?
BUN: No, sir, I'm not at home.
WOOD: This information is distressing;
                        If you will shortly be returning,
                          My soul is burning
                        With keen anxiety to know?
BUN: I've gone abroad on business pressing;
                        When home from places foreigneering
                          I shall be steering
                        Is quite uncertain! Go!
WOOD *(doubtfully):*   Uncertain? Oh!
BUN: It's quite uncertain! Go!

SOLO—WOODPECKER

From the Marchioness's,
Whom nobody guesses
    To be of the rank of a peeress or peer—
In courtesy lacking

> They sent us all packing,
>   And each with a very fine flea in his ear.
> Those Johnnies and Jackies
> The overfed lackies
>   They "went for" the bride and her guests with a rush—
> The combat was heated
> But we were defeated
>   By insolent armies of powder and plush.
> And Mister Maguire,
> Who's raging with ire,
>   Has taken an oath by the powers that he,
> That restaurant-keeper
> Shall not close a peeper
>   Until she has published an apologee!
> Ha! ha! ha! ha!
>   Until she has published an apologee!

BUN: Well, sir, what's all that to me, sir? Will you go, sir?

WOOD: Oh, I see *(Raising blanket)*, you're taking a footbath.

BUN *(furious):* I won't listen to you. I'm not well. I've got a headache! Who are you?

WOOD: Woodpecker Tapping—married this morning: the wedding party is at your door, in eight cabs.

BUN: I don't know you, sir! What do you want?

WOOD: Your wife.

BUN *(rising):* My wife! Do you know my wife?

WOOD: Not at all, but she possesses something that I am most anxious to purchase.

BUN: We don't sell it. Will you go?

WOOD: Not till I've seen Mrs. Bunthunder.

BUN: She's not at home.

WOOD: Nonsense, I know better! I dare say she's in here—at all events, I mean to look.

*(*WOODPECKER *closes screen round* BUNTHUNDER, *concealing him from the audience, and leaving his boots outside.* WOODPECKER *then runs into room at right)*

BUN: He's a thief! He's a burglar! Wait one moment—only one moment, until I've finished dressing!

(Enter MAGUIRE, *limping)*

MAG: My son-in-law is a most remarkable person; he invites us to his house and when we get there, he shuts the door in our faces! Fortunately the lock didn't catch and here I am. Now, now I shall be able to take off these confounded tight boots which have been bothering me all day!

BUN *(behind screen, taking his trousers, which are hanging over the top):* One moment—only one moment!

MAG: Hallo, Woodpecker! He's in here. Ha! *(Seeing* BUNTHUNDER's *boots)* The very thing; that's uncommonly lucky! *(Takes off his own boots and puts on* BUNTHUNDER's*)* The very thing! *(They are much too large for him)* Dear me, what a relief! *(Puts his own boots by screen, where* BUNTHUNDER's *were)*

BUN *(reaching round screen for his boots, takes* MAGUIRE's*):* Now for my boots—wait one moment—only one moment!

MAG: I say, my boy, your wife's below.

BUN: Oh, my wife's below, is she? Just one moment—I'm nearly ready!

MAG: All right! I'll go downstairs and tell them all to come up.

(Exit MAGUIRE. *At the same moment enter* BOPADDY*)*

BUN *(in screen):* My feet seem much swollen, I can scarcely get my boots on; but no matter. Now, then! *(Coming out of screen sees* BOPADDY, *whom he mistakes for* WOODPECKER, *swings him round)* Now, you scoundrel, I've got you!

BO: Don't—I don't want to dance—I'm quite tired out!

BUN: It's not the same—it's another of the gang! *(Noise heard within)* He's in there! *(Rushes off)*

BO: Another wedding guest, and in regimentals, too! Dear, dear—Woodpecker is certainly doing it uncommonly well!

(Music, "Haste to the Wedding." Enter MAGUIRE, FOODLE, MARIA *and the wedding party, all dancing on in couples. They dance round the stage, and range themselves at back)*

MAG: That's right, my dears—stop there, because Woodpecker hasn't quite finished dressing—he's behind the screen and he won't be a minute and you mustn't look, any of you. *(The screen is now open)* Woodpecker, my boy, your wife is here; and while you're completing your toilet, I'll give you both a bit of matrimonial advice, drawn from my own experience.

SONG—MAGUIRE

If you value a peaceable life,
This maxim will teach you to get it

In all things give in to your wife—
   I didn't—I lived to regret it.
My wife liked to govern alone,
   And she never would share with another;
Remarkably tall and well grown,
She had plenty of muscle and bone,
With an excellent will of her own—
   And my darling takes after her mother!
     Oh, if early in life
       I had happily known
     How to humor a wife
       With a will of her own,
     We should not have been snarling
       All day at each other—
     And, remember, my darling
       Takes after her mother!

Never wake up her temper—I did—
   And smash went a window, instanter;
Invariably do as you're bid—
   I didn't—bang went a decanter.
Give in to each whim—I declined—
   At my head went a vinegar-cruet.
Whatever inducement you find,
Never give her advice of a kind
That is known as "a bit of your mind"—
   I did—and the crockery knew it!
     Oh, if early in life
       I had happily known, &c.

Though her aspect was modest and meek,
   She could turn on the steam in a minute:
Her eruptions went on for a week—
   Vesuvius, my boy, wasn't in it.
Give your wife of indulgence her fill,
   Though your meals be unpleasantly scrappy—
Never look at her milliner's bill;
Gulp down that extravagant pill,
And you may, and you probably will,
   Be bankrupt—and thoroughly happy!
     Oh, if early in life
       I had happily known, &c.

(Music, "Haste to the Wedding." Wedding party all dance off. Enter WOOD-
PECKER *with several hats in one hand and the specimen in the other)*

DUET—WOODPECKER *and* BUNTHUNDER

WOOD: I've come across hats of all colors and sorts,
          But none like this specimen, demme!

(Enter BUNTHUNDER*)*

BUN *(seizing him):* Thief! Burglar! Away to the Criminal Courts,
          With your skeleton keys and your jemmy!
WOOD: Excuse me, you're really mistaken in that—
          I'll prove it, if patient you'll be, sir:
          This morning my horse ate a young lady's hat—
BUN: Well, what does that matter to me, sir?
WOOD: But she's now at my lodgings—and leave them she won't
          Until I've produced her another!
BUN: By all that is prudent and proper, why don't
          The young lady go home to her mother?
          Already too long she has tarried—
          Why don't the young widow withdraw?
WOOD: Young widow? good gracious, she's married,
          And her husband can claim her by law!

BUN *(tickled):*   Ha, ha! Ho, ho!
              Sly dog! *(Digging* WOODPECKER *in the ribs)*
WOOD *(same business):* Sly dog!
BOTH: Ha, ha! Ho, ho!

WOOD: Now, her husband's a jealous old fellow,
          A savage old Tartar, no doubt,
          A middle-class white-washed Othello—
          One leg in the grave, and one out!

BUN *(much amused):* Ha, ha! Ho, ho!
              Sly dog!
WOOD: Sly dog!
BOTH: Ha, ha! Ho, ho!

WOOD: Now, you'd think he'd abuse her or thrash her,
          Just to give her a kind of a fright.
(Spoken) My dear sir, he'd simply and silently smash her!

BUN *(emphatically):* And, by George, he'd be perfectly right!
                    Ha, ha! Ho, ho!
                    Sly dog!
WOOD: Sly dog!
BOTH: Ha, ha! Ho, ho!

WOOD: Now, assist me if you could be brought to,
            We'd hoodwink Othello, I bet—
BUN: No, really I don't think I ought to,
            I *don't* think I ought to—and yet—

                    Ha, ha! Ho, ho!
                    Sly dog!
WOOD: Sly dog!
BOTH: Ha, ha! Ho, ho!

WOOD *(with specimen):*   Here are the fragments—decorated they,
                            With choicest gifts of Flora's.
BUN *(recognizing them):* By all the blighting tricks that devils play,
                            This hat is Leonora's!
(Pointing to name in hat)   Her name, sir—Leonora's!
WOOD: Quite right, it's Leonora's!

                    Ha, ha! ho, ho!
                    Sly dog!

BUN: Be quiet, sir! The married lady
            For whom, with motives base and shady,
            A furnished lodging you've provided,
            Turns to be my wife misguided!
WOOD: What!
BUN *(seizing him):* Scoundrel, villain, scurvy traitor!
            Peace of mind exterminator!
            So, for private *tater-tater,*
                With my wife you've made a fixture!
WOOD: Let me go, sir—you're mistaken,
            Or my anger you'll awaken;
            I object thus to be shaken
                Like an eighteenpenny mixture!

BUNTHUNDER:	WOODPECKER:
Fire and fury!	Cease your fury!
Judge in ermine	Judge in ermine
(With a jury)	My injury
Shall determine	Shall determine!
How to treat this social wrong,	Your remarks are clearly wrong,
sir—	sir—
Come along, sir—come along,	Much too strong, sir—much too
sir!	strong, sir!

(BUNTHUNDER *drags* WOODPECKER *off. Music changes to "Haste to the Wedding." The wedding party enter, dance in couples across the stage, after them,* BOPADDY *last with the doll's head.*)

Scene Two

A street, with Square in the distance. A rainy night. WOODPECKER*'s house left, another house beyond it. Police station right. A lamp center supported by brackets from each side of the stage, a lamp post left. Window of first floor of police station is practicable. Doorsteps to* WOODPECKER*'s house, a light in one window. A gutter crosses the stage. Music, "Haste to the Wedding." Wedding party enter, dancing in couples round stage, with umbrellas up.* BOPADDY *politely holding umbrella over doll's head.*

MAG *(leading them):* This way, my friends—this way! Hallo! look out for the gutter! *(He jumps over it—all the wedding party follow, jumping over it in succession)*

MARIA: Oh, papa, where's Woodpecker?

MAG: Eh? Isn't he here? Why, he has given us the slip again!

MARIA: Papa dear, I'm so tired—I can't go any farther! *(Sits on step of* WOODPECKER*'s house)*

FOOD: And my new boots hurt me so that I must sit down! *(Crosses and sits by her)*

MAG *(stamping about in* MAJOR-GENERAL*'s boots):* Ha, ha! so did mine, but I've changed 'em!

MARIA: Oh, papa, why did you send away the cabs?

MAG: Why? I've paid 'em eleven pounds fifteen already—isn't that enough? But where are we?

ALL: I don't know!

MARIA: Woodpecker told us to follow him to his house. No. 8 Little Pickleboy Gardens, Mulberry Square.

MAG: Perhaps this is Mulberry Square. (*To* BOPADDY) Your great grandfather used to live in London—is this Mulberry Square?

BO: Yes—yes, it is—splendid—splendid weather for ducks and peas! Ha, ha! Oh, yes—for ducks and peas!

MAG: He's doting—doting!

(*Enter* WILKINSON, *a policeman. He sneezes*)

MAG: Here's a policeman, I'll ask him. (*Very politely*) I beg your pardon, but will you be so polite as to tell me if this is Little Pickleboy Gardens, Mulberry Square?

WILK (*sternly*): Move on! (*Exit*)

MAG: And I pay taxes to support that overbearing underling! I feed him, I clothe him, I lodge him, and I pay him; and in return he tells me to move on! Insupportable bureaucrat!

FOOD (*who has climbed up lamp post and read name of street*): Hurrah! Little Pickleboy Gardens. It's all right—here we are!

MAG: And here is No. 8. (*To* MARIA, *who is sitting on the doorstep*) Get up, my dear.

MARIA: Papa dear, it's no use—I must sit down somewhere.

MAG: Not in a muddy road, in a thirty-seven and sixpenny wedding dress, my love. Why don't they come? (*Knocks*)

FOOD: There's a light in the first floor.

MAG: Then Woodpecker must have arrived before us. (*Calls*) Woodpecker! Woodpecker!

ALL: Woodpecker! Woodpecker!

(*Re-enter* WILKINSON)

WILKINSON (*to* BOPADDY, *who has fallen asleep on step*): Now, then, can't have that noise here! (*Shakes him*) Move on! Move on, will you? (*Pushing his shoulder, which is muddy*)

BO: Thank you, my dear friend; don't you trouble to brush it off; I'll do that when I go in.

(*Exit* WILKINSON. JACKSON *opens door of* WOODPECKER's *house*)

MAG: Hurrah! Here we are! Come in!

(*Music commences "Haste the Wedding" as the wedding party dance into the house*)

JACK: Stop. (*All stop suddenly in arrested attitudes*) Out of the question!

MAG: Eh?

JACK: Impossible! more than my place is worth. Why, the lady is still upstairs! (*Movement*)

MAG: A lady! What lady?

JACK: The lady who is stopping with master—the lady without a hat.

MAG: A lady stopping with your master!

FOOD: On his wedding day!

MARIA: And without a hat! *(Faints into* FOODLE's *arms)*

MAG *(furiously):* It's off! It's off! I'll get you divorced, my dear. Foodle shall have you!

FOOD: Maria!

MAG: Come along back to Pettytwiddlllm. There's a train at eleven; we shall just catch it.

MARIA: Oh, papa—papa——

MAG: What is it, my child?

MARIA *(tragically):* Am I never—never to see Woodpecker again?

MAG: Never!

MARIA: Woodpecker, whom I loved so fondly, and who was the very music of my little life?

MAG: Never!

MARIA: Oh! Then hadn't I better take back my wedding presents?

MAG: My dear, you're a very sensible girl. To be sure you had. *(To* JACKSON) Go and bring out all my daughter's wedding presents—mind—every one!

(Exit JACKSON *into house. Enter* WOODPECKER, *as if pursued)*

ALL: Here is the monster!

MAG: It's off! It's off! You—you serpent!

WOOD: Hold your tongue—be quiet! I hear him—he's coming!

MAG: Who's coming?

WOOD: Major-General Bunthunder. *(Listening)* No—he's missed me— he's got tight boots and he can't run. There'll be time to get Leonora out of the house before he arrives.

MAG: Oho! So, sir, you own to Leonora?

WOOD: Of course I own to Leonora!

ALL: Oho! He owns to Leonora!

(Enter JACKSON *from house with his arms full of wedding presents, done up in parcels)*

JACK: Here are the wedding presents.

MAG: My friends, let us each take a parcel. (JACKSON *gives a parcel to each,* MAGUIRE *gets the bandbox given by* BOPADDY *in Act I)* And now off we go to Pettytwiddlllm!

WOOD: What's all this?

JACK: Wedding presents, sir.

WOOD: Oh, this won't do! Drop those things directly! *(All drop their parcels)*

MAG: Nonsense—pick them all up again!

(All pick up parcels. WOODPECKER *and* MAGUIRE *struggle for the bandbox)*

BO: Take care—you'll crush it! It's a Leghorn hat worth twenty pounds!

WOOD: What!

BO: It's my little present—I'm in the trade. I sent to Florence for it, for my little niece!

WOOD: Give it here. *(Takes bandbox from* MAGUIRE—*takes out straw hat and compares it with the fragments)* Good heavens, it's the very thing! Here's the cockatoo—and the armadillo's claw—and the mackerel—and the peach—why, it's the very thing I've been looking for all day!

(Shakes hands with BOPADDY, *holding the bandbox under his arm)*

MAG *(aside):* A hat worth twenty pounds! He sha'n't have it, the scamp!

(Takes hat out of bandbox unobserved and shuts box again)

WOOD *(who believes that the hat is in the box):* Wait one moment—I'll give her the hat and then we'll all go in and enjoy ourselves. *(Exit into house)*

MAG *(who has watched him off):* Now, my friends—off we go to Pettytwid-dllm.

(All going. Enter WILKINSON*)*

WILK: Hallo! what's all this? What are you doing with these parcels?

MAG: We—we are moving.

WILK: What! at this time o' night? This won't do, you know—I know you!

MAG: Sir!

WILK: What have you got here, eh?

MAG: That? Oh, that's a—a carriage clock.

WILK *(opens muff-box and finds a muff):* That's very like a carriage clock! Come along—all on yer, in yer go!

(Music, "Haste to the Wedding." They all dance into stationhouse, except BOPADDY *who is walking off slowly, talking to his doll's head)*

BO *(to doll's head):* It was a nice ickle gal! It was a very nice ickle gal! Don't know that I ever saw a nicer ickle gal!

WILK *(coming out of stationhouse, crosses to* BOPADDY*)* Now, then—come along—in yer go!

*(*WILKINSON *taps* BOPADDY *on the shoulder and points to station.* BOPADDY

mildly expostulates and resumes his flirtation with the doll's head. WILKINSON *seizes him roughly.* BOPADDY *again remonstrates.* WILKINSON *shakes him,* BOPADDY *suddenly turns furious, flies at* WILKINSON, *knocks him down, seizes his staff, thrashes him soundly and finally drags him off triumphantly into station. Enter* WOODPECKER, CAPTAIN BAPP, *and* LEONORA *from house)*

WOOD: Come along, you are saved! I've found the hat! Make haste, put it on and be off before your husband arrives!

(He gives them the bandbox. They open it)

ALL: Empty!

WOOD: It *was* there—I'll swear it was! My old villain of a father-in-law has stolen it! *(Enter* WILKINSON *from stationhouse)* Where is my father-in-law?

WILK: Where? Station-'us.

WOOD: And my wedding party?

WILK: Station-'us. Run 'em all in. *(Exit* WILKINSON*)*

WOOD: And they've got the hat! What is to be done?

BAPP: Wait a moment—I know the inspector—he'll give it to me if I explain the facts. *(Exit into stationhouse)*

BUN *(without):* Stop! Cabman! Hi! Put me down here!

LEO: Heavens! my husband! I'll run and hide in your house!

WOOD: Not for worlds! He's coming to search it!

LEO: But what shall I do?

WOOD: I know! I'll give you in charge. Hi! policeman. *(Re-enter* WILKINSON*)* Take this woman away. Drunk and disorderly. *(Tipping him)*

WILK *(crossing to her):* What, agin? Come along—I know yer!

(Walks her into station. Enter BUNTHUNDER, *hobbling)*

BUN: So, here you are! Open your door! I'll blow her brains out, and your brains out, and my own brains out!

WOOD: By all means—only take me last!

(Exit BUNTHUNDER *into house.* CAPTAIN BAPP *appears at window of stationhouse, first floor)*

BAPP: Quick! quick! here's the hat!

WOOD: Throw it out—make haste!

*(*BAPP *throws hat, which rests on the lamp—just out of reach)*

WOOD: Confound it!

(Tries to unhook it with his umbrella, but in vain. Re-enter BUNTHUNDER *from house)*

BUN: She's not there! Forgive me, I've been unjust!

WOOD: You have. Come under my umbrella.

(Takes BUNTHUNDER*'s arm and puts up umbrella to conceal hat. They both stand under the lamp)*

BUN: No, no—it doesn't rain! Put the umbrella down. It's quite fine over-head.

WOOD: But it's so wet underfoot.

BUN: That's true. I've made a great fool of myself, sir.

WOOD: You have.

(He jumps to unhook the hat with his umbrella and makes BUNTHUNDER *jump, too)*

BUN: I apologize, sir.

WOOD: I think you should, sir. *(Jumps)*

BUN: Forgive me, sir.

WOOD: I do, sir. *(Jumps)*

BUN: What are you jumping for?

WOOD: Violent cramp—indigestion. Can't help it—always takes me so.

BUN: Indeed! Have you tried—— (WOODPECKER *jumps again and comes down on* BUNTHUNDER*'s toes)* Don't, sir! I won't be trodden on by bride-grooms!

(Enter LEONORA *from station, followed by* MAGUIRE, BOPADDY *and all the guests—one of whom unhooks the hat, which falls to the ground)*

MAG: It's all right—it's all right! The Captain has squared the Inspector and we leave the Court without a stain on our characters! Oh, it's a great country!

FINALE

CHORUS

Free, free! Hurrah!
Free, free! Hurrah!
False charges fade into thin air—
(This is a great Countree!)
When English justice, nobly fair—
(This is a great Countree!)
Is freely tipped with English gold!
For then the wicked oppressor is sold,
And all stray lambs come back to the fold—
This is a great Countree!

Yes—
This is a great Countree!

LEO *(coming forward wearing the hat):*
So, sir—I've found you out at last!
WOOD *(aside, astonished):*   She's got the hat!
LEO: At your assurance I'm aghast!
BUN *(aside astonished):*   She's got the hat!
LEO: While you've been on clandestine jaunts—
BO *(aside):*   She's got my hat!
LEO: I've waited for you—at my aunt's!
I've waited, waited, waited, waited—
All day I've waited for you—at my aunt's!

CHORUS

She's got the hat—she's got the hat!
(We don't know how, but never mind that)—
It's tat for tit, and tit for tat—
She's got the hat, she's got the hat!

BUN: Forgive me—I have been unjust!
ALL: She's got the hat!
BUN: You'll overlook the past, I trust?
ALL: She's got the hat!
BUN: But, stop! The gate of Heaven shuts!
ALL: She's got the hat.
BUN: Where are the Barcelona nuts!
The Barcelona—lona—lona—
You have *not* got the Barcelona nuts!

CHORUS

Well, what of this and what of that—
Somehow or other she's got the hat—
It's tat for tit, and tit for tat—
She's got the hat, she's got the hat!

FINAL CHORUS

Ring, ye joybells, long and loudly,
Happy hearts together tied—

Bridegroom's bosom swelling proudly
As he takes his blushing bride!

(During these lines the bride and bridegroom bid farewell to the guests and go towards the house. All the others gradually move off except BOPADDY *who, still carrying his doll's head, proposes to enter the house with the bridal couple. He is brought back by* MAGUIRE *as the curtain falls.)*

THE MAN WHO MARRIED A DUMB WIFE

by
Anatole France
Translated by Curtis Hidden Page

Jacques-Anatole-François Thibault, better known as ANATOLE FRANCE (1844–1924), was the son of a Parisian bookseller. His numerous short stories and novels, which include *Penguin Island* and "The Procurator of Judaea" (possibly the most devastating "conte cruelle" ever penned), earned him the Nobel Prize for Literature in 1921.

France wrote THE MAN WHO MARRIED A DUMB WIFE as a prank when he was sixty years old. Once enormously popular with amateur theatre companies, it might give modern theatre producers qualms, considering its deliciously meanspirited view of marriage in general and corrupt lawyers, judges and doctors in particular.

CAST OF CHARACTERS

MASTER LEONARD BOTAL, judge
MASTER ADAM FUMÉE, lawyer
MASTER SIMON COLLINE, doctor
MASTER JEAN MAUGIER, surgeon
MASTER SERAFIN DULAURIER, apothecary
GILES BOISCOURTIER, secretary
A BLIND FIDDLER
CATHERINE, Botal's wife
ALISON, Botal's servant
MADEMOISELLE DE LA GARANDIÈRE
MADAME DE LA BRUINE
THE CHICKWEED MAN
THE WATERCRESS MAN
THE CANDLE MAN
PAGE TO MADEMOISELLE DE LA GARANDIÈRE
FOOTMAN TO MADAME DE LA BRUINE
FIRST DOCTOR'S ATTENDANT
SECOND DOCTOR'S ATTENDANT
A CHIMNEY SWEEP
FIRST APOTHECARY'S BOY
SECOND APOTHECARY'S BOY

Scene One

A large room in JUDGE LEONARD BOTAL'*s house in Paris.*

Left: Main entrance, from the rue Dauphine; when the door is open, vista to the Pont-Neuf.

Right: Door to the kitchen.

At the rear of the stage: A wooden stairway, leading to the upper rooms.

On the walls are portraits of magistrates, in gown and wig and, along the walls, great cabinets or cupboards full of books, papers, parchments and bags of legal documents, with more piled on top of the cabinets. There is a double stepladder on castors with flat steps on each side, used to reach the top of the cabinets.

A writing table, small chairs, upholstered armchairs, and a spinning wheel.

The street door of the house opens on a hallway, from which a door leads off to the kitchen and a short stairway leads up, in a direction parallel with the front of the stage, past a double lattice window open to the street, to an upper room in which most of the action takes place.

This room has a large balcony and window seat, and stands entirely open to the street. The writing table, bookcase (instead of cabinets), and stepladder are seen within it. There is a bench or form, long enough to seat two or three people, in front of the table. A door at the right rear corner of the room is supposed to open on a stairway leading to the rooms above.

GILES *is discovered sitting on a small form in front of the table; on the rise of the curtain he turns to the audience, bows in flamboyant style, and then sits down again, with his back to the audience.*

The CHICKWEED MAN *goes by, calling:* "Chickweed! Chickweed! Good birdseed, good birdseed, good birdseed for saäle!"

Enter ALISON, *with a large basket under each arm. She curtsies to the audience.* GILES, *as soon as he spies her, runs to the street door and stands quiet beside it, so that she does not notice him. As she starts to enter the house, he jumps at her and snatches a bottle from one of the baskets.*

ALISON: Holy Mary, don't you know better than to jump at anybody like a bogie man, here in a public place?

GILES *(pulling a bottle of wine out of the other basket):* Don't scream, you little goose. Nobody's going to pluck you. You're not worth it.

(Enter MASTER ADAM FUMÉE. *He bows to the audience)*

ALISON: Will you let the Judge's wine alone, you rascal! *(She sets down her baskets, snatches back one of the bottles, cuffs the secretary, picks up her baskets and goes off to the kitchen. The kitchen fireplace is seen through the half-open door)*

MASTER ADAM *(slightly formal in manner and speech at first):* Is this the dwelling of Mr. Leonard Botal, Judge in civil and criminal cases?

GILES *(with bottle behind his back, and bowing):* Yes, sir; it's here, sir; and I'm his secretary, Giles Boiscourtier, at your service, sir.

MASTER ADAM: Then, boy, go tell him his old schoolfellow, Master Adam Fumée, lawyer, wishes to see him on business.

GILES: Here he comes now, sir.

(LEONARD BOTAL *comes down the stairs.* GILES *goes off into the kitchen)*

MASTER ADAM: Good day, master Leonard Botal, I am delighted to see you again.

LEONARD: Good morning, Master Adam Fumée, how have you been this long time that I haven't set eyes on you?

MASTER ADAM: Well, very well. And I hope I find you the same, Your Honor.

LEONARD: Fairly so, fairly so. And what good wind wafts you hither, Master Adam Fumée? *(They come forward in the room)*

MASTER ADAM: I've come from Chartres on purpose to put in your own hands a statement on behalf of a young orphan girl . . .

LEONARD: Master Adam Fumée, do you remember the days when we were law students together at Orleans University?

MASTER ADAM: Yes, yes; we used to play the flute together, and take the ladies out to picnics, and dance from morning to night. . . . But I've come, Your Honor, my dear old schoolfellow, to hand you a statement on behalf of a young orphan girl whose case is now pending before you.

LEONARD: Will she give good fees?

MASTER ADAM: She is a young orphan girl. . . .

LEONARD: Yes, yes, I know. But, will she give good fees?

MASTER ADAM: She is a young orphan girl who's been robbed by her guardian, and he left her nothing but her eyes to weep with. But if she wins her suit, she will be rich again, and will give plentiful proof of her gratitude.

LEONARD *(taking the statement which* MASTER ADAM *hands him):* We will look into the matter.

MASTER ADAM: I thank you, Your Honor, my dear old schoolfellow.

LEONARD: We will look into it, without fear or favor.

MASTER ADAM: That goes without saying. . . . But, tell me: is everything going smoothly with you? You seem worried. And yet, you are well placed here . . . the judgeship's a good one?

LEONARD: I paid enough for it to be a good one—and I didn't get cheated.

MASTER ADAM: Perhaps you are lonely. Why don't you get married?

LEONARD: What, what! Don't you know, Master Adam, that I *have* just been married? *(They sit down on the form in front of the table)* Yes, only last month, to a girl from one of our best country families, young and handsome, Catherine Momichel, the seventh daughter of the Criminal Court Judge at Salency. But alas! she is dumb. Now you know my affliction.

MASTER ADAM: Your wife is dumb?

LEONARD: Alas, yes.

MASTER ADAM: Quite, quite dumb?

LEONARD: As a fish.

MASTER ADAM: And you didn't notice it till after you'd married her?

LEONARD: Oh, I couldn't help noticing it, of course, but it didn't seem to make so much difference to me then as it does now. I considered her beauty and her property, and thought of nothing but the advantages of the match and the happiness I should have with her. But now these matters seem less important, and I do wish she could talk; that would be a real intellectual pleasure for me and, what's more, a practical advantage for the household. What does a Judge need most in his house? Why, a good-looking wife, to receive the suitors pleasantly and, by subtle suggestions, gently bring them to the point of making proper presents, so that their cases may receive—more careful attention. People need to be encouraged to make proper presents. A woman, by clever speech and prudent action, can get a good ham from one and a roll of cloth from another; and make still another give poultry or wine. But this poor dumb thing Catherine gets nothing at all. While my fellow judges have their kitchens and cellars and stables and store-rooms running over with good things, all thanks to their wives, I hardly get wherewithal to keep the pot boiling. You see, Master Adam Fumée, what I lose by having a dumb wife. I'm not worth half as much. . . . And the worst of it is, I'm losing my spirits, and almost my wits, with it all.

MASTER ADAM: There's no reason in that, now, Your Honor. Just consider the thing closely and you will find some advantages in your case as it stands, and no mean ones neither.

LEONARD: No, no, Master Adam; you don't understand. Think!—When I hold my wife in my arms—a woman as beautiful as the finest carved statue, at least so I think—and quite as silent, that I'm sure of—it makes me feel queer and uncanny; I even ask myself if I'm holding a graven image or a mechanical toy or a magic doll made by a sorcerer, not a real human child of our Father in Heaven; sometimes, in the morning, I am tempted to jump out of bed to escape from bewitchment.

MASTER ADAM: What notions!

LEONARD: Worse yet! What with having a dumb wife, I'm going dumb myself. Sometimes I catch myself using signs, as she does. The other day on the Bench, I even pronounced judgment in pantomine and condemned a man to the galleys, just by dumb show and gesticulation.

MASTER ADAM: Enough! Say no more! I can see that a dumb wife may be a pretty poor conversationalist! There's not much fun in talking yourself, when you get no response.

LEONARD: Now you know the reason why I'm in low spirits.

MASTER ADAM: I won't contradict you; I admit that your reason is full and sufficient. But perhaps there's a remedy. Tell me: is your wife deaf as well as dumb?

LEONARD: Catherine is no more deaf than you and I are; even less, I might say. She can hear the very grass growing.

MASTER ADAM: Then the case is not hopeless. When the doctors and surgeons and apothecaries succeed in making the deaf and dumb speak, their utterance is as poor as their ears; for they can't hear what they say themselves, any more than what's said to them. But it's quite different with the dumb who can hear. 'Tis but child's play for a doctor to untie their tongues. The operation is so simple that it's done every day to puppies that can't learn to bark. Must a countryman like me come to town to tell you that there's a famous doctor, just around the corner from your own house in Buci Square at the Sign of the Dragon, Master Simon Colline, who has made a reputation for loosing the tongues of the ladies of Paris? In a turn of the hand, he'll draw from your wife's lips a full flood of mellifluous speech, just as you'd turn on a spigot and let the water run forth like a sweet-purling brook.

LEONARD: Is this true, Master Adam? Aren't you deceiving me? Aren't you speaking as a lawyer in court?

MASTER ADAM: I'm speaking as a friend and telling you the plain truth.

LEONARD: Then I'll send for this famous doctor—and that right away.

MASTER ADAM: As you please. . . . But before you call him in, you must reflect soberly and consider what it's really best to do. For, take it all in all, though there are some disadvantages in having a dumb wife, there are some advantages, too. . . . Well, good day, Your Honor, my dear old schoolfellow. (*They go together to the street door*) Remember, I'm truly your friend—and read over my statement, I beg you. If you give your just judgment in favor of the orphan girl robbed by her grasping guardian, you will have no cause to regret it.

LEONARD: Be back this afternoon, Master Adam Fumée; I will have my decision ready. (*They bow low to each other. Exit* MASTER ADAM) Giles! Giles! . . . The rogue never hears me; he is in the kitchen, as usual, upsetting the soup and the servant. He's a knave and a scoundrel. Giles! . . . Giles! . . . Here, you rapscallion! You reprobate! . . .

GILES *(entering)* Present, your Honor.

LEONARD *(taking him by the ear):* Sirrah! Go straight to the famous doctor, Master Simon Colline, who lives in Buci Square at the Sign of the Dragon, and tell him to come to my house at once, to treat a dumb woman. . . .

GILES: Yes, Your Honor. (GILES *starts off, running, to the right)*

LEONARD: Go the nearest way, not round by the New Bridge, to watch the jugglers. I know you, you slowpoke; there's not such another cheat and loafer in ten counties.

(GILES comes back slowly across stage and stops)

GILES: Sir, you wrong me. . . .

LEONARD: Be off! and bring the famous doctor back with you.

GILES *(bolting off to the left):* Yes, Your Honor.

LEONARD *(going up and sitting down at the table, which is loaded with brief-bags):* I have fourteen verdicts to render today, besides the decree in the case of Master Adam Fumée's ward. And that is no small labor because a decree, to do credit to the Judge, must be cleverly worded, subtle, elegant and adorned with all the ornaments both of style and of thought. The ideas must be pleasingly conceived and playfully expressed. Where should one show one's wit, if not in a verdict?

(The WATERCRESS MAN enters from the right and crosses to the left singing: "Good watercress, fresh from the spring! Keeps you healthy and hearty! Six farthings a bunch. Six farthings a bunch." When the WATERCRESS MAN is well on, enter the CANDLE MAN from left to right, singing: "Candles! Cotton-wick candles! Burn bright as the stars!" While he is passing, CATHERINE enters from the upper stairway door; she curtsies to the audience and then sits on the window seat, embroidering. As the street cries die away, LEONARD looks up from his work at the table and, seeing CATHERINE, goes to her and kisses her as she rises to meet him. She makes a curtsy, kisses him in return and listens with pleased attention.)

Good morning, my love. . . . I didn't even hear you come down. You are like the fairy forms in the stories that seem to glide upon air; or like the dreams which the gods, as poets tell, send down to happy mortals. *(CATHERINE shows her pleasure in his compliments)* My love, you are a marvel of nature and a triumph of art; you have all charms but speech. *(CATHERINE turns away, sobbing slightly)* Shouldn't you be glad to have that, too? *(She turns back, intensely interested)* Shouldn't you be happy to let your lips utter all the pretty thoughts I can read in your eyes? Shouldn't

you be pleased to show your wit? *(She waves her handkerchief in glee)*
Shouldn't you like to tell your husband how you love him? Wouldn't it be
delightful to call him your treasure and sweetheart? Yes, surely! . . .
(They rise. CATHERINE *is full of pleased animation)*

Well, I've a piece of good news for you, my love. . . . A great doctor is
coming here presently, who can make you talk. . . . (CATHERINE *shows
her satisfaction, dancing gracefully up and down)* He will untie your tongue
and never hurt you a bit.

(CATHERINE*'s movements express charming and joyous impatience. A* BLIND
MAN *goes by in the street playing a lively old-fashioned country dance. He
stops and calls out in a doleful voice:* "Charity, for the love of God, good
gentlemen and ladies." LEONARD *motions him away, but* CATHERINE *pleads
for him by her gestures, indicating that he is blind.* LEONARD *yields and goes
back to his writing table. She stands at the window listening while the* BLIND
MAN *sings)*

BLIND MAN:

> There's lots of good fish in the sea,
> La dee ra, la dee ra;
> Now who will come and fish with me?
> La dee ra, la dee ra;
> Now who'll with me a-fishing go?
> My dainty, dainty damsel, O!
> Come fish the livelong day with me,
> La dee ra, la dee ra,
> And who will then be caught?—we'll see!
> La dee ra, dee ra, day.

(Toward the end of the verse CATHERINE *glances at* LEONARD *and sees that she
is unobserved; she steals to the street door as the* BLIND MAN *begins the second
verse there; during this verse she dances to him and frolics around the stage
as he sings.)*

BLIND MAN:

> Along the rippling river's bank,
> La dee ra, la dee ra,
> Along the wimpling water's bank,
> La dee ra, la dee ra,
> Along the bank so shady O
> I met the miller's lady, O
> And danced with her the livelong day

> La dee ra, la dee ra,
> And oh! I danced my heart away!
> La dee ra, dee ra, day.

(The BLIND MAN *stops playing and singing, and says in a hollow and terrifying voice:* "Charity, for the love of God, good gentlemen and ladies.")

LEONARD *(who has been buried in his documents and noticed nothing, now drives the* BLIND MAN *off the stage with objurgations):* Vagabond, robber, ruffian! *(And throws a lot of brief-bags and books at his head; then speaks to* CATHERINE, *who has gone back to her place)* My love, since you came downstairs, I haven't been wasting my time; I have sentenced fourteen men and six women to the pillory; and distributed among seventeen different people—*(he counts up)*—six, twenty-four, thirty-two, forty-four, forty-seven; and nine, fifty-six; and eleven, sixty-seven; and ten, seventy-seven; and eight, eighty-five; and twenty, a hundred and five—a hundred and five years in the galleys. Doesn't that make you realize the great power of a judge? How can I help feeling some pride in it?

*(*CATHERINE, *who has stopped her work, leans on the table and smilingly watches her husband. Then she sits down on the table, which is covered with brief-bags)*

LEONARD *(making as if to pull the bags from under her):* My love, you are hiding great criminals from my justice. Thieves and murderers. But I will not pursue them, their place of refuge is sacred.

(A CHIMNEY SWEEP *passes in the street, calling:* "Sweep your chimneys, my ladies; sweep them clear and clean." LEONARD *and* CATHERINE *kiss across the table. But, seeing the* DOCTORS *arriving,* CATHERINE *runs off up the stairs. Enter, in formal procession,* GILES, *leading the line and imitating a trumpeter, then the two* DOCTORS' ATTENDANTS, *then* MASTER SIMON *and* MASTER JEAN. *The* ATTENDANTS, *one carrying the case of instruments, take their stand on either side of the door. The* DOCTOR *and* SURGEON *bow formally to the audience)*

GILES: Your Honor, here's the great doctor you sent for.

MASTER SIMON *(bowing):* Yes, I am Master Simon Colline himself. . . . And this is Master Jean Maugier, surgeon. You called for our services?

LEONARD: Yes, sir, to make a dumb woman speak.

MASTER SIMON: Good! We must wait for Master Serafin Dulaurier, apothecary. As soon as he comes we will proceed to operate according to our knowledge and understanding.

LEONARD: Ah! You really need an apothecary to make a dumb woman speak?

MASTER SIMON: Yes, sir; to doubt it is to show total ignorance of the relations of the organs to each other, and of their mutual interdependence. Master Serafin Dulaurier will soon be here.

MASTER JEAN MAUGIER *(suddenly bellowing out in stentorian tones):* Oh! how grateful we should be to learned doctors like Master Simon Colline, who labor to preserve us in health and comfort us in sickness. Oh! how worthy of praise and of blessings are these noble doctors who follow in their profession the rules of scientific theory and of long practice.

MASTER SIMON *(bowing slightly):* You are much too kind, Master Jean Maugier.

LEONARD: While we are waiting for the apothecary, won't you take some light refreshment, gentlemen?

MASTER SIMON: Most happy.

MASTER JEAN: Delighted.

LEONARD: Alison! . . . So then, Master Simon Colline, you will perform a slight operation and make my wife speak?

MASTER SIMON: Say, rather, I shall order the operation. I command, Master Jean Maugier executes. . . . Have you your instruments with you, Master Jean?

MASTER JEAN: Yes, Master. *(He claps his hands; the* ATTENDANTS *run forward into the room and, each holding one side, they unfold the large cloth case of instruments and hold it up, disclosing a huge saw with two-inch teeth and knives, pincers, scissors, a skewer, a bit-stock, an enormous bit, etc.)*

LEONARD: I hope, sirs, you don't intend to use all those?

MASTER SIMON: One must never be caught unarmed by a patient.

(The ATTENDANTS *fold up the case and give it to* MASTER JEAN; *then run back to their positions by the door as* ALISON, *with a large tray, bottles, and glasses, enters from the kitchen)*

LEONARD: Will you drink, gentlemen?

*(*COLLINE *and* MAUGIER *take glasses from* ALISON *and drink, after* ALISON *has kissed* COLLINE's *glass)*

MASTER SIMON: This light wine of yours is not half bad.

LEONARD: Very kind of you to say so. It's from my own vineyard.

MASTER SIMON: You shall send me a cask of it.

LEONARD *(to* GILES, *who has poured himself a glass full to the brim):* I didn't tell you to drink, you reprobate.

MASTER JEAN *(looking out of the window):* Here is Master Serafin Dulaurier, the apothecary.

(*Enter* MASTER SERAFIN. *He trots across the stage, stopping to bow to the audience*)

MASTER SIMON (*peering into the street*): And here is his mule! . . . Or no— 'tis Master Serafin himself. You never can tell them apart. (MASTER SERAFIN *joins the group in the room*) Drink, Master Serafin. It is fresh from the cellar.

MASTER SERAFIN: Your good health, my Masters!

MASTER SIMON (*to* ALISON): Pour freely, fair Hebe. Pour right, pour left, pour here, pour there. Whichever way she turns, she shows new charms. Are you not proud, my girl, of your trim figure?

ALISON: For all the good it does me, there is no reason to be proud of it. Charms are not worth much unless they are hidden in silk and brocade.

MASTER SERAFIN: Your good health, my Masters! (*They* ALL *drink, and make* ALISON *drink with them*)

ALISON: You like to fool with us. But free gratis for nothing.

MASTER SIMON: Now we are all here, shall we go see the patient?

LEONARD: I will show you the way, gentlemen.

MASTER SIMON: After you, Master Maugier, you go first.

MASTER MAUGIER (*glass in one hand, case of instruments in the other*): I'll go first, since the place of honor is the rear. (*He crosses to the left and goes behind the table toward the door, following* BOTAL)

MASTER SIMON: After you, Master Serafin Dulaurier.

(MASTER SERAFIN *follows* MAUGIER, *bottle in hand.* MASTER SIMON, *after stuffing a bottle into each pocket of his gown and kissing the servant,* ALISON, *goes up stage, singing*)

MASTER SIMON:

> Then drink! and drink! and drink again!
> Drink shall drown our care and pain.
> Good friends must drink before they part,
> To warm the cockles of the heart!

(ALISON, *after cuffing* GILES, *who was trying to kiss her, goes up last*)

ALL (*singing in chorus as they go out by the right upper door*):

> Then drink! and drink! and drink again!

(*Curtain.*)

Scene Two

Scene:—the same. Four or five hours have elapsed.

MASTER ADAM: Good afternoon, Your Honor. How are you this afternoon?

LEONARD: Well, fairly well. And how are you?

MASTER ADAM: Well as can be. Excuse my besieging you, Your Honor, my dear comrade. Have you looked into the case of my young ward who's been robbed by her guardian?

LEONARD: Not yet, Master Adam Fumée. . . . But what's that you say? You've been robbing your ward?

MASTER ADAM: No, no, never think it, Your Honor. I said "my" out of pure interest in her. But I am not her guardian, thank God! I'm her lawyer. And if she gets back her estate, which is no small estate neither, then I shall be her husband; yes, I've had the foresight to make her fall in love with me already. And so, I shall be greatly obliged to you if you'll examine her case at the earliest possible moment. All you have to do is to read the statement I gave you; that contains everything you need to know about the case.

LEONARD: Your statement is there, Master Adam, on my table. I should have looked through it already, if I hadn't been so besieged. But I've been entertaining the flower of the medical faculty here. *(Suddenly seizing him by the shoulders and shaking him)* 'Twas your advice brought this trouble upon me.

MASTER ADAM: Why, what do you mean?

LEONARD: I sent for the famous doctor you told me about, Master Simon Colline. He came with a surgeon and an apothecary; he examined my wife, Catherine, from head to foot to see if she was dumb. Then the surgeon cut my dear Catherine's tongue-ligament, the apothecary gave her a pill—and she spoke.

MASTER ADAM: She spoke? Did she need a pill to speak?

LEONARD: Yes, because of the interdependence of the organs.

MASTER ADAM: Oh! Ah! . . . Anyhow, the main point is, she spoke. And what did she say?

LEONARD: She said: "Bring me my looking glass!" And, seeing me quite overcome by my feelings, she added, "You old goose, you shall give me a new satin gown and a velvet-trimmed cape for my birthday."

MASTER ADAM: And she kept on talking?

LEONARD: She hasn't stopped yet.

MASTER ADAM: And yet you don't thank me for my advice; you don't thank me for having sent you to that wonderful doctor? Aren't you overjoyed to hear your wife speak?

LEONARD *(sourly):* Yes, certainly. I thank you with all my heart, Master Adam Fumée, and I am overjoyed to hear my wife speak.

MASTER ADAM: No! You do not show as much satisfaction as you ought to. There is something you are keeping back—something that's worrying you.

LEONARD: Where did you get such a notion?

MASTER ADAM: From your face. . . . What is bothering you? Isn't your wife's speech clear?

LEONARD: Yes, it's clear—and abundant. I must admit, its abundance would be a trial to me if it kept up at the rate which it started at.

MASTER ADAM: Ah! . . . I feared *that* beforehand, Your Honor. But you mustn't be cast down too soon. Perhaps this flood of words will ebb. It is the first overflow of a spring too long bottled up. . . . My best congratulations, Your Honor. My ward's name is Ermeline de la Garandière. Don't forget her name; show her favor and you will find proper gratitude. I will be back later in the day.

LEONARD: Master Adam Fumée, I will look into your case at once.

(Exit MASTER ADAM FUMÉE. CATHERINE *is heard off-stage singing the* BLIND MAN's *song;* LEONARD *starts, shakes his head, hurries to his writing table and sits down to work.* CATHERINE, *still singing, enters gaily, and goes to him at the table)*

LEONARD *(reading):* "Statement, on behalf of Ermeline-Jacinthe-Marthe de la Garandière, gentlewoman."

CATHERINE *(standing behind his chair and first finishing her song: "La dee ra, dee ra, day," then speaking with great volubility).* What are you doing, my dear? You seem busy. You work too much. *(She goes to the window seat and takes up her embroidery)* Aren't you afraid it will make you ill? You must rest once in a while. Why don't you tell me what you are doing, dear?

LEONARD: My love, I . . .

CATHERINE: Is it such a great secret? Can't I know about it?

LEONARD: My love, I . . .

CATHERINE: If it's a secret, don't tell me.

LEONARD: Won't you give me a chance to answer? I am examining a case and preparing to draw up a verdict on it.

CATHERINE: Is drawing up a verdict so very important?

LEONARD: Most certainly it is. *(CATHERINE sits at the window singing, humming to herself and looking out)* In the first place, people's honor, their liberty and sometimes even their life may depend on it; and further-more, the Judge must show therein both the depth of his thought and the finish of his style.

CATHERINE: Then examine your case and prepare your verdict, my dear. I'll be silent.

LEONARD: That's right. . . . "Ermeline-Jacinthe-Marthe de la Garandière, gentlewoman . . ."

CATHERINE: My dear, which do you think would be more becoming to me, a damask gown or a velvet suit with a Turkish skirt?

LEONARD: I don't know, I . . .

CATHERINE: *I* think a flowered satin would suit my age best, especially a light-colored one, with a *small* flower pattern.

LEONARD: Perhaps so. But . . .

CATHERINE: And don't you think, my dear, that it is quite improper to have a hoop skirt very full? Of course, a skirt must have *some* fullness . . . or else you don't seem dressed at all; so, we mustn't let it be scanty. But, my dear, you wouldn't want me to have room enough to hide a pair of lovers under my hoops, now would you? That fashion won't last, I'm sure; some day the court ladies will give it up, and then every woman in town will make haste to follow their example. Don't you think so?

LEONARD: Yes! Yes! But . . .

CATHERINE: Now, about high heels. . . . They must be made just right. A woman is judged by her foot-gear—you can always tell a real fine lady by her shoes. You agree with me, don't you, dear?

LEONARD: Yes, yes, *yes,* but . . .

CATHERINE: Then write out your verdict. I shan't say another word.

LEONARD: That's right. *(Reading, and making notes)* "Now, the guardian of the said young lady, namely Hugo Thomas of Piédeloup, gentleman, stole from the said young lady her—"

CATHERINE: My dear, if one were to believe the wife of the Chief Justice of Montbadon, the world has grown very corrupt; it is going to the bad; young men nowadays don't marry; they prefer to hang about rich old ladies; and meanwhile the poor girls are left to wither on their maiden stalks. Do you think it's as bad as all that? Do answer me, dear.

LEONARD: My darling, won't you please be silent one moment? Or go and talk somewhere else? I'm all at sea.

CATHERINE: There, there, dear; don't worry. I shan't say another word! Not a word!

LEONARD: Good! *(Writing)* "The said Piédeloup, gentleman, counting both hay crops and apple crops . . ."

CATHERINE: My dear, we shall have for supper tonight some minced mutton and what's left of that goose one of your suitors gave us. Tell me, is that enough? Shall you be satisfied with it? I hate being mean and like to set a good table, but what's the use of serving courses which will only be sent back to the pantry untouched? The cost of living is getting higher all the time. Chickens and salads and meats and fruit have all gone up so, it will soon be cheaper to order dinner sent in by a caterer.

LEONARD: I beg you . . . *(Writing)* "An orphan by birth . . ."

CATHERINE: Yes, that's what we're coming to. No home life any more. You'll see. Why, a capon or a partridge or a hare cost less all stuffed and roasted than if you buy them alive at the market. That is because the cook-shops buy in large quantities and get a big discount; so they can sell to us at a profit. I don't say we ought to get our regular meals from the cook-shop. We can do our everyday plain cooking at home and it's better to; but when we invite people in, or give a formal dinner party, then it saves time and money to have the dinner sent in. Why, at less than an hour's notice, the cook-shops and cake-shops will get you up a dinner for a dozen or twenty or fifty people; the cook-shop will send in meat and poultry, the caterer will send galantines and sauces and relishes, the pastry-cook will send pies and tarts and sweets and desserts; and it's all so convenient. Now, don't you think so yourself, Leonard.

LEONARD: Please! please!

(LEONARD *tries to write through the following speech, murmuring:* "An orphan by birth, a capon by birth, an olla podrida," *etc.)*

CATHERINE: It's no wonder everything goes up. People are getting more extravagant every day. If they are entertaining a friend, or even a relative, they don't think they can do with only three courses, soup, meat and dessert. No, they have to have meats in five or six different styles, with so many sauces or dressings or pasties that it's a regular olla podrida. Now, don't you think that is going too far, my dear? For my part, I just cannot understand how people can take pleasure in stuffing themselves with so many kinds of food. Not that I despise a good table; why, I'm even a bit of an epicure myself. "Not too plenty, but dainty," suits *my* taste. Now, what I like best of all is capons' kidneys with artichoke hearts. But you, Leonard, I suspect you have a weakness for tripe and sausages. Oh, fie! Oh, fie! How can anyone enjoy sausages?

LEONARD *(his head in his hands):* I shall go mad! I know I shall go mad.

CATHERINE *(running to the table behind him):* My dear, I just shan't say another word—not a single word. For I can see that my chattering *might* possibly disturb your work.

LEONARD: If you would only do as you say!

CATHERINE *(returning to her place):* I shan't even open my lips.

LEONARD: Splendid!

CATHERINE (*busily embroidering*): You see, dear, I'm not saying another word.

LEONARD: Yes.

CATHERINE: I'm letting you work in perfect peace and quiet.

LEONARD: Yes.

CATHERINE: And write out your verdict quite undisturbed. Is it almost done?

LEONARD: It never will be—if you don't keep still. (*Writing*) "Item, One hundred twenty pounds a year, which the said unworthy guardian stole from the poor orphan girl . . ."

CATHERINE: Listen! Ssh-sh! Listen! Didn't you hear a cry of fire? (LEONARD *runs to the window, looks out and then shakes his head at* CATHERINE) I thought I did. But perhaps I may have been mistaken. Is there anything so terrifying as a fire? Fire is even worse than water. Last year I saw the houses on Exchange Bridge burn up. What confusion! What havoc! The people threw their furniture into the river and jumped out of the windows. They didn't know what they were about; you see, fear drove them out of their senses.

LEONARD: Lord, have mercy upon me!

CATHERINE: Oh! What makes you groan so, dear? *Tell* me, tell me what is the matter?

LEONARD: I can't endure it another minute.

CATHERINE: You must rest, Leonard. You mustn't work so hard. It isn't reasonable. You have no right to . . .

LEONARD: Will you never be still?

CATHERINE: Now, don't be cross, dear. I'm not saying a word.

LEONARD: Would to Heaven!

(MADAME DE LA BRUINE, *followed by her* FOOTMAN, *crosses the stage during the following speech*)

CATHERINE (*looking out of the window*): Oh! Here comes Madame de la Bruine, the attorney's wife! She's got on a silk-lined hood and a heavy puce-colored cape over her brocade gown. And she has a lackey with a face like a smoked herring. Leonard, she's looking this way; I believe she's coming to call. Hurry and arrange the chairs and bring up an armchair for her; we must show people proper respect according to their rank and station. She is stopping at our door. No, she's going on. She's going on. Perhaps I was mistaken. Perhaps it was somebody else. You can't be sure about recognizing people. But if it wasn't she, it was somebody like her and even very much like her. Now I think of it, I'm sure it was she, there simply couldn't be another woman in Paris so like Madame de la Bruine. My dear. . . . My dear. . . . Would you have liked to have Madame de la Bruine call on us? *(She sits down on his table)* I know you don't like rattle-tongued women; it's lucky for you that you didn't marry *her;* she jabbers like a magpie; she does nothing but gabble from morning to night. What a chatterbox! And sometimes she tells stories which are not to her credit. (LEONARD, *driven beyond endurance, climbs upon his stepladder, sits down on one of the middle steps and tries to write there)* In the first place, she always gives you a list of all the presents her husband has received. It's a dreadful bore to hear her tell them over. *(She climbs up on the other side of the double stepladder and sits down opposite* LEONARD) What is it to us, if the Attorney de la Bruine receives presents of game or flour or fresh fish or even a sugar-loaf? But Madame de la Bruine takes good care *not* to tell you that one day her husband received a great Amiens pasty and when he opened it he found nothing but an enormous pair of horns.

LEONARD: My head will burst! *(He takes refuge on top of one of the cabinets, with his writing-case and papers)*

CATHERINE *(at the top of the ladder):* And did you see my fine lady, who's really no lady at all, wearing an embroidered cape, just like any princess? Don't you think it's ridiculous! But there! Nowadays everybody dresses above his station, men as well as women. Your court secretaries try to pass for gentlemen; they wear gold chains and jewelry and feathers in their hats; all the same, anyone can tell what they are.

LEONARD *(on top of his cupboard):* I've got to the point where I can't answer for the consequences; I feel capable of committing any crime. *(Calling)* Giles! Giles! Giles! The scoundrel! Giles! Alison! Giles! Giles! *(Enter* GILES) Go quick and find the famous doctor in Buci Square, Master Simon Colline, and tell him to come back here at once for a matter far more needful and urgent than before.

GILES: Yes, Your Honor. *(Exit)*

CATHERINE: What's the matter, my dear? You seem excited. Perhaps the air is close. No? It's the east wind then, don't you think?—or the fish you ate for dinner?

LEONARD *(frantically gesticulating on top of his cupboard): Non omnia possumus omnes.* It is the office of servants to clean crockery, of mercers to measure ribbon, of monks to beg, of birds to drop dirt around everywhere and of women to cackle and chatter like mad. Oh! How I regret, you saucy baggage, that I had your tongue loosed. Don't you worry, though—the famous doctor shall soon make you more dumb than ever you were. *(He catches up armfuls of the brief-bags which are piled on his cupboard of refuge and throws them at* CATHERINE'*s head; she jumps nimbly down from the ladder and runs off in terror, crying)*

CATHERINE: Help! Murder! My husband's gone mad! Help! help!

LEONARD: Alison! Alison!

(Enter ALISON*)*

ALISON: What a life! Sir, have you turned murderer?

LEONARD: Alison, follow her, stay by her and don't let her come down. As you value your life, Alison, don't let her come down. For if I hear another word from her, I shall go raving mad, and God knows what I might do to her—and to you. Go! Off with you!

*(*ALISON *goes upstairs. Enter* MASTER ADAM, MLLE DE LA GARANDIÈRE *and a* LACKEY *carrying a basket.* LEONARD *is still on top of the cabinet or bookcase.* MASTER ADAM *and* MLLE DE LA GARANDIÈRE *climb up on each side of the stepladder. The* LACKEY, *with an enormous basket on his head, kneels in front, center)*

MASTER ADAM: Permit me, Your Honor, with the object of softening your heart and arousing your pity, to present before you this young orphan girl, despoiled by a grasping guardian, who implores you for justice. Her eyes will speak to your heart more eloquently than my voice. Mlle de la Garandière brings you her prayers and her tears; she adds thereunto one ham, two duck pies, a goose and two goslings. She ventures to hope in exchange for a favoring verdict.

LEONARD: Mademoiselle, you arouse my interest. . . . Have you anything to add in defense of your case?

MLLE DE LA GARANDIÈRE: You are only too kind, sir; I must rest my case on what my lawyer has just said.

LEONARD: That is all?

MLLE DE LA GARANDIÈRE: Yes, sir.

LEONARD: She knows how to speak—and to stop. The poor orphan touches my heart. *(To the* LACKEY*)* Carry that package to the pantry. *(Exit* LACKEY. *To* MASTER ADAM*)* Master Adam, when you came in, I was just drawing up the decree which I shall presently render in this young lady's case. *(He starts to come down from his cabinet)*

MASTER ADAM: What, up on that cupboard?

LEONARD: I don't know where I am; my head is going round and round. Do you want to hear the decree? I need to read it over myself. *(Reading)* "Whereas, Mlle de la Garandière, spinster and an orphan by birth, did fraudulently, deceitfully and with injurious intent steal, filch and subtract from her lawful guardian, Squire Piédeloup, gentleman, ten loads of hay and eighty pounds of freshwater fish, and whereas, there is nothing so terrifying as a fire, and whereas, the State's Attorney did receive an Amiens pasty in which were two great horns . . ."

MASTER ADAM: What in Heaven's name are you reading?

LEONARD: Don't ask me. I don't know myself. I think my brains have been brayed in a mortar for two hours running by the very devil himself for a pestle. *(He breaks down and weeps on their shoulders)* I'm a driveling idiot. . . . And all your fault, too, Master Adam Fumée. . . . If that fine doctor of yours hadn't restored my wife's speech . . .

MASTER ADAM: Don't blame me, Master Leonard. I forewarned you. I told you right enough that you must think twice before untying a woman's tongue.

LEONARD: Ah, Master Adam Fumée, how I long for the time when my Catherine was dumb. No! Nature has no scourge more fearsome than a rattle-tongued female. . . . But I count on the doctors to recall their cruel gift. I have sent for them. Here's the surgeon now.

(Enter MASTER JEAN MAUGIER)

MASTER JEAN MAUGIER: Your Honor, I bid you good day. Here is Master Simon Colline coming forward upon his mule, followed by Master Serafin Dulaurier, apothecary. About him crowds the adoring populace: chambermaids, trussing up their petticoats, and scullions with hampers on their heads form his escort of honor. *(Enter MASTER SIMON COLLINE and MASTER SERAFIN DULAURIER followed by the TWO APOTHECARY'S BOYS)* Oh! how justly does Master Simon Colline command the admiration of the people when he goes through the city clad in his doctor's robe, his square cap, his cassock and bands. Oh! how grateful we should be to those noble doctors who labor to preserve us in health and comfort us in sickness. Ohhhh! how . . .

MASTER SIMON *(to MASTER JEAN MAUGIER)*: Have done; 'tis enough.

LEONARD: Master Simon Colline, I was in haste to see you. I urgently beg for your services.

MASTER SIMON: For yourself? What is your disease? Where is the pain?

LEONARD: No! for my wife; the one who was dumb.

MASTER SIMON: Has she any trouble now?

LEONARD: None at all. I have all the trouble now.

MASTER SIMON: What? The trouble is with you and it's your wife you want cured?

LEONARD: Master Simon Colline, she talks too much. You should have given her speech, but not so much speech. Since you've cured her of her dumbness, she drives me mad. I cannot bear another word from her. I've called you in to make her dumb again.

MASTER SIMON: 'Tis impossible!

LEONARD: What's that? You can't take away the power of speech which you gave her?

MASTER SIMON: No! That I cannot do. My skill is great, but it stops short of that.

(LEONARD *in despair turns to each of them in succession*)

MASTER JEAN MAUGIER: We cannot do it.

MASTER SERAFIN: Our greatest efforts would have not the slightest result.

MASTER SIMON: We have medicines to make women speak; we have none to make them keep silence.

LEONARD: You haven't? Is that your last word? You drive me to despair.

MASTER SIMON: Alas, Your Honor! *(He advances to the center, claps his hands for attention and declaims)* There is no elixir, balm, magisterium, opiate, unguent, ointment, local application, electuary nor panacea that can cure the excess of glottal activity in woman. Treacle and orvietano would be without virtue and all the herbs described by Dioscorides would have no effect.

LEONARD: Can this be true?

MASTER SIMON: Sir, you dare not so offend me as to doubt it.

LEONARD: Then I am a ruined man. There's nothing left for me to do but tie a stone around my neck and jump into the Seine. *(He rushes to the window and tries to jump out, but is held back by the* DOCTORS*)* I cannot live in this hubbub. *(The* DOCTORS *drag him back, set him down and, with* MASTER ADAM, *stand in a circle in front of him)* If you don't want me to drown myself straightway, then you doctors must find me some cure.

MASTER SIMON: There is none, I tell you, for your wife. But there might be one for you, if you would consent to take it.

LEONARD: You give me a little hope. Explain it, for Heaven's sake.

MASTER SIMON: For the clack of a wife, there's but one cure in life. Let her husband be deaf. 'Tis the only relief.

LEONARD: What do you mean?

MASTER SIMON: Just what I say.

MASTER ADAM: Don't you understand? That's the finest discovery yet. Since he can't make your wife dumb, this great doctor offers to make you deaf.

LEONARD: Make me really deaf? Oh! . . . *(He starts to rise, but is pushed back by* MASTER SIMON, *who stands directly in front of him)*

MASTER SIMON: Certainly. I can cure you at once, and for all time, of your wife's verbal hypertrophy by means of cophosis.

LEONARD: By cophosis? What is cophosis?

MASTER SIMON: 'Tis what is vulgarly called deafness. Do you see any disadvantages in becoming deaf?

LEONARD: Certainly I do!

MASTER JEAN MAUGIER: You think so?

MASTER SERAFIN: For instance?

MASTER SIMON: You are a Judge. What disadvantage is there in a Judge's being deaf?

MASTER ADAM: None at all. Believe me; I am a practicing lawyer. There is none at all.

MASTER SIMON: What harm could come to justice thereby?

MASTER ADAM: No harm at all. Quite the contrary. Master Leonard Botal could then hear neither lawyers nor prosecutors and so would run no risk of being deceived by a lot of lies.

LEONARD: That's true.

MASTER ADAM: He will judge all the better.

LEONARD: Maybe so.

MASTER ADAM: Never doubt it.

LEONARD: But how do you perform this . . .

MASTER JEAN MAUGIER: This cure.

MASTER SIMON: Cophosis, vulgarly called deafness, may be brought about in several ways. It is produced either by otorrhoea or by sclerosis of the ear or by otitis or else by anchylosis of the ossicles. But these various means are long and painful.

LEONARD: I reject them! . . . I reject them absolutely.

MASTER SIMON: You are right. It is far better to induce cophosis by means of a certain white powder which I have in my medicine-case; a pinch of it, placed in the ear, is enough to make you as deaf as Heaven when it's angry, or as deaf as a post.

LEONARD: Many thanks, Master Simon Colline; keep your powder. I will not be made deaf.

MASTER SIMON: What? You won't be made deaf? What? You refuse cophosis? You decline the cure which you begged for just now? Ah, 'tis a case but too common, and one calculated to make a judicious physician grieve, to see a recalcitrant patient refuse the salutary medicament . . .

MASTER JEAN MAUGIER: And flee from the care, which would cure all his ailments . . .

MASTER SERAFIN: And decline to be healed. Oh!

MASTER ADAM: Do not decide too quickly, Master Leonard Botal; do not deliberately reject this slight affliction which will save you from far greater torment.

LEONARD: No! I will not be deaf; I'll have none of your powder.

ALISON (*rushes in from the stairs, stopping her ears*): I can't stand it. My head will burst. No human creature can stay and listen to such a clatter. There's no stopping her. I feel as if I'd been caught in the millwheel for two mortal hours.

(CATHERINE *is heard off-stage singing the* BLIND MAN's *song*)

LEONARD: Wretch! Don't let her come down. Alison! Giles! Lock her in.

MASTER ADAM: Oh! Sir!

MLLE DE LA GARANDIÈRE: Oh! Sir, can your heart be so cruel as to want to lock the poor lady up all alone?

(CATHERINE *is heard singing again.* LEONARD *starts for the ladder and climbs it as she enters*)

CATHERINE: What a fine large assembly! I am your humble servant, gentlemen. *(She curtsies)*

MASTER SIMON COLLINE: Well, madam? Aren't you pleased with us? Didn't we do our work well in loosing your tongue?

CATHERINE: Fairly well, sirs; and I'm truly grateful to you. At first, to be sure, I could speak but haltingly and bring out only a few words; now, however, I have some degree of facility; but I use it with great moderation, for a garrulous wife is a scourge in the house. Yes, gentlemen, I should be in despair if you could so much as suspect me of loquacity or if you think for a moment that any undue desire to talk could get hold on me. (LEONARD, *on top of the cabinet, laughs wildly*) And so, I beg you to let me justify myself here and now in the eyes of my husband who, for some inconceivable reason, has become prejudiced against me and taken it into his head that my conversation bothered him while he was drawing up a decree. . . . Yes, a decree in favor of an orphan girl deprived of her father and mother in the flower of her youth. But no matter for that. *(She crosses to the ladder and starts to go up one side of it.* LEONARD *climbs down the other side, goes first to one doctor, then to another and finally sits down on the bench in front of the table)* I was sitting beside him and hardly saying a single word to him. My only speech was my presence. Can a husband object to that? Can he take it ill when his wife stays with him and seeks to enjoy his company, as she ought? *(She goes to her husband and sits down beside him. During the rest of the speech all those present, one after another, sink down in exhaustion at listening to her)* The more I think of it, the less I can understand your impatience. What can have caused it? You must stop pretending it was my talkativeness. That idea won't hold water one moment. My dear, you must have some grievance against me which I know nothing about; I *beg* you to tell me what it is. You *owe* me an explanation, and as soon as I find out what displeased you I will see to it that you have no reason to complain of the same thing again—if only you'll tell me what it is. For I am eager to save you from the slightest reason for dissatisfaction. My mother used to say: "Between husband and wife, there should be no secrets." And she was quite right. Married people have only too often brought down terrible catastrophes on themselves or their households just because they didn't tell each other everything. That is what happened to the Chief Justice of Beaupréau's wife. To give her husband a pleasant surprise, she shut up a little sucking pig in a chest in her room. Her husband heard it squealing and thought it was a lover, so he out with his sword and ran his wife through the heart, without even waiting to hear the poor lady's explanation. You can imagine his surprise and despair when he opened the chest. And that shows you must never have secrets, even for good reasons. My dear, you can speak freely before these gentlemen. I know I have done nothing wrong, so whatever you say can only prove the more clearly how innocent I am.

LEONARD *(who has for some time been trying in vain by gestures and excla-mations to stop* CATHERINE's *flow of words and has been showing signs of extreme impatience):* The powder! Give me the powder! Master Simon Colline, your powder—your white powder, for God's sake!

MASTER SIMON: Never was a deafness-producing powder more needed, that's sure. Be so kind as to sit down, Your Honor. Master Serafin Dulaurier will inject the cophosis powder in your ears.

(The DOCTORS *crowd about* LEONARD *and inject the powder first in one ear and then in the other)*

MASTER SERAFIN: Gladly, sir, gladly.

MASTER SIMON: There! 'Tis done.

CATHERINE *(To* MASTER ADAM FUMÉE): Master Adam, you are a lawyer. Make my husband hear reason. Tell him that he must listen to me, that it's unheard of to condemn a wife without letting her state her case; tell him it's not right to throw brief-bags at your wife's head—yes, he threw brief-bags at my head—unless you are forced to it by some very strong feeling or reason. . . . Or no!—no, I'll tell him myself. *(To* LEONARD) My dear, answer me, have I ever failed you in anything? Am I a naughty woman? Am I a bad wife? No, I have been faithful to my duty; I may even say I have loved my duty . . .

LEONARD *(his face expressing beatitude, as he calmly twirls his thumbs):* 'Tis delicious. I can't hear a thing.

CATHERINE: Listen to me, Leonard, I love you tenderly. I will open my heart to you. I am not one of those light, frivolous women who are afflicted or consoled by airy nothings and amused by trifles. *(She puts her arms about him and they rock back and forth,* LEONARD *grinning from ear to ear)* I need companionship. I need to be understood. That is my nature—I was born so. When I was only seven years old I had a little dog, a little yellow dog. . . . But you're not listening to me . . .

MASTER SIMON: Madam, he can't listen to you, or to anyone else. He can't hear.

CATHERINE: What do you mean he can't hear?

MASTER SIMON: I mean just that. He can't hear, as the result of a cure he has just taken.

(The BLIND MAN *is heard again, playing the same air)*

MASTER SERAFIN: A cure which has produced in him a sweet and pleasant cophosis.

CATHERINE: I'll make him hear, I tell you.

MASTER SIMON: No, you won't, madam; it can't be done.

CATHERINE: You shall see. *(To her husband, affectionately)* My dear, my beloved, my pretty one, my sweetheart, my better half. . . . You don't hear me? *(She shakes him)* You monster, you Herod, you Bluebeard, you old cuckold.

LEONARD: I can't hear her with my ears, but I hear her only too well with my arms and with my shoulders and back.

MASTER SIMON: She is going mad.

MASTER MAUGIER: She has gone mad! Stark staring mad!

LEONARD: Oh! How can I get away? (CATHERINE *bites his neck)* Oh! She has bitten me, I feel myself going mad, too.

(The BLIND MAN *has come forward, playing and singing the first verse of his song. Meanwhile* CATHERINE *and* LEONARD *go singing and dancing about and bite the others, who likewise go mad and sing and dance wildly, all at the front of the stage. The other characters of the play come in—the* CANDLE MAN, CHIMNEY SWEEP, MADAME DE LA BRUINE, *etc.; all are caught and bitten, and join in the song and the dance which resolves itself into the old-fashioned country "right and left," as they sing the second verse)*

ALL:

Along the rippling river's bank,
La dee ra, la dee ra,
Along the wimpling water's bank
La dee ra, la dee ra,
Along the bank so shady O
I met the miller's lady O
And danced with her the livelong day,
La dee ra, la dee ra,

> And oh! I danced my heart away
> La dee ra, dee ra, day.

(As LEONARD BOTAL *reaches the center of the front stage, the dance stops a moment for him to say to the audience)*

LEONARD: Good gentlemen and ladies, we pray you to forgive the author all his faults.

(The dance re-commences and the curtain falls as all dance off, singing the refrain)

ALL *(diminuendo):*

> I danced with her the livelong day,
> La dee ra, la dee ra,
> And oh! I danced my heart away
> La dee ra, dee ra, day.

(Curtain.)

THE LAND OF COUNTERPANE

by
M. Ellis Grove

I save the final spot in my anthologies for personal favorites: The place of honor this time is reserved for a delightfully wacky fantasy by my late lamented friend MURRAY ELLIS GROVE who, as Associate Professor, General Education in the Arts, was one of The Pennsylvania State University's most popular teachers and critics of theatre and the media.

THE LAND OF COUNTERPANE is an amusing nondescript whose last line, however, leaves few eyes dry. (I know this for a fact; when the play was originally produced at Penn State, I played Somersault.)

THE LAND OF COUNTERPANE was first performed in New York on November 9, 1981, at the Bruno Walter Auditorium, Lincoln Center, with the following cast:

HILDEGARDE, a witch . . . . June Miller
PRINCESS GLORIANNA . . . . . . Rosalind Salzberg
SOMERSAULT, a clown . . . . . . Howard Roller
TOMMY, a hero . . . . Toby Sanders

CAST OF CHARACTERS

TOMMY, a hero
HILDEGARDE (Hildy), a witch
GLORIANNA (Glory), a princess
SOMERSAULT, a clown
A distant voice

The setting is simple and stylized. At rear of the stage is an extra-large door, which opens offstage. Scattered around the stage are many blocks of various sizes and colors. There should be several down left and a few put together up right, together with a variety of props, as specified later. In the center of the stage is a large black pot with some foul substance boiling in it.

At rise: HILDEGARDE (HILDY) *is busy stirring the content of the pot. She is dressed in black shirt and sweater with a silver belt. She also wears a tall, pointed witch's hat. Down right on one of the blocks sits* GLORIANNA (GLORY). *She is dressed in a long white robe with gold trimmings. She has long blonde hair and is bound and gagged.*

HILDY *(singing):* That old black magic's going to cast a spell. That old black magic that I weave so well.

GLORY *(trying to talk through gag):* Mumble, rumble, bumble, fumble.

HILDY: Quiet, deary, don't be so impatient. The love potion is almost ready. Hee, hee, hee. Now let me see, what else do I need? *(She crosses to rear right and gets book from behind blocks)* One puppydog's tail . . . check . . . one crushed spider . . . I put that in . . . one beetle's tongue . . . did that and . . . ah yes . . . finally, stir in one beautiful princess. Well, deary, where do you think I'm going to get her, eh? Hee, hee, hee.

GLORY: Mumble, mumble, mumble.

HILDY: Oh, but you are beautiful . . . and rich . . . and pure . . . and in love with Sir Tommy . . . Sir Tommy, the handsome knight . . . and you love him and he loves you. But you'll never see him again, for when your handsome hero comes looking for you, you'll be in the brew and the brew will be in me and it will transform me into you and he will see me as you and he will love me and marry me and we'll live happily ever after. Hahahahahaha. *(She goes to kettle and tests it with her elbow)* Ah, just right. And now is the final ingredient ready? *(She crosses to* GLORY, *pinching her arm and feeling her forehead)* Ah, just at room temperature. Now to prepare the beautiful princess for her warm tub. *(She pulls* GLORY *to her feet and pushes her to "kitchen," rear stage right.* GLORY *struggles. Her gag slips)*

GLORY: Help. Help. Tommy. Oh, save me. Save me, save—

*(*HILDY *clamps hand over* GLORY'S *mouth and fixes gag again)*

HILDY: It's too late, lovely princess. Your bath awaits. But first, we must rub your body with the finest butter in all Araby . . . *(She sits* GLORY *on block and brushes her with butter)* And just a bit of salt and pepper to make you palatable. *(She applies salt and pepper)* A touch of nutmeg

. . . *(She adds this)* And finally, a sprig of parsley. *(She puts this into* GLORY's *hair)* Ah, just right. Now to the pot.

(As HILDY *leads* GLORY *to the pot,* SOMERSAULT *appears down left. He is a clown with a feather in his hair. He creeps commando fashion toward* HILDY *and is about to leap upon her when she sees him, turns, and freezes him with a gesture)*

HILDY: Ah, the noble Somersault, the brave Sir Tommy's friend and faithful clown companion. Then freeze, dog. That's better—better. Now I don't think we'll be disturbed for a while. If the nine-headed dragon doesn't slow Sir Tommy up, the magic maze will certainly do so. Only a simpleton like this frozen Eskimo pie here could pass through the Woeful Woods without getting lost. So I shall dispose of you first, clown, and then give my fair lady her bath. After all, a few more minutes will only make the potion stronger. Goodbye for now, my pretty. I shall return, never fear. *(She crosses to* SOMERSAULT*)* Now how shall I eradicate you, fool? Feed you to my pet bats? No, you might give them indigestion. Turn you into a petunia? No, you're already a blooming idiot. Heeheeeheeeh. I think voodoo will do for you. *(She goes to kitchen area and gets a clown doll and removes hat pin from her hair)* Pin, pin, go right in. Then die, fool, die. Oh me, oh my. *(She jabs the pin home with the gesture and throws the doll away. Then she frees* SOMER-SAULT *from the spell. He grabs his stomach and begins staggering around the stage in an exaggerated death scene.* HILDY *ignores him, turns, check's* GLORY's *bonds and goes to kitchen to consult book)* I wonder, did I put in the salamander's toenail or didn't I? Or is that part of the formula for the Hallowe'en hash? I'd better check.

*(*SOMERSAULT *falls left.* TOMMY *enters. He is tall, handsome, wears a white silk long-sleeved shirt, black trousers, white scarf tied round neck in an ascot. He carries two six guns [water pistols] and a gun belt.* TOMMY *sees* GLORY *and starts toward her, but hears* SOMERSAULT *groaning. He goes to him)*

TOMMY: Somersault, old friend, what has befallen you, kimo sabe?

SOMER: She got me, Sir Tommy, she got me. I'm going fast. I'm sorry that I failed you, but she was too smart for me.

TOMMY: You failed me? Oh, no, dear friend, I failed you. Had I only followed you through the magic maze, we would have arrived together, but now . . .

SOMER: Don't cry, comrade. Smile. You arrived in time to save the beautiful Glorianna. I'm thankful for that and I can die happy.

TOMMY: No, no, old friend, don't say that. I'll pull you through.

SOMER: It's too late, Tommy. I'm heading for that big circus in the sky, where there's always cotton candy and no matinées. All I ask of you, old friend, is, don't forget faithful old Somersault. *(He dies)*

TOMMY: Goodbye, old friend, good friend, true friend, I will avenge you. *(He lays* SOMERSAULT *down gently, rises and, jaw working, checks his guns and leaps to top of the nearest block)*

VOICE *(from offstage, behind the big door):* Tommy. Tommy? Where are you?

*(*TOMMY *stops, puzzled)*

HILDY *(to* GLORY*):* Do you think he heard that? *(*GLORY *shakes her head no)* I hope not. *(She returns to the cookbook)*

TOMMY: Ah-ha, Hildegarde Witch, at last.

*(*HILDY *whirls, makes freezing gesture. It doesn't work. She tries again. It still doesn't work. She blows out end of fingers)*

HILDY: The handsome Sir Tommy. We meet again. *(She gestures)* Then freeze, knight. What? Freeze, knight. It doesn't work. My spell has failed me. What happened?

TOMMY: Your spell would work on an ordinary mortal, but I am protected by this. *(He thrusts his badge at her)*

HILDY: Aaaah, a Hopalong Cassidy straight shooter badge. I'm finished.

TOMMY: Yes, Hildegarde Witch, you are finished. Prepare to die. *(He draws a gun)*

HILDY: No, Sir Tommy, no. You cannot kill a woman. You are a knight. You are pledged to protect all womankind.

TOMMY: Yes, witch, you are right. Although every fiber in my body wishes your death, I cannot bring myself to rid the world of you.

HILDY: Oh, thank you, Sir Tommy, thank you. *(She kneels before him and kisses his hand up to his elbow)*

TOMMY: But I must rid this fair land of your curse once and for all, so turn in your union card or else I'll . . . *(He gestures with badge)*

HILDY: All right, Sir knight, I'll get it. *(She reaches behind block as* TOMMY *goes to* GLORY *and unties her)*

TOMMY: My princess, forgive me for not freeing you at once, but I had to attend to that evil woman first.

GLORY: My beloved, I understand. *(*GLORY *sees* HILDY *draw gun)* Oh, look out!

HILDY: Now die, knight. A straight shooter badge can't stop a bullet.

*(*TOMMY *whirls and fires first with his water pistols)*

TOMMY: And a witch can't stand water. Take that.

HILDY: Aaaaaaaaah, no. Water. Water. I'm clean. Clean. I'll die. I'll die.

Aaaaaaagh. *(She staggers around the stage and dies, finally falling on top of* SOMERSAULT)

GLORY: My hero. *(She runs to* TOMMY's *arms)*

TOMMY: And we shall live happily ever after.

(They kiss. Both HILDY *and* SOMERSAULT *jump up and begin applauding and cheering)*

SOMER.: Bravo. Bravo.

HILDY: Author. Author.

SOMER.: Tremendous. What excitement.

HILDY: Wonderful. Wonderful performance, Tommy.

*(*TOMMY *and* GLORY *break clinch. They bow to each other and to* SOMERSAULT *and* HILDY)

GLORY: Oh, Tommy, that was your best production yet. It was magnificent.

TOMMY: No, my friends, it was you who were wonderful. You were so lovely, Glory. And Hildy, that was the best witch you've ever played. Somersault, I really loved your death scene. I would have cried, if it wasn't against the code of the good guys.

GLORY: But, Tommy, you held us together. You made the play go, especially those love scenes. I think that last one was the very best we've ever played.

HILDY *(to* SOMERSAULT*)*: I wish I could play a love scene with him. Just once. I'd show her something. Him, too.

SOMER.: And I wish I could play one of these stories just once without dying in the end. I'm getting tired of dying, Tommy. I'm not as young as I used to be.

TOMMY: I know it's hard on you, Somersault, but someone has to die in every story. That's the way it is.

SOMER.: Well, just for once I'd like to be a live coward . . . just once. That's all I ask.

HILDY *(to* TOMMY*)*: I do want to thank you, Tommy, for letting me die normally for once. I hate falling into the boiling pot all the time. It takes all the wave out of my hair.

GLORY: I don't see any in there now, dear. Don't tell me the water straightened it out.

HILDY: No, the water didn't straighten it. And while I'm on the subject, sweet, next time cut your fingernails. I bet there's at least a pound of me under them.

GLORY: Not that you couldn't use it.

HILDY: I heard that, honey. Just you wait till the next scene. I'll pull every bit of that bleached mop out . . .

TOMMY: Ladies. Ladies, please. We mustn't fight. There's plenty of time for us to do another play, before supper. So let's clean off this set and set up for another one.

SOMER.: Right, Tommy. Hildy, get rid of the props. Glory and I'll clean up here.

TOMMY: I'll help you, Hildy.

(TOMMY *strikes kettle.* HILDY *clears kitchen area of props*)

HILDY *(as she works):* Don't you think the heroine of the next play could be a little taller and maybe a brunette . . . I mean, just this once?

(TOMMY *and* HILDY *exit*)

GLORY *(to* SOMERSAULT*):* You had to open your big mouth. Now that . . . witch is back there all alone with him.

SOMER.: Ssssshhh. I wanted to talk with you alone, Glory. Come here.

(They cross down left)

GLORY: What's wrong, Somersault?

SOMER.: Look, Glory, I don't like to butt into anyone's business, but that last kiss was a little too much. You'll be giving him ideas before he's ready for them, and we can't have that. You know what happens to us then.

GLORY: I know. I'm sorry about that kiss, but I just couldn't help it. He was so close and I love him so very much.

SOMER.: I'm not blaming you. I understand. But just be careful.

GLORY *(crying):* Oh, Somersault, he'll be leaving soon and I don't want him to go. I love him.

SOMER. *(puts her head on his shoulder):* All right, honey, cry it out, but hurry up. You can't let him see you crying.

GLORY: Yes, Somersault. *(She dries her eyes on his sleeve)*

SOMER.: Let's make the most of the time we have left.

GLORY: But I can't let him go. I can't. (SOMERSAULT *hushes her*)

TOMMY *(enters):* Well, that's all done. Now what will we play?

HILDY *(enters minus witch makeup):* Just getting rid of that nose makes me feel so good that I'm ready to do another play. What'll it be?

TOMMY: Do you have any ideas?

HILDY: Do I? *(She moves toward* TOMMY, *but* SOMERSAULT *stops her)*

SOMER. *(to* HILDY*):* Not that kind. *(To* TOMMY*)* Well, we could play Hansel and Gretel.

GLORY: Or Jack the Giant Killer.

SOMER.: No, I'm sick of falling down the beanstalk. My back can't take it any more.

HILDY: How about Beauty and the Beast?

SOMER.: Or Tom Sawyer?

HILDY: Oh, I'd have to play Aunt Polly, then.

VOICE *(offstage):* Tommy. Tommy. Where are you, Tommy? Come here, please.

TOMMY: What was that?

GLORY: What was what? I didn't hear anything. Did you, Somersault?

SOMER.: Nope, not a thing.

TOMMY *(looking around, bewildered):* It came from behind that big door over there. That big door? Huh? Has that been there all the time? I never noticed it before. *(He goes over to it and feels it)* It's funny, but right here I feel so strange. *(Crosses to* SOMERSAULT*)* What's wrong with me, Somersault? Do you know? (SOMERSAULT *gestures that he doesn't know)* I feel like something's pulling me back to that door . . . that I have to go through it. But I don't want to go. I want to stay here with you and Hildy and Glory and play. I'm so afraid. I don't know why. Help me, Somersault. Help me.

SOMER.: Sure, Tommy, sure. Glory, pull up a couple of blocks for you and Tommy. (GLORY *gets them)* And now, if you'll be seated, sir and madam, Hildegarde Witch and I will do our unique specialty dance that has been performed before the crowned heads of Europe and the bald heads of America. *(He bows and falls flat on his face.* TOMMY *laughs and claps)* I'm ready. Are you, Madam Witch?

HILDY: Somersault, you know I can't dance a step. Are you trying to make a fool out of me?

SOMER.: Shut up and dance. It's our only chance. Music, please.

(SOMERSAULT *gestures and* GLORY *begins to play "By the Light of the Silvery Moon" on tissue paper and comb. They dance a soft shoe, badly, with jokes on the break—)*

SOMER.: How many hairs on a monkey's chin?

HILDY: I don't know.

SOMER.: Next time you shave, count 'em.

(HILDY *swings at* SOMERSAULT, *who ducks. She falls.* TOMMY *laughs.* HILDY *goes to him—)*

HILDY: How many hairs on a monkey's chin?

TOMMY: I don't know.

HILDY: Next time I shave, I'll count 'em.

(TOMMY *laughs.* HILDY *rejoins her dancing partner. On exit,* SOMERSAULT *kicks* HILDY *and she falls. The dance is over)*

TOMMY: Oh, wonderful. Wonderful. When you fell, Hildy, I thought I'd
. . . *(He trails off into gales of laughter. When he is wiping his eyes,* HILDY
kicks SOMERSAULT *in the seat of the pants, while he is bowing. He falls.*
TOMMY *laughs more)* Oh, my, that was fun. Now what'll we play?

GLORY: We could play House or Doctor and Nurse.

SOMER.: What did I tell you, Glory?

TOMMY: Oh, no. Let's play something exciting . . . with lots of blood.

HILDY: Cowboys and indians, anyone?

TOMMY: No, I'm tired of that. *(Thinks)* I know. Let's play War.

GLORY: Oh, not again. I'm sick of War.

SOMER.: Yes, Tommy, couldn't we play something else? Anything, just so it
isn't War. I always get blown to bits.

TOMMY: No, I want to play War and that's what we're going to play. I want
to play War. I want to play War.

SOMER.: All right, Tommy, we'll be glad to play War. If that's what you
want.

GLORY: Sure, Tommy, we like playing War. What part am I going to play?
The beautiful nurse who saves your life and who falls in love with you?

TOMMY: No, this time we'll do something different.

HILDY: Right. This time I'm going to play the beautiful nurse. Oh, Tommy,
that's so sweet of you.

TOMMY: No one is going to play the beautiful nurse. We're all going to be
men.

GLORY: What?

HILDY: Why, the idea . . .

GLORY: Well, I'm not going to cut my hair, just for your old war play.

HILDY: And I don't want to wear slacks. I hate slacks. They make me—

GLORY:—look bunchy. I know, dear, you do have your problems. But then,
I'm the only one here who really looks good in slacks.

HILDY: The word is sacks, dear. With potatoes in them. Dirty, lumpy
potatoes. And I must say—

(SOMERSAULT *puts his hand over her mouth)*

SOMER.: That we'll be glad to do the play. Tell us about it, Tommy.

TOMMY: Well, it takes place in France in 1916. We're all flying for the
Lafayette Escadrille . . .

(They go into a huddle, then set up stage. All exit, TOMMY *right, others left.
Then* HILDY *enters and begins the play)*

HILDY *(pacing behind desk made of orange crates):* Where is that idiot,
Major Tommy Steeljaws? Where is he? He's ten hours overdue now.
And just when I'm sure he's dead and that I'm rid of him forever, he'll

come back to show me up again. He does it all the time and I'm sick of it. Sick, sick, sick. Oh, where is he? I just know he's going to get through. And it was such an impossible mission. One small red Spad with all the guns and armor removed and carrying one ten-ton bomb, hedge-hopping over France to bomb the big ammo dump at Weisbaden. Any other fool would stay home, but only Major Tommy Steeljaws would dare try. *(Does a Bette Davis imitation)* And I'm sick of it. Sick. Sick. Sick . . . oops, wrong play. (SOMERSAULT *knocks*) Yes, come in. (SOMERSAULT *and* GLORY *enter*) What is it, Blinky?

SOMER. *(salutes):* Colonel Fatzpitrick?

HILDY: That's Fitzpatrick, idiot.

SOMER. *(salutes):* Colonel, sir, this here's the new recruit, sir.

HILDY *(salutes):* At ease, Lieutenant. What's your name, son?

GLORY *(salutes):* Glorianna, sir.

HILDY: Glorianna? What kind of a name is that for a fighting man?

GLORY: But that's the only name he ever gave me.

HILDY: Who?

GLORY: Tommy, when he was telling us about the play. You know what I'm talking about, Hildy.

HILDY: Silence in the ranks.

SOMER.: For Pete's sake, Glory, play the part, will you? We've got to keep Tommy from thinking about that Voice.

HILDY: Come on, girl, get with it.

GLORY: Oh, all right. My name is . . . er . . . ah . . . Philip Greenway, sir.

HILDY: Good. Well, Greenway, how much money do you have with you?

GLORY: About ten dollars, sir.

HILDY: Excellent. As commander of this post, I fine you ten dollars for reporting out of uniform.

GLORY: Oh, Hildy, for crying out loud, you know we didn't have time to change before this silly play started.

HILDY: No alibis, Lieutenant. Fork it over.

GLORY: Oh, if I must, I must. *(She reaches into bosom of dress and takes out money.* SOMERSAULT *tries to peek and gets a finger in his eye)* Here you are, sir.

HILDY: Very good. Blinky?

SOMER.: Sir?

HILDY: Two bottles of your best cognac, on the double. *(She hands him money)*

SOMER. *(salutes):* Yes, sir. *(He exits)*

HILDY: Sit down, Greenway. Have any combat experience?

GLORY: No, sir, I just got my wings yesterday.

HILDY: Fine. Excellent. We'll just give you some light scouting work until you get used to the Boche.

GLORY: Oh, peachy.

HILDY: Do you know how to handle a Sopwith Camel?

GLORY: No, but I taught a puppydog to roll over and play dead.

HILDY: Idiot, I'm talking about an airplane.

GLORY: Oh, sir, I don't know anything about airplanes. I just got my wings. I did pass the orals with an excellent, though.

HILDY: Well, don't worry. It's really very simple. You just turn on the ignition and keep the nose up and the plane'll do the rest. That's all there is to it. (SOMERSAULT *enters, carrying two bottles*) Ah, Blinky's here. Say, Lieutenant, would you like a taste of real French cognac?

GLORY: Oh, yes, sir.

HILDY: Have you any more money?

GLORY: No, sir.

HILDY: Well, the barman in the canteen will take your chit. *(She whirls on* SOMERSAULT*)* Is that alcohol you're carrying, Sergeant?

SOMER.: Yes, sir.

HILDY: You know the rules of the post, Sergeant. Why the idea, carrying alcohol around. I'll confiscate it at once. Hand that filthy stuff over. (SOMERSAULT *gives her bottles*) And you're fined ten dollars. (SOMERSAULT *gives her money*) Well, it looks like I'll have to dispose of this rotten stuff. Can't let it poison the men. *(She kills half a bottle)* Now, Lieutenant, I think I'll send you over Berlin for a little scouting. What do you say?

GLORY: Wonderful, sir. I'm ready any time.

HILDY: Good. You'll leave immediately.

SOMER.: But sir, that mission's sheer suicide.

HILDY: Hold your tongue, Sergeant. Warm up old ninety-seven.

SOMER.: Yes, sir.

(SOMERSAULT *salutes and exits as* TOMMY *enters right, pretending to be an airplane. He flies around the stage, making motor noises)*

TOMMY: Steeljaws to airdrome. Steeljaws to airdrome. Do you read me?

SOMER. *(enters left, on apron):* Loud and clear, Tommy. Where are you?

TOMMY: About two minutes away. Coming in for a landing.

SOMER.: Roger. What is your condition?

TOMMY: Wheels shot off. Tail blown off. Wings dropped off over No Man's Land.

SOMER.: Bail out, Tommy. We don't need the ship that bad.

TOMMY: Not as long as I have my propeller and motor. I'm going to try a stomach landing.

SOMER.: Stomach landing?

TOMMY: Yes. Mother said it wasn't nice to say belly.

SOMER.: Tommy, don't try it. Bail out.

TOMMY: I see you now. Tommy Steeljaws coming in.

SOMER. *(exits):* No, no, I can't watch this.

(TOMMY *flies along apron, collapses in center of stage. He gets to his feet and dusts himself off*)

TOMMY *(crosses to* HILDY): Pretty smooth landing, if I do say so myself. *(He salutes)* Major Steeljaws reporting, sir. Mission accomplished, sir.

HILDY: I might have known. Details, please, Major.

TOMMY: Weisbaden is no more, sir. A direct hit. I had to fight my way in and out, sir. That was difficult, since I had no guns, sir. Got two Boches anyway, sir.

HILDY: Good gracious, man, how?

TOMMY: Hard bricks. Good aim. I also dropped a note to Baron von Seitzinger and his Grey Ghosts on the way back, sir, to challenge him to a duel. End of report.

HILDY: Well done, I suppose. Do you think there's a chance that Seitzinger might accept your challenge?

TOMMY: I hope so, sir.

HILDY: So do I. Who's Seitzinger?

TOMMY: My Boche rival. *(Sees* GLORY) By the way, who are you? A replacement?

HILDY: Yes. This is Lieutenant Greenway, Major.

GLORY *(salutes):* Pleased to meet America's greatest air ace, sir.

TOMMY: Yes, I know. *(He kisses her in exaggerated Hollywood fashion)*

HILDY: You can't kiss her, Tommy. She's a boy.

TOMMY *(dropping her):* Oh, I forgot. Force of habit, I guess.

SOMER. *(enters, carrying an orange crate):* Major, you made it. I'm glad, sir. *(He puts down the crate)*

TOMMY: Thanks to you, Blinky. As soon as I heard your voice on the radio, I knew I'd make it. I couldn't let down the man who taught me all I know about flying, now could I? Thanks, friend.

HILDY: Sergeant, is Lieutenant Greenway's plane ready?

SOMER. *(gesturing at the crate):* Yes, sir, there it is.

GLORY: Oh, how exciting. And it's so cute. *(Pause)* Is that all there is to it?

TOMMY: Wait a minute, Fitzpatrick, I'm not going to let you send the kid up in an old crate like that.

HILDY: You're interfering again, Steeljaws. Remember what I said I'd do if you . . .

SOMER.: Listen. There's a plane coming.

HILDY: Where?

SOMER.: There. *(He points left)*

HILDY: Then I'll go hide there. *(She points right, then hides behind a block)*

TOMMY: Can you make out what it is yet?

SOMER.: Yes, it's a grey Fokker.

GLORY *(slaps him):* Smutty Mouth!

TOMMY: It must be Seitzinger repaying my call.

GLORY: He's waving his wings. *(She waves back)*

TOMMY: He's dropping something.

(With a groan, SOMERSAULT *clutches his head and falls)*

SOMER.: Oooooooh. He got me with that monkey wrench he dropped from his plane. I'm a goner.

GLORY: There's a note attached to it. What does it say?

TOMMY: Never mind that now. Can't you see old Blinky's dying?

GLORY *(crying):* Oh, no.

TOMMY: Get hold of yourself, man. This is no time to go to pieces. *(He slaps her)*

GLORY: Yes, sir. Thank you, sir. I needed that.

TOMMY: And don't just stand there. Hum "Tipperary." (GLORY *begins humming.* HILDY *crawls out and joins her)* I'm sorry, old friend, it's my fault. I shouldn't have challenged von Seitzinger to a duel.

SOMER.: That's all right, Tommy. I'm proud that you did. I know you'll get him.

TOMMY: Not I, Blinky. Because we'll both be riding the ship that sends the Grey Ghost of Gitzhagen down to a flaming death. This is one flight you're going to make.

SOMER.: Only in spirit, Tommy. There's another flight I'll have to make first . . . to that big airfield in the sky, where all the officers are privates and the mess hall's open twenty-four hours a day. And I don't mind going, Tommy. I know I've been a part of Something Big and Good and Noble, and that I've Made the World Safe for Democracy. Goodbye, sir. *(He struggles to his feet, salutes and dies.* GLORY *and* HILDY *hum "Taps")*

TOMMY: He was a good grease monkey. His fingernails were never clean. And now to take care of von Seitzinger. *(To* GLORY) Lieutenant, I want you to—

VOICE: Tommy. Tommy. Where are you?

TOMMY: I'm here. Right here.

VOICE: Then come here. To me. Right away. Tommy.

*(*TOMMY *starts toward door.* GLORY *tries to hold him back)*

GLORY: No, Tommy, don't. Stay here. Stay with us. You won't like it over there. Please, Tommy, please, I love you. Please stay . . . for me, please.

HILDY: Stay. Tommy, we need you.

TOMMY: But I can't help myself. I can't stop. I don't want to go. I want to stay here with you. It's fun here. I like our plays. I want to stay. Help me. I don't want to go. I don't want to go.

(SOMERSAULT *rises and crosses to him, pushing* GLORY *and* HILDY *aside*)

SOMER.: Listen to me, boy, don't fight it; go with it. It's really not so bad over there. And you can come back and see us. We'll be right here waiting. Any time you want to see us, we'll be right here. Now go along with you and don't cry. Look at me. Silly old Somersault isn't crying . . . and you know what a softie I am. So you know it can't be so terrible.

TOMMY: Honest, Somersault?

SOMER.: Honest, Tommy.

TOMMY: Well, you've always known best, Somersault.

SOMER.: That's a good boy. (*He wipes* TOMMY's *nose*) Don't cry.

VOICE: Tommy, come on, Tommy.

TOMMY: I'm coming. I'm coming. (*He runs happily to the door, reaches it and turns knob, starts through, but stops, turns and runs back. He goes to* HILDY *and kisses her on the cheek*) Goodbye, Hildegarde. You're the nicest witch I know.

HILDY (*touching cheek*): After all these years . . . goodbye, Tommy.

TOMMY: Goodbye, Glorianna. I love you. (*He kisses her*)

GLORY: And I love you, Tommy. (*She turns away, crying*)

(TOMMY *goes to* SOMERSAULT, *starts to hug him but, embarrassed, shakes hands, instead*)

TOMMY: Goodbye, Somersault. Good old Somersault, the best friend I've ever had.

SOMER.: So long, Tommy. Now off with you. (*He pushes* TOMMY *away*)

TOMMY (*runs toward open door, stops, waves goodbye*): Goodbye. Goodbye, my friends. I'll be back.

(TOMMY *exits quickly. The three rush toward the door, but it closes in their faces*)

SOMER. (*turning away from the door*): No, Tommy, you'll never be back. That door only works one way.

(They all move down to the blocks. The lights begin a slow dim toward a blackout at Curtain. All movements begin to slow down)

HILDY *(as she sits):* I wonder what Tommy's doing now?

SOMER.: Forgetting us.

GLORY: Are you sure?

SOMER.: That's the way it's always been. Tommy won't change it.

HILDY: Do you think he'll ever think about us?

SOMER.: No. We're behind him and the world's stretching out ahead of him. A witch, a princess and a clown aren't big enough to compete with that.

HILDY: Maybe he'll be different. Maybe he'll remember.

SOMER.: Maybe.

HILDY: I'm getting so sleepy. Guess I'm not as young as I used to be. *(She barely gets this out and she's asleep)*

SOMER.: Rest well, Hildy. *(He turns to GLORY)* Now don't cry, dear Glory. A princess isn't supposed to cry, you know.

GLORY: I know, but I did love him so.

SOMER.: So did I. That's why I made him go.

GLORY: I know you had to. I'm happy for him, I guess, but . . . Somersault, Somersault, look at me. Why, you're crying. Clowns aren't supposed to cry, you know that. Come on, where's the old Somersault? It's not that bad. Why, just think, soon another little boy will imagine us all over again. And then you and I and Hildegarde will be together again and awake and alive and happy and we'll put on the same wonderful plays for him, just like we did for Tommy and we'll make him happy, too. And we'll all be together forever and ever. Won't we? Won't we?

SOMER.: Sure we will, Glorianna. And it'll be even better than now.

GLORY: He's forgetting me, too . . . now. I can feel it. I'm getting so tired. Goodnight, good, sweet friend. (GLORY *sleeps, too)*

SOMER.: Goodnight, my lovely princess. Sleep well. You're so lovely and so lucky, too. Surely another child will dream of a beautiful princess named Glorianna someday, and then you'll be awake and alive again. That's nice to think about. *(He kisses her, then goes to HILDY)* And maybe some child might even imagine a clumsy witch named Hildegarde who can't dance a step, but who's pretty and gracious. Just the right kind of a witch for a small child. *(Moving very slowly, he sits down)* But no one's ever . . . going to dream up a silly old clown named Somersault . . . ever again. *(Pause. SOMERSAULT listens to something)* I thought I heard him laugh. That's a good sound to hear . . . before I . . .

(SOMERSAULT sleeps, too. The lights dim down with his last word. A moment's pause. Curtain.)